IMAGES
of America

MOUNT HOLLY

This book is lovingly dedicated to all the people who help make Mount Holly a better place by working for the common good of all in our historic town. We dedicate this volume to those who fight to preserve our remaining historic treasures and history, so generations beyond ours may enjoy Mount Holly's architecture and heritage. Finally, to all those who quietly volunteer their time to improve and be a part of our town, we present Mount Holly.

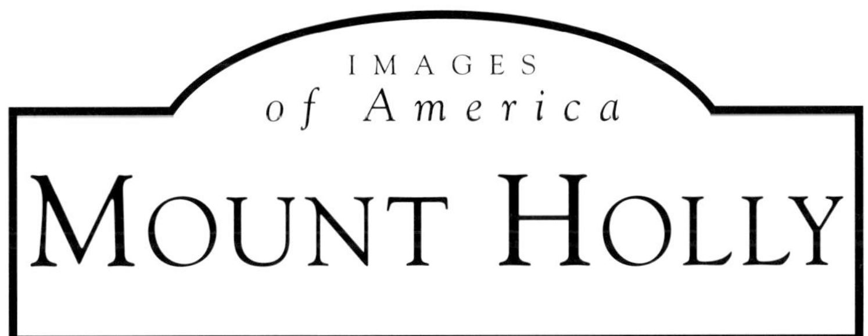

Heidi J. Winzinger and Mary L. Smith

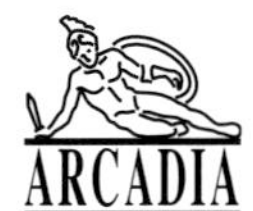

ISBN 0-7385-0908-6

First published 2001

Published by Arcadia Publishing,
Charleston SC, Chicago IL, Portsmouth NH, San Francisco CA

Printed in Great Britain

Library of Congress Catalog Card Number: 2001090998

For all general information, contact Arcadia Publishing:
Telephone 843-853-2070
Fax 843-853-0044
E-mail sales@arcadiapublishing.com
For customer service and orders:
Toll-free 1-888-313-2665

Visit us on the Internet at www.arcadiapublishing.com

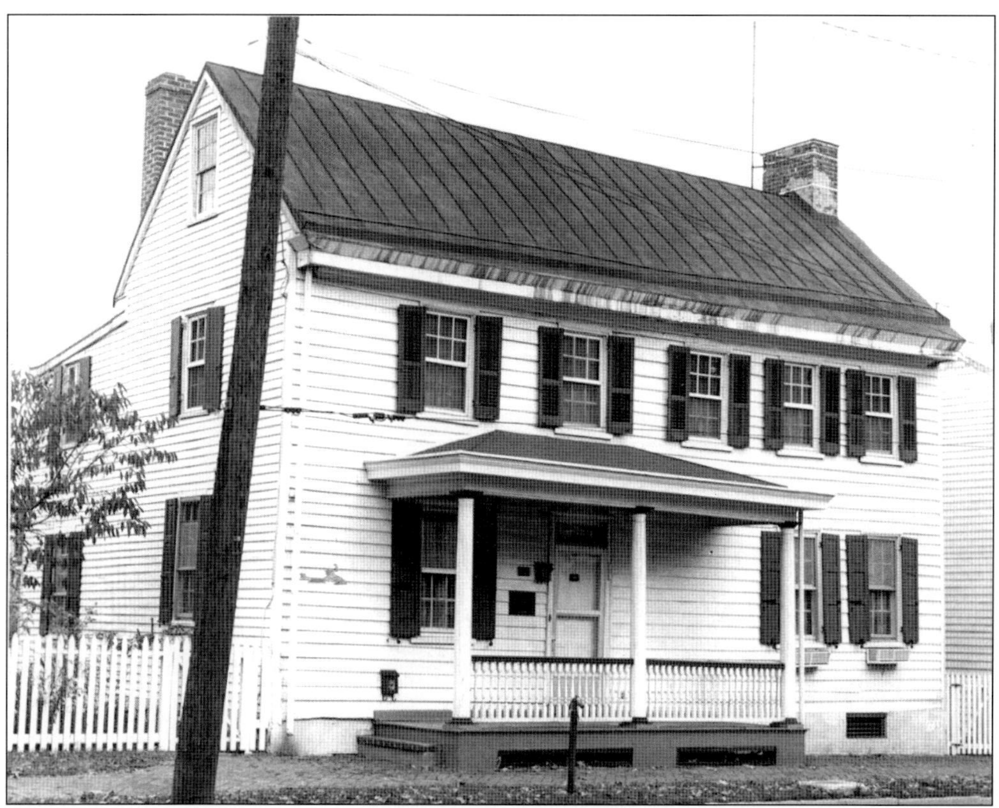

The Stephen Girard House is located at 211 Mill Street. This was Girard's home and where he operated a store. He was the founder of Girard College and Girard Bank in Philadelphia.

Contents

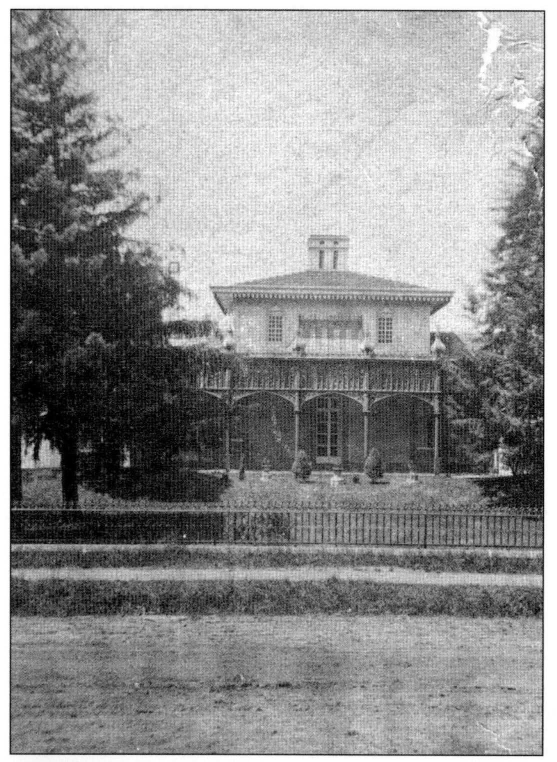

The Nathan Dunn Chinese Cottage is probably one of Mount Holly's best-kept secrets and was one of the community's most beautiful buildings in its prime. Nathan Dunn was the curator for the Chinese Museum of Art in Philadelphia and made his home here on a large estate in this cottage. The building was modified (below) to include an upper floor. The building is currently the Sacred Heart School and Church rectory and has been modernized, removing lots of great character.

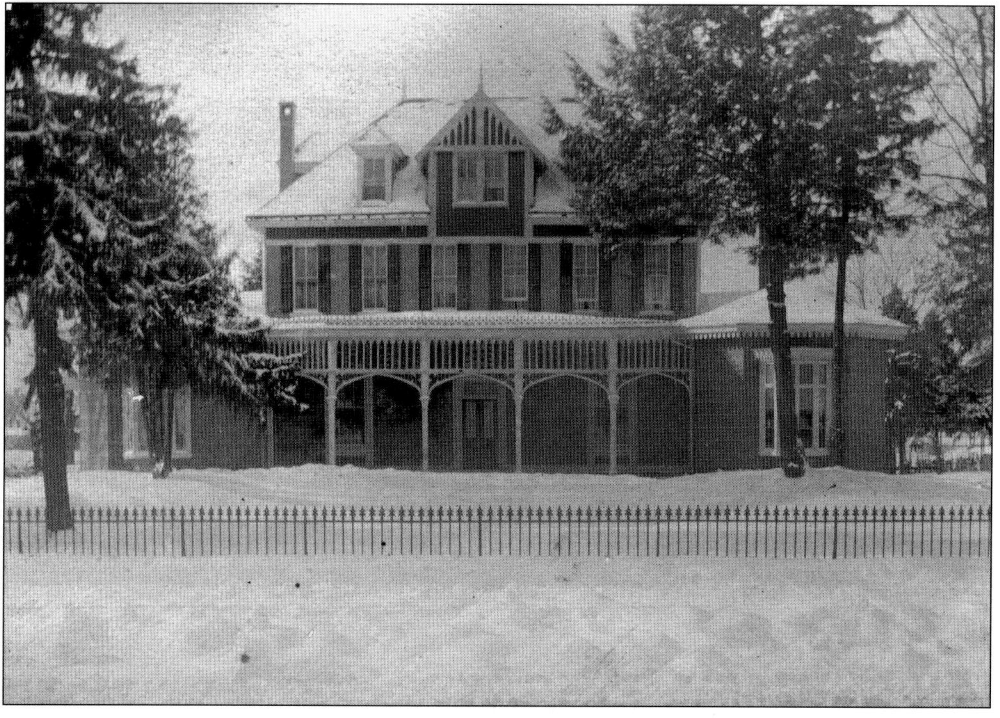

INTRODUCTION

As Mary Smith creeps into her eighties and Heidi Winzinger tops the hill of her mid-thirties, they have both found themselves on common ground, working to preserve the history of their hometown. During her lifetime, Mary has witnessed the once grand town of Mount Holly take many turns for the worse and for the better, but one thing remains constant: slowly, Mount Holly's history and architecture, year by year, bit by bit, are lost, forgotten, burned, demolished, covered with vinyl, or thrown out in the trash.

This book is a reminder of all that was and all that remains in Mount Holly—a wake-up call for all to recognize the splendor of this town and its significance as the seat of Burlington County, New Jersey.

The history of Mount Holly predates the American Revolution by nearly 100 years. Walter Reeves acquired land, by payment or by squatters rights, from local Native Americans even before the Friends (Quakers) had made settlement in Burlington in 1677. At first, Mount Holly was called Bridgetown, named for its bridges allowing travelers to cross the Rancocas Creek along the Great Road to Philadelphia (now Route 537). Eventually, the town took on the name Mount Holly, undoubtedly for the large hill, or mount, standing 185 feet above sea level—a dramatic difference compared to the center of town, which stands a mere 15 feet above sea level. The mount in Mount Holly can be seen for many miles around, along with other mounts dotting the flatlands of southern New Jersey.

Around 1723, Edward Gaskill, another Mount Holly pioneer, was the first to use the Rancocas Creek for more than transportation. He harnessed its power by hand-digging the millrace to power the first great mill in Mount Holly. Surely without the millrace and the mills that came after, Mount Holly would not have grown into the thriving business community that it became.

In 1776, Mount Holly became entrenched in an important skirmish between Hessian soldiers and American regiments aiding George Washington in the battle of Trenton by keeping opposing troops occupied. During the Battle of Iron Works Hill, as it was known, the Hessians fought from the mount on one side of town and the Americans from the top of Iron Works Hill on the other side of the Rancocas Creek just off Pine Street. Today, the only remnants of this battle can be seen in the Friends Meetinghouse, where cleaver marks still adorn the wooden seats from a time when Hessian troops used this place as a commissary. During the American Revolution, Mount Holly became the temporary capital of New Jersey when Trenton was threatened and the state legislature was forced to meet here in 1779.

Mount Holly is home to the oldest continually active fire company in the United States, the Burlington County Prison Museum (designed by Robert Mill, architect of the Washington Monument), the oldest schoolhouse on its original site in the state, and the Burlington County Court House (designed by Samuel Lewis, architect for Congress Hall in Philadelphia).

Among Mount Holly's most noted people are Bessie Pease Guteman (1876–1960), one of America's most famous children's artists in the 1920s and 1930s. Of the great capitalists from Mount Holly are Isaac H. Clothier (1838–1921) and Justus Strawbridge (1838–1911), founders of the retail giant Strawbridge & Clothier, and Stephen Girard (1750–1831), founder of Girard College and Girard Bank in Philadelphia. John Woolman (1721–1772) was one of the greatest Quakers of all time. He is noted as a staunch abolitionist. The John Woolman Memorial is still operated and is open to the public.

As you will see in the pages to come, Mount Holly may be small (2.9 square miles), but it is big on history. History is being preserved in all forms, and dedicated residents work to share Mount Holly's history with all who live and visit here. Mary Smith is actively researching Mount Holly's connection to the Underground Railroad, documenting the stories of the Strawbridge and Clothier families, and actively supports the Mount Holly Historical Society and their museum, the Shinn Curtis Log Cabin. She has written a book about important women in Mount Holly's history. Heidi Winzinger works for her family business developing and restoring the oldest part of Mount Holly along White and Church Streets, now called the Mill Race Village, that includes 11 artisan shops and the Robin's Nest Restaurant.

In addition, the authors and others have been actively involved with creating and supporting the Historic Rancocas Valley Tourism Association (HRVTA), promoting Mount Holly and the surrounding towns (Hainesport, Lumberton, Medford, Burlington City, Eastampton, Westampton, Rancocas Woods, and portions of Mount Laurel and Vincentown) as a one- and two-day destination for visitors interested in history.

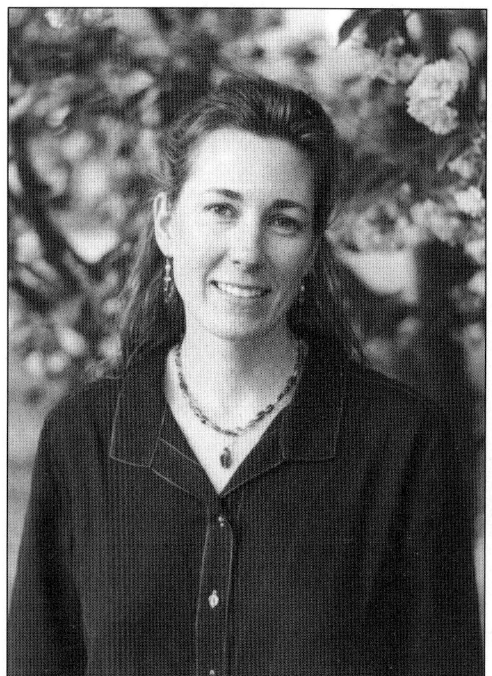

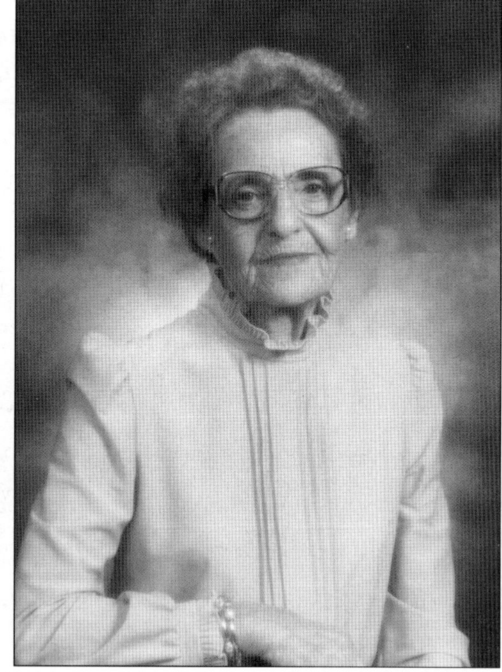

Pictured are authors Heidi Winzinger (left) and Mary Smith.

One

Fires and Firemen

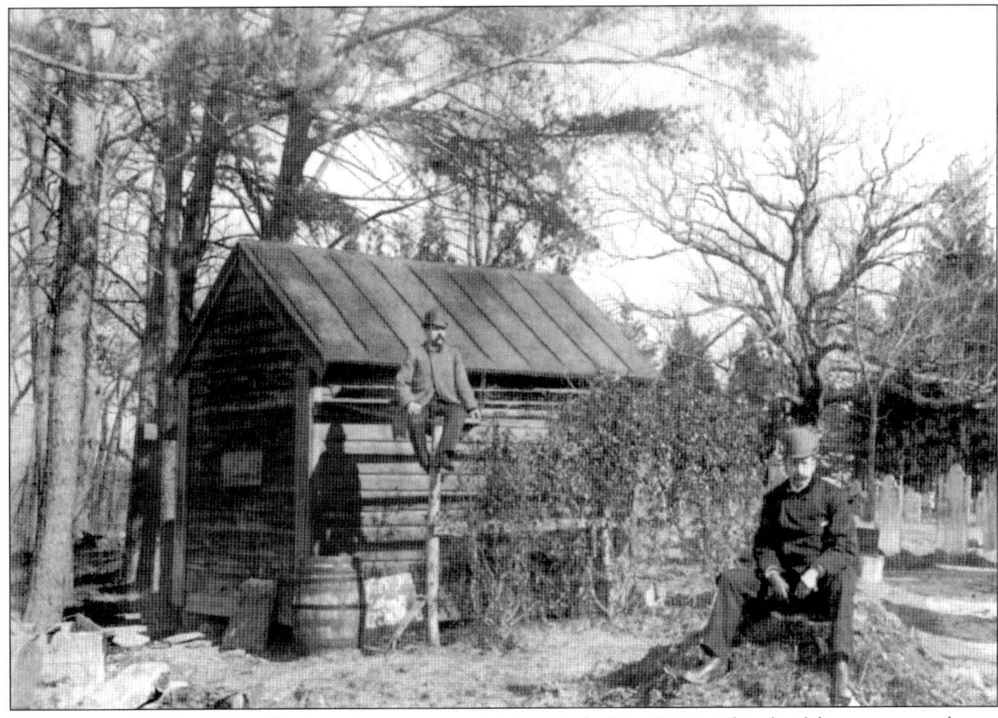

The original Relief Fire Company was organized on July 11, 1752. This building was used as a tool house at St. Andrew's cemetery until the late 1900s, when it was moved to another location near the current Relief Firehouse, closer to downtown along Pine Street.

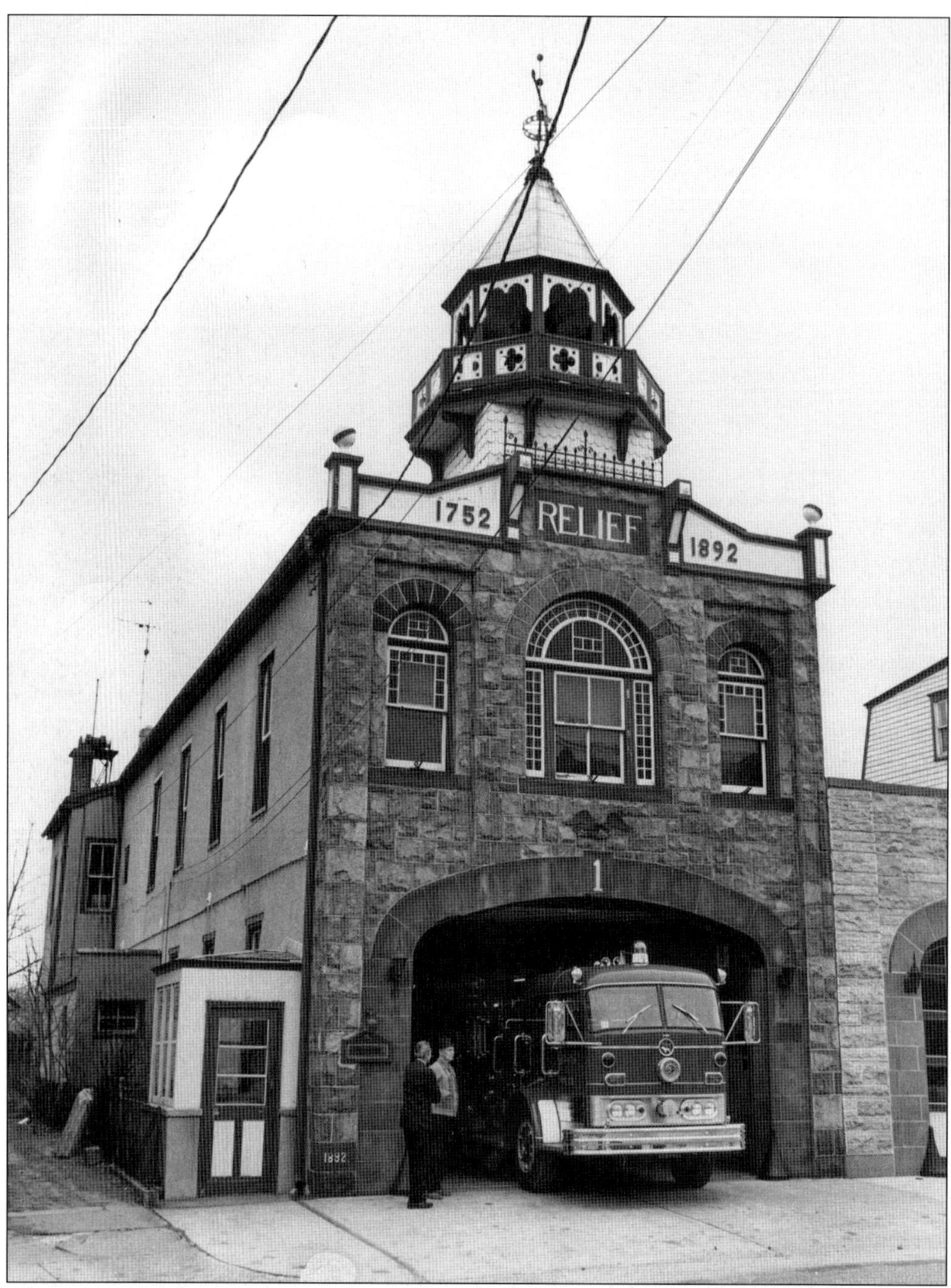

The Relief Fire Company is the oldest active volunteer fire company in the United States. The name has changed over the years. In 1787, it was changed from the Britannia Fire Company to the Mount Holly Fire Company. Finally, after 1805, it was known as the Relief Fire Company.

This is another building of the Relief Firehouse, *c.* 1870, on Pine Street near the current firehouse. Frank Garbarino is the boy in the front on the far left and Ted Wescott is on the top rail on the right.

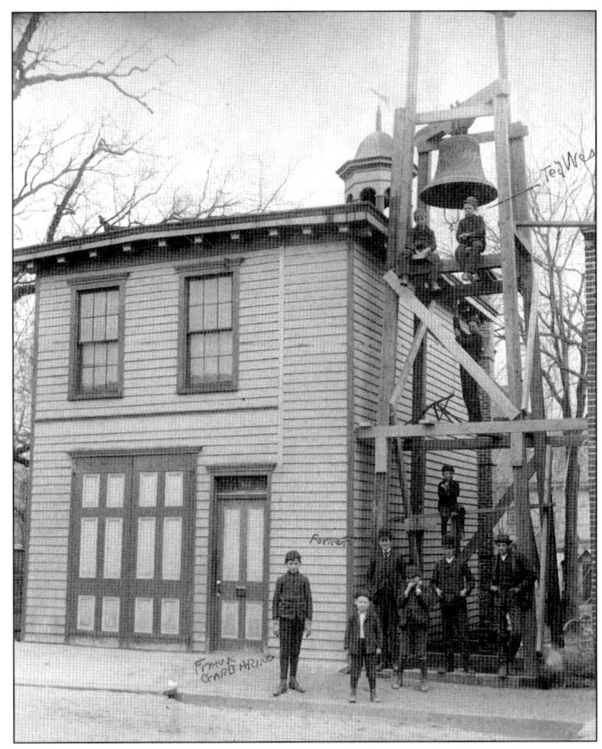

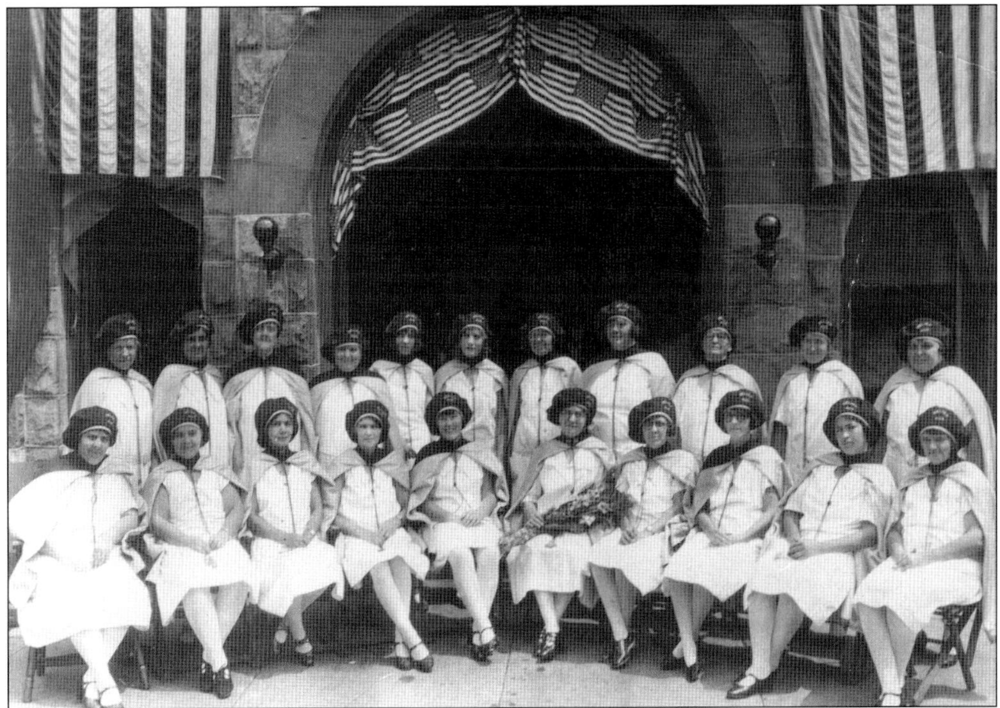

In front of the Relief Fire Company are, from left to right, the following: (front row) six unidentified people, Clara Warner, Elsie Barber, and Ignore Powell; (back row) five unidentified people, Florence Beverland, Cassie Gaskill, and Dorothy Frake.

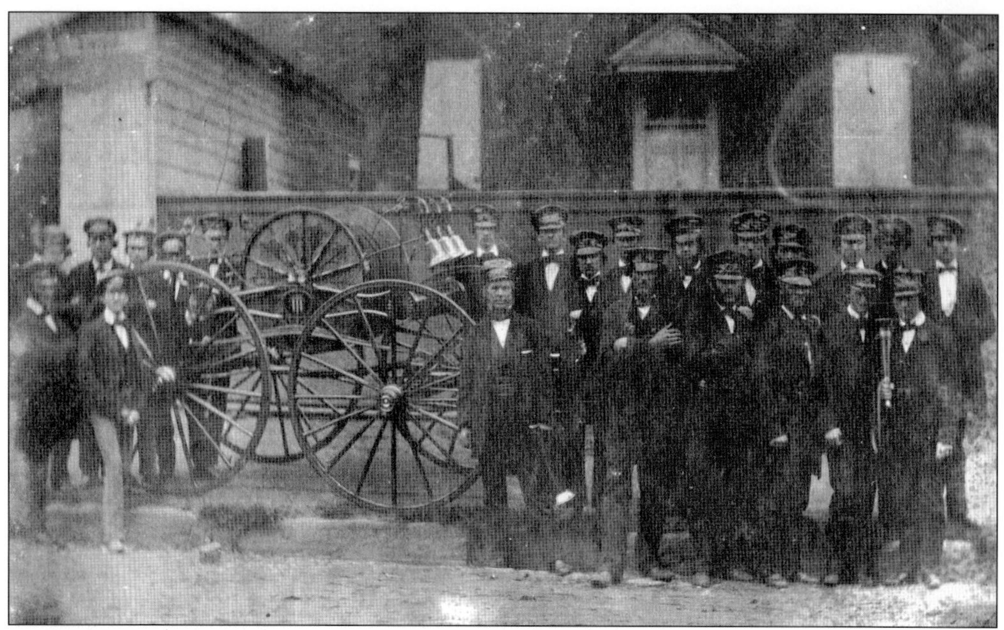

The original members of the American Fire Company pose in front of the original Union Firehouse, where they kept their firefighting apparatus. The company was organized in 1858 and erected its own station on Main Street (now High Street) and later moved to the corner of Mount Holly Avenue and Mill Street.

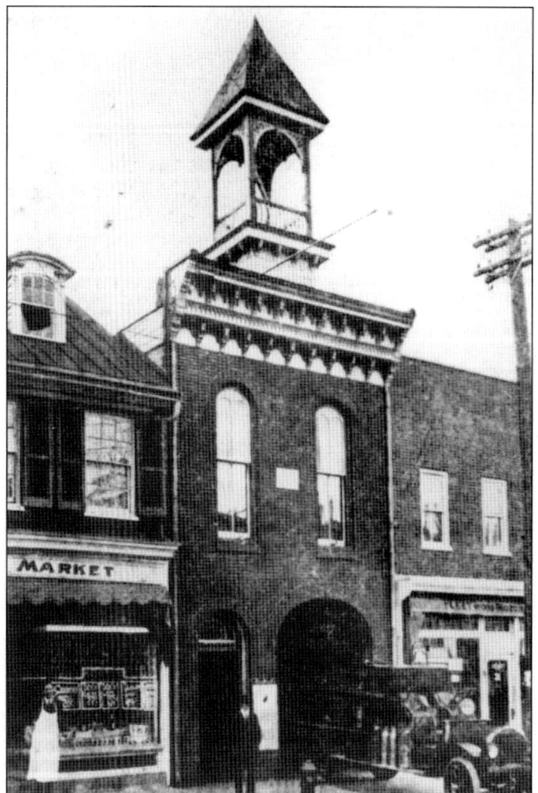

The company's firehouse, built in 1871, was where the company resided until 1956, when they moved to a modern building on Mill Street. This old firehouse has gone through many transformations and was the home of David's Jewelers for many years. It currently maintains its modernization but unfortunately has lost the bell tower.

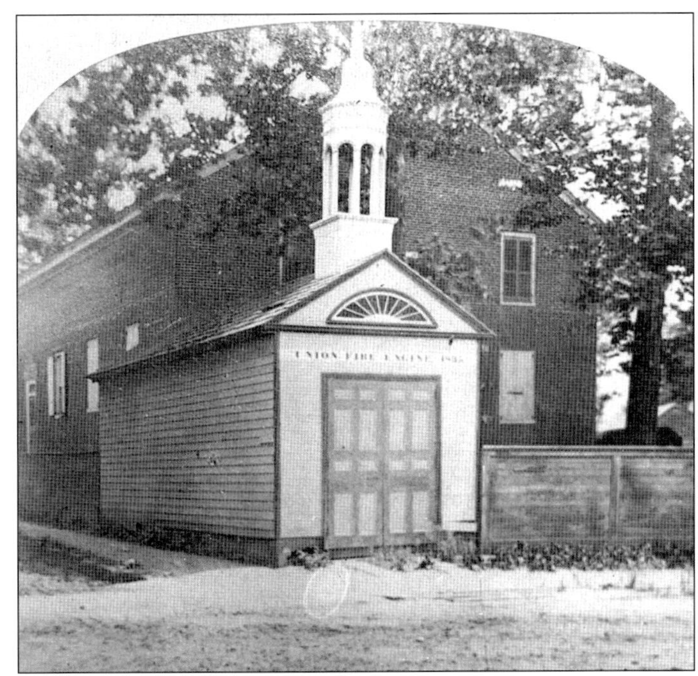

The Union Hose Company was organized in 1805 at Griffith Owen's Tavern. This small house was built at the corner of Main and Garden Streets in front of the Friends Meetinghouse. After a few years, the building was enlarged and moved to the Garden Street side of the Friends burial ground.

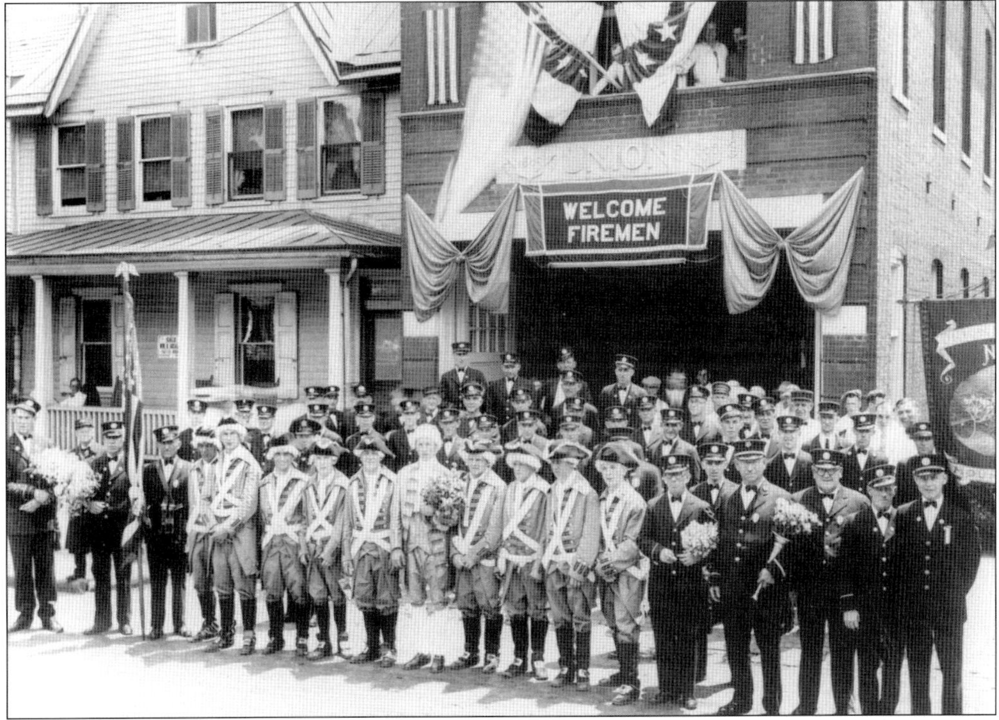

The newest Union Firehouse on Washington Street is shown decked out for a parade. The house on the left is Mrs. Clothier's home, where she operated a small dance studio in the 1920s. The home was demolished to make room for a modern addition to the Union Fire Company. John Hayfield is the sixth person from the right in front, and Benjamin Bozarth is the third from the right in front.

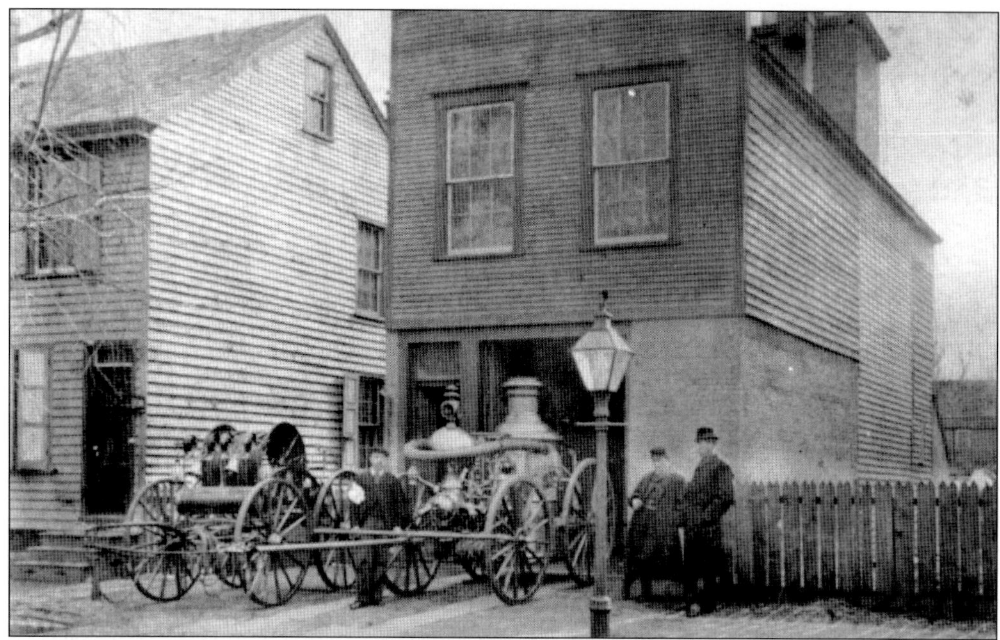

Around 1864, the Good Intent Firehouse was located on Mount Holly Avenue on a lot donated by William N. Risdon. Before the company constructed this building, its hand engine was kept in the arsenal at the head of Grant Street, but that building was demolished. In 1878, the Good Intent Fire Company purchased Mount Holly's first steam engine.

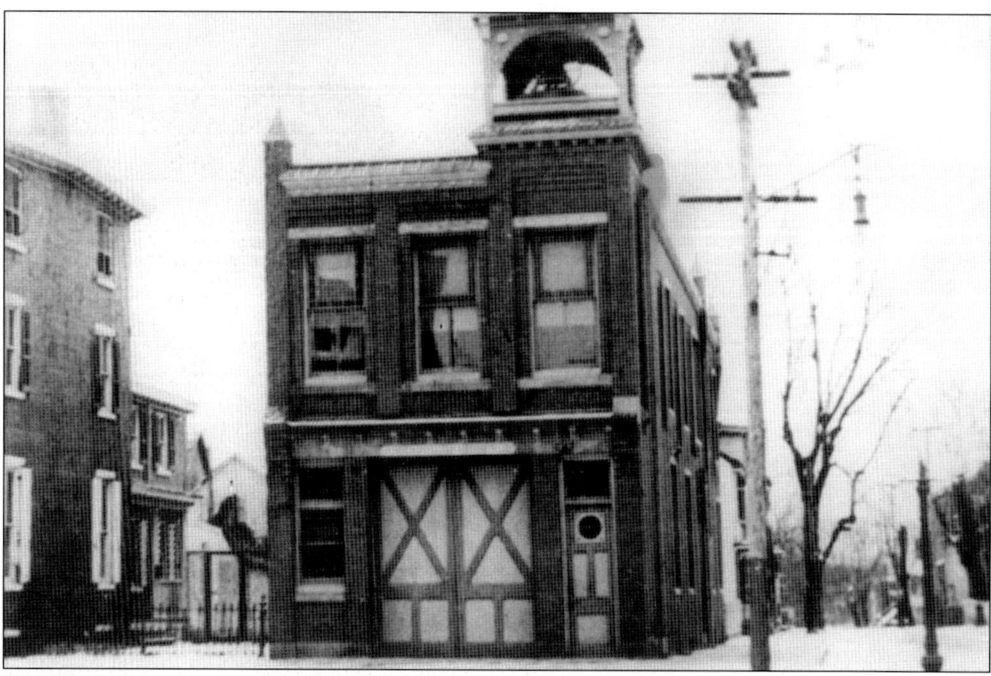

Here is the Good Intent Firehouse close to how it stands today on the corner of Buttonwood and Gardens Streets. The company organized *c.* 1850 as the Delaware Hose Company and adopted the name Good Intent in 1860.

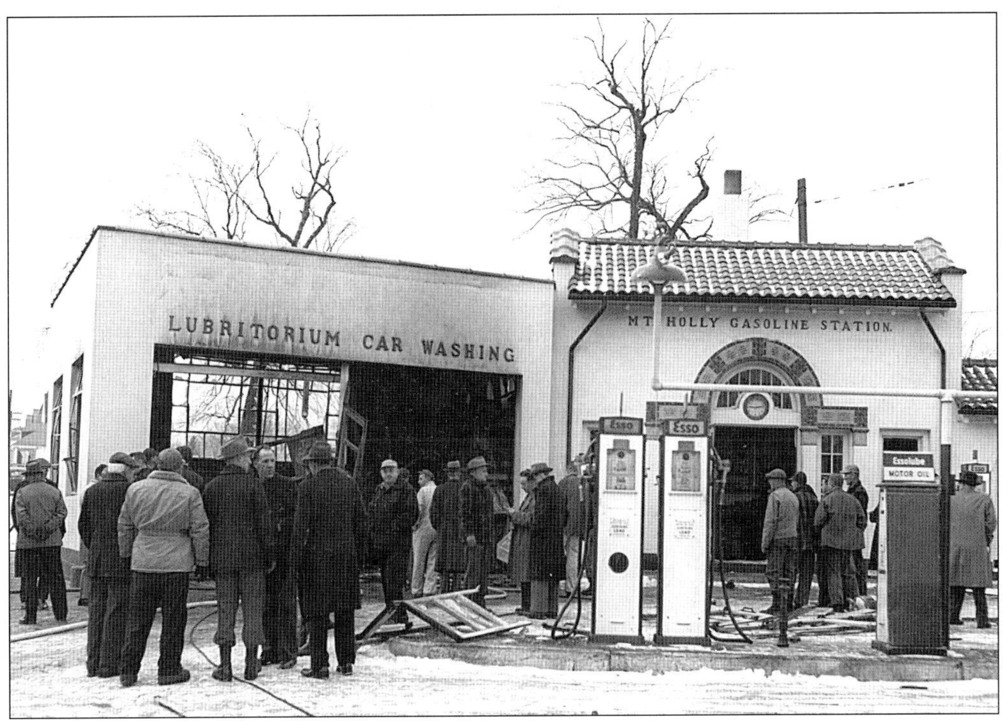

William A. Jones's Mount Holly gasoline station suffered damage during an unexpected explosion. This station was located at the corner of Madison Avenue and Washington Street, where the old Madison Hotel was located (see photographs on page 16). The blast sent doors and windows flying and bent the window frames outward (left side of building).

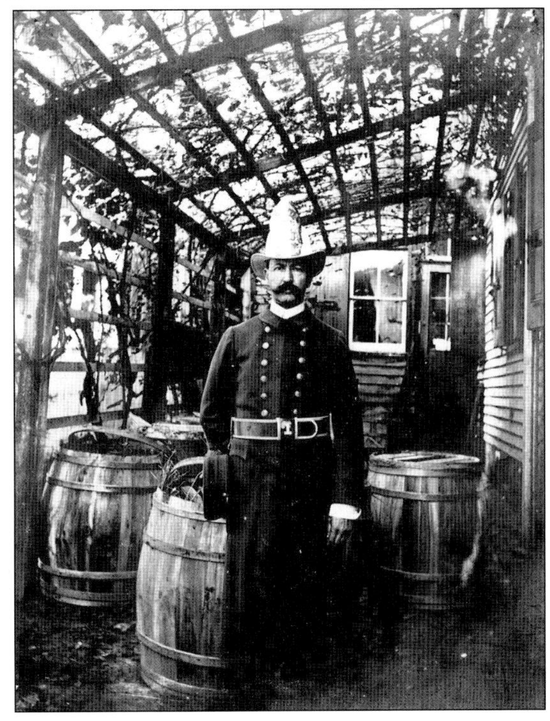

Joseph C. Cowgill was a member of the Relief Fire Company and was recognized as a town historian. He also built a three-story brick building on Main Street on the east side and operated a grocery store there. Joe Ward took this photograph.

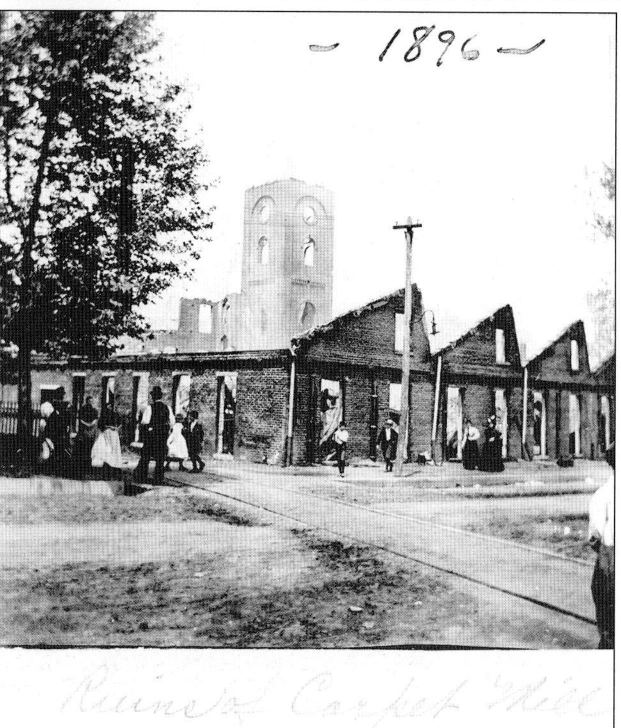

Mount Holly was once known for its thriving industry, including manufacturing plants, mills, hotels, and shops. This huge carpet factory was located on the corner of King and Washington Streets, thereby benefiting from Mount Holly's prime location for workers and train service. As the second photograph shows, this place was destroyed by fire in May 1896.

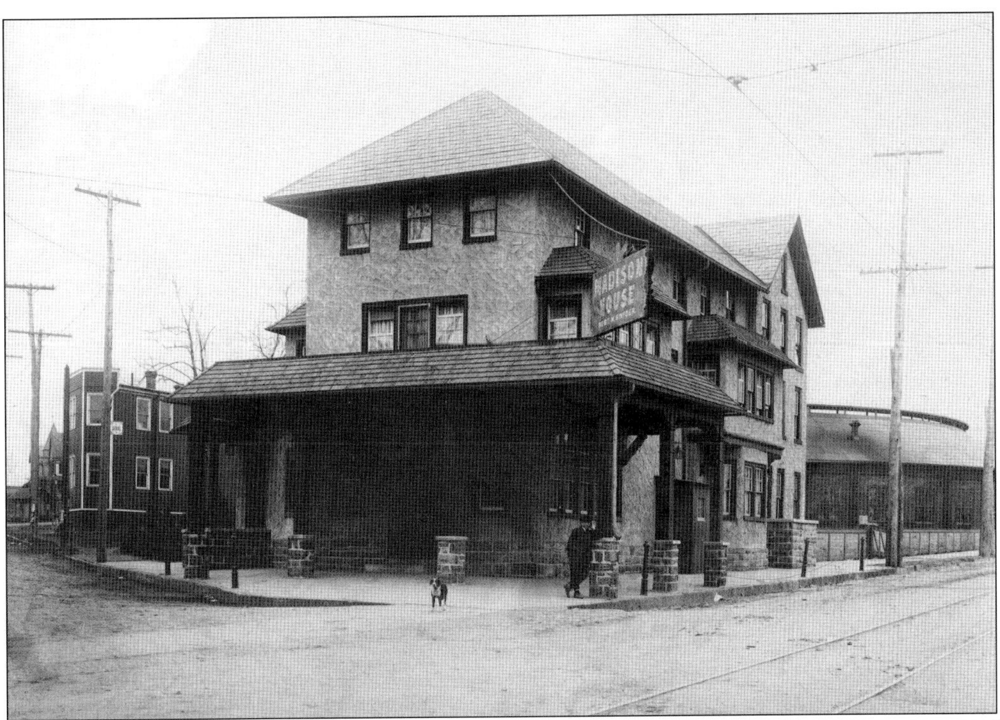

The Madison House Hotel (shown in ruins below) was located at the southwest corner of Madison Avenue and Washington Street. The photograph above was taken in 1914 before the gas explosion, which killed two people in 1916. After the debris was cleared, William Jones built the Mount Holly gas station (page 15), also the victim of an explosion. More recently, this lot has been the home of a Wawa Food Market and now houses various restaurants in a modern building.

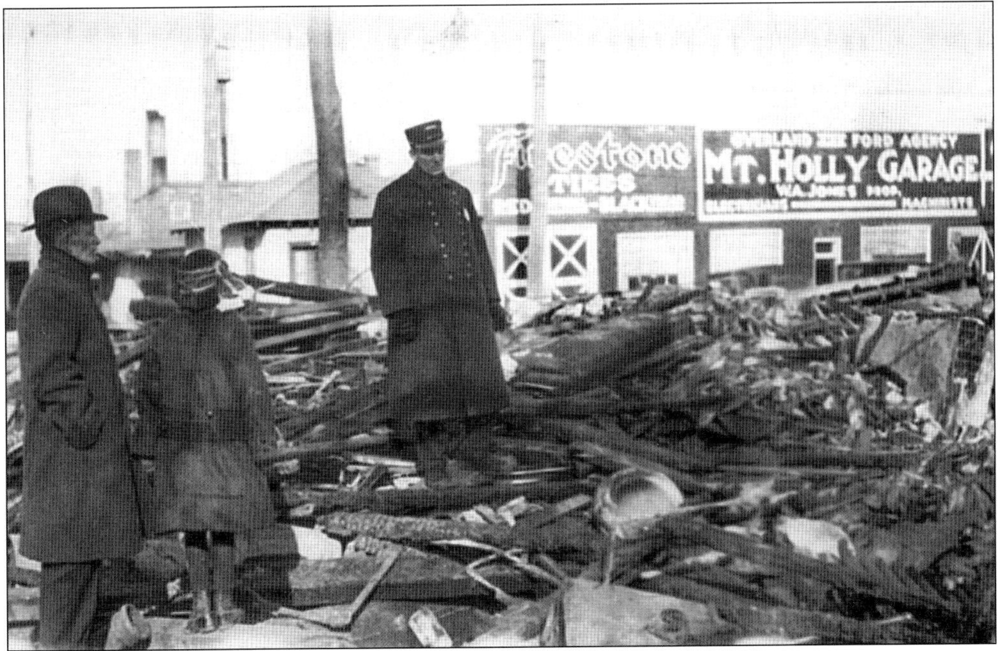

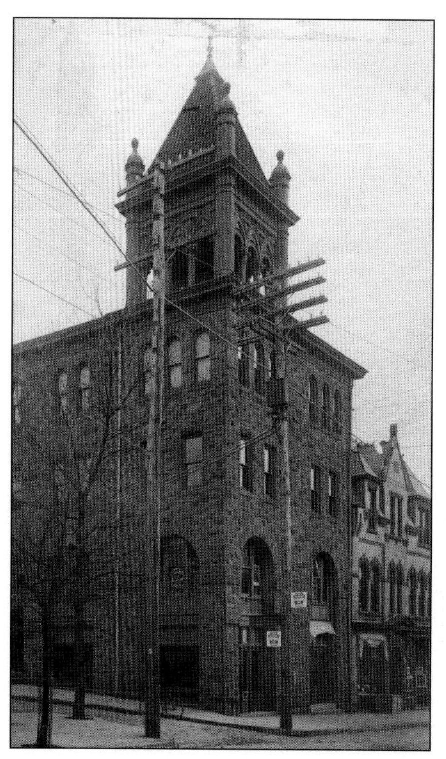

The Masonic Lodge was originally located on Water Street (now Rancocas Road) in a building once occupied by Thomas Butcher as a home. The Masons built a new hall with a brick front on Water Street and held meetings there until March 1887. This building was erected in 1891 of brownstone at the corner of Main Street and Brainerd Street. Unfortunately, the expense of building the place became excessive, and the Masons ended up as tenants instead of owners. It was destroyed by fire on January 28, 1925, despite attempts to put out the fire on that freezing day. The new Masonic Lodge was built in 1930 and stands on Garden Street.

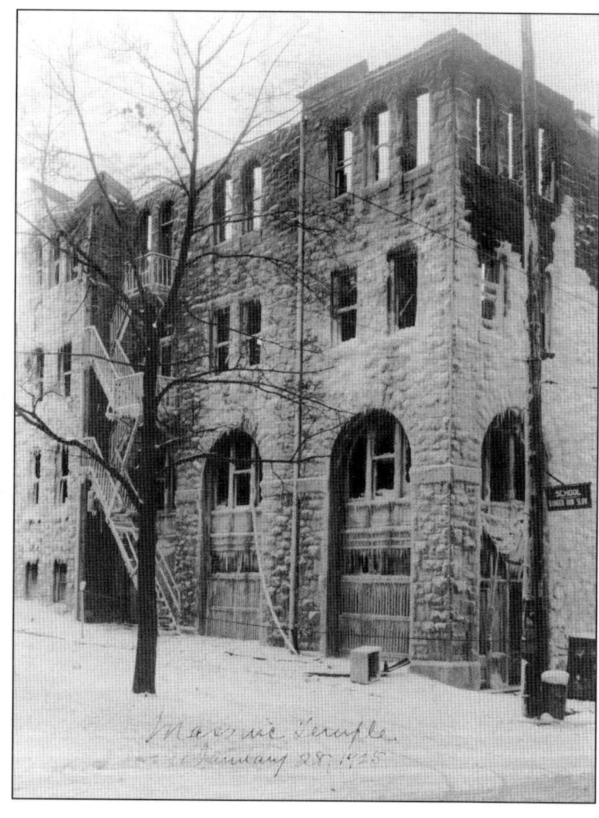

Two

Business, Commerce, and Government

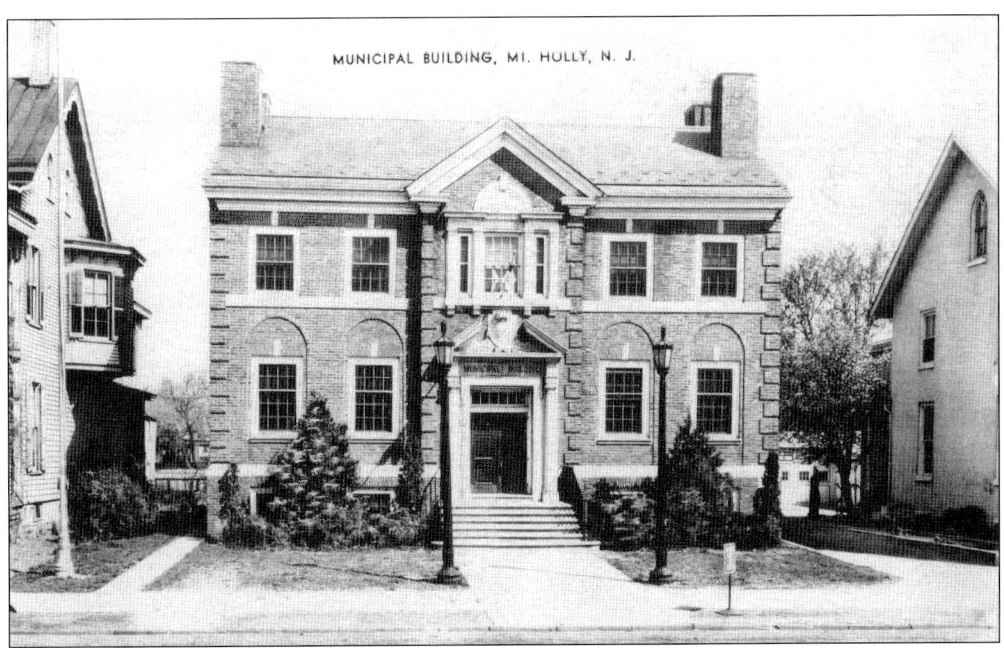

The Mount Holly Township Municipal Building, located at 23 Washington Street, was built in 1932. A rear addition was added in 1975. The building to the left is no longer extant, and a paved street now runs along the left of the municipal building. At one time, a wrought-iron fence was added and later removed. The old wooden front doors have been removed and replaced with painted metal with fake stained glass.

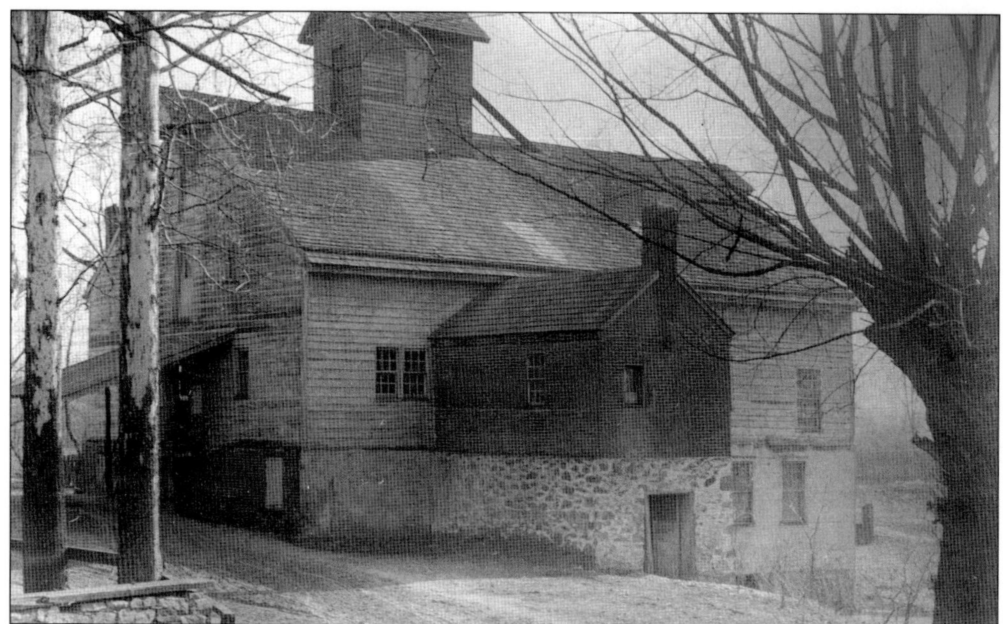

The first gristmill was built in 1723 by Edward Gaskill, James Lippincott, Abraham Bickley, and Samuel Brian. A second was built in 1735 and a third in 1796. All utilized the waterpower gained from the millrace, which had been hand dug by Edward Gaskill. The mill built in 1796 (by Richard Cox and Robert Davidson) was destroyed by fire in 1910. All of the mills were located near the millrace around the area of the current Mount Holly Water Company.

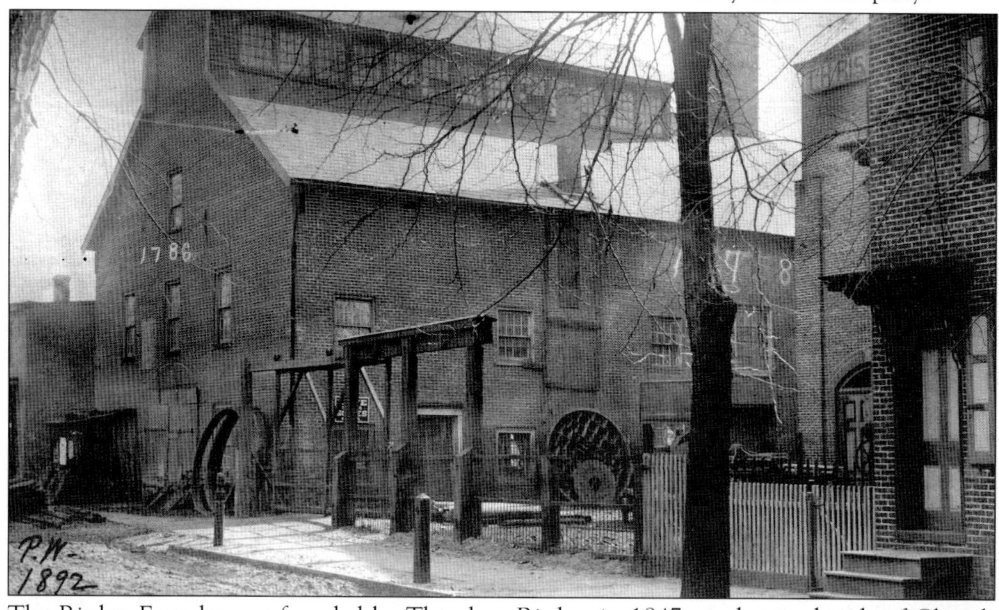

The Risdon Foundry was founded by Theodore Risdon in 1847 on the south side of Church Street; its original name was the Eagle Foundry Company. It began as a blacksmith shop in 1832 on Pine Street. The foundry received great praise for its turbine wheel design at the Centennial Exhibit in Philadelphia (1876). In the 1930s, it was used by the Roosevelt Cottages Company, which made outhouses for local farms. It later became Cooney's welding shop and was eventually demolished.

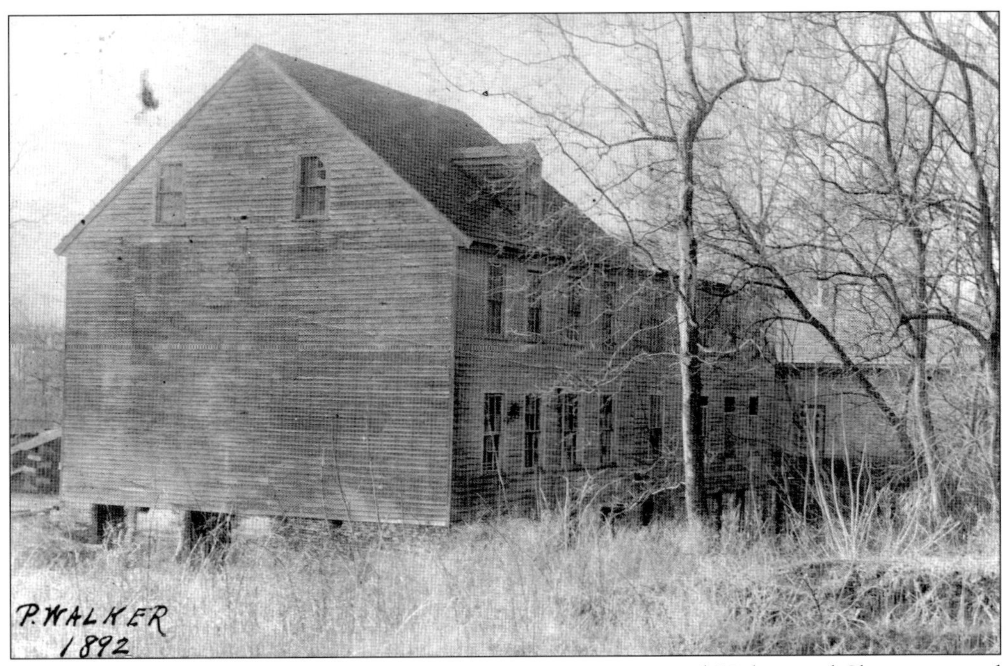

Semple's Cotton Mill was started here in 1856. Two men named Hulme and Shreve erected a building west of the Levis Mills near the site of the old gristmill. The Semple and Burnett Company manufactured cotton thread here and moved to a new building in 1867 on the northwest corner of Washington and King Streets. The Levis Mills were operated by Samuel T. Levis.

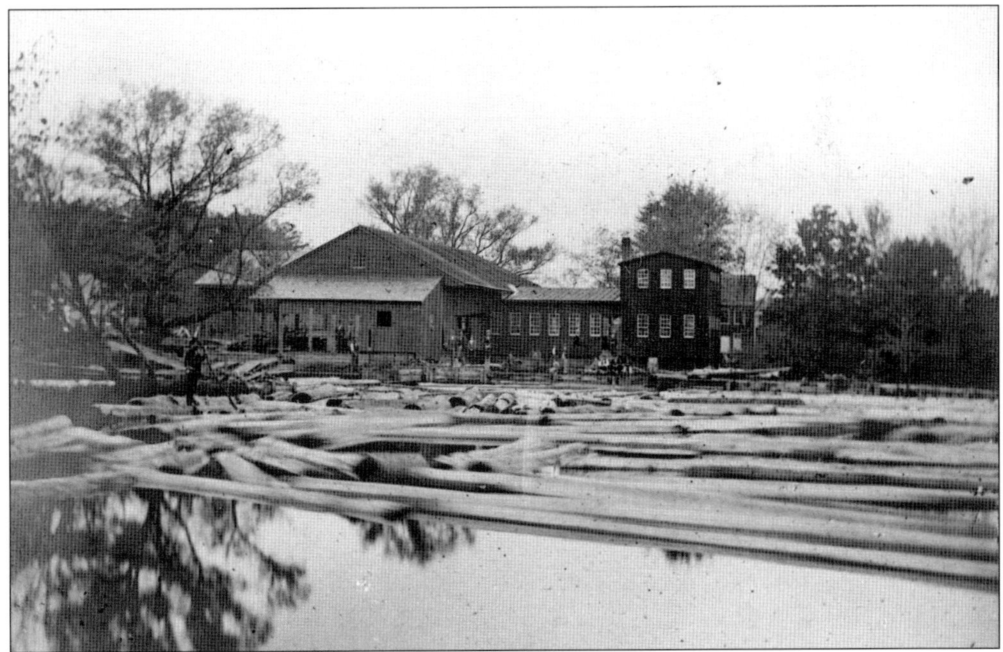
The old sawmill on Pine Street utilized the Rancocas Creek to move huge logs. This was one of the first industrial uses of waterpower and helped Mount Holly to develop its business base in the early 1700s.

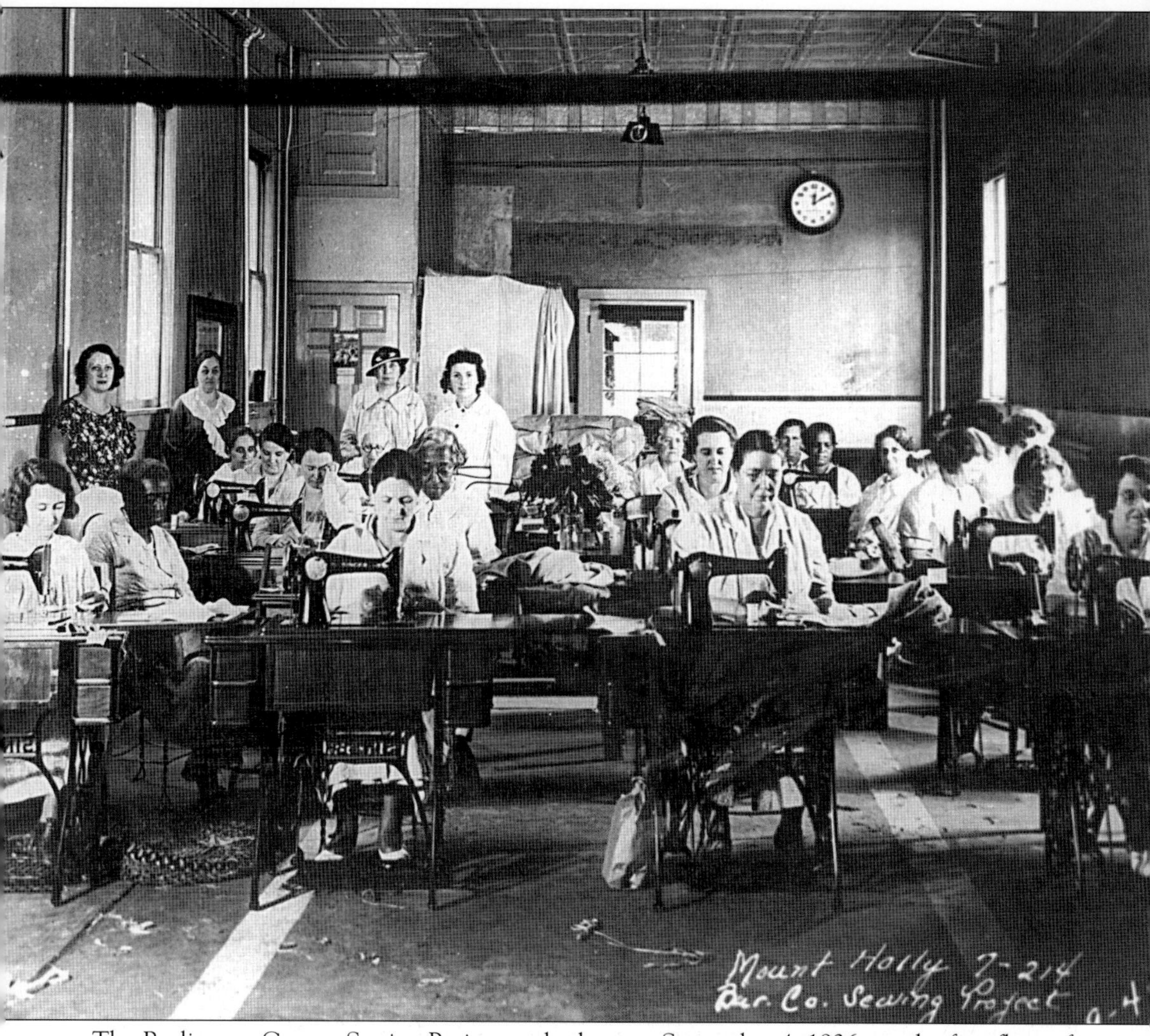

The Burlington County Sewing Project took place on September 4, 1936, on the first floor of the Union Fire Company on Mill Street. Shown from left to right are the following: (front row) unidentified, ? Webb, and two unidentified participants; (second row) two unidentified participants, ? Frake, and ? Baker; (third row) all unidentified; (fourth row) Ann Faile and two unidentified participants; (fifth row, standing in rear) ? Keley, Miriam Green, ? Gauntt, and Ann Lee.

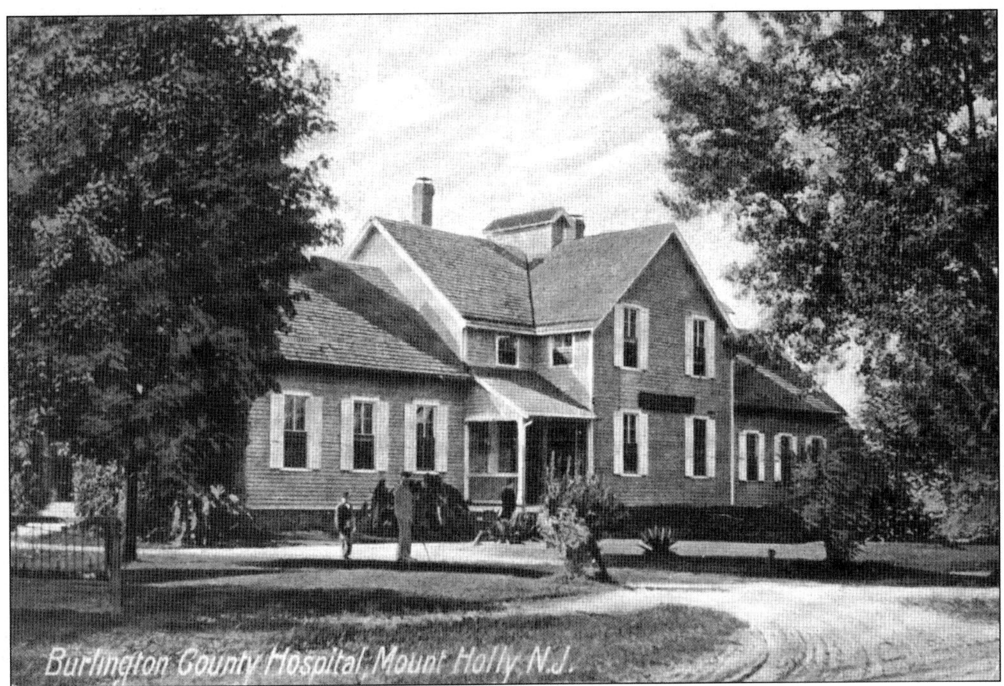

The Burlington County Hospital was originally located on Mount Holly Avenue. The postcard shows a small structure that was built later on the west side of Madison Avenue. Eventually this building too was outgrown and the larger structure was built on the opposite side of Madison Avenue, where the hospital still stands (and continues to grow) today.

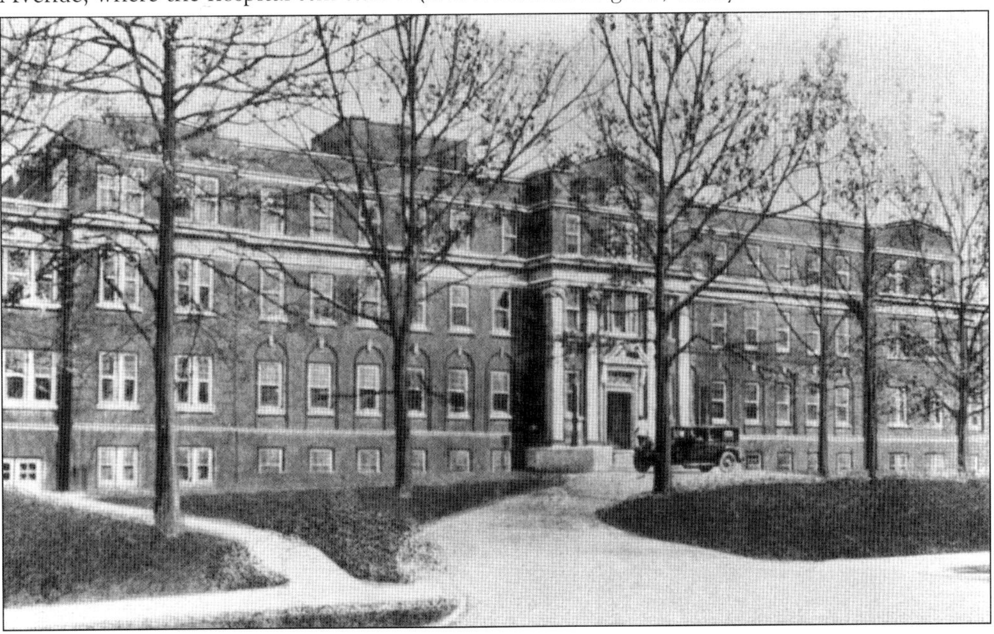

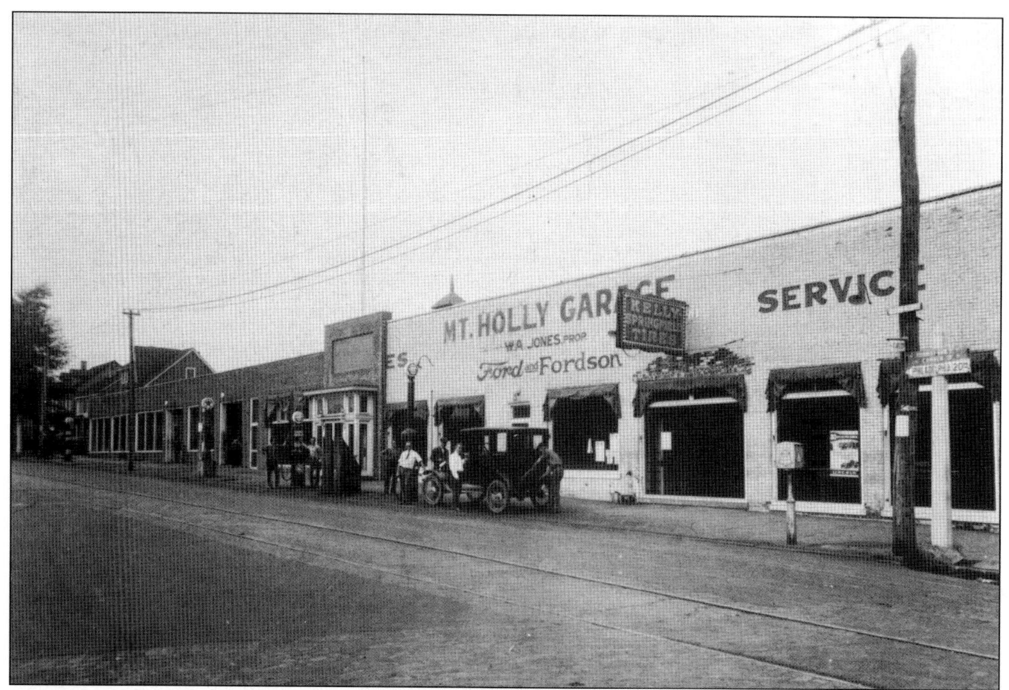

The Mount Holly Garage, located at the corner of Washington and King Streets, was founded and built by William A. Jones in 1912. After Jones died in 1940, it was operated by Charles Miller, John Archer, and Eckard Cox. After Cox's death in 1958, it was operated by Miller, who continued the business after moving to a larger location on Route 38 in Mount Holly, where Miller Ford still operates today.

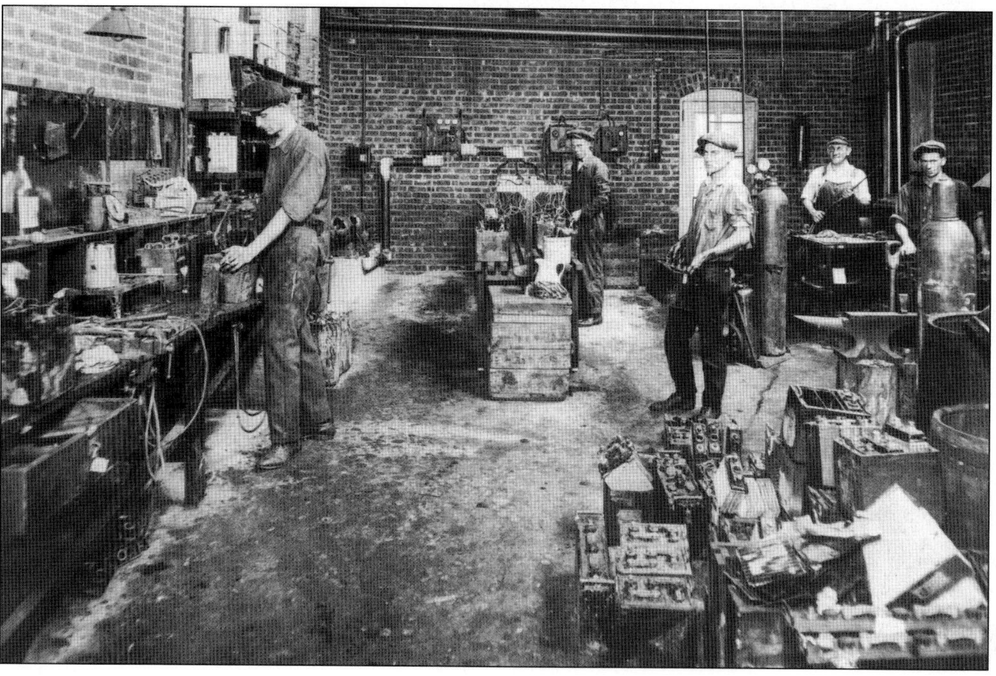

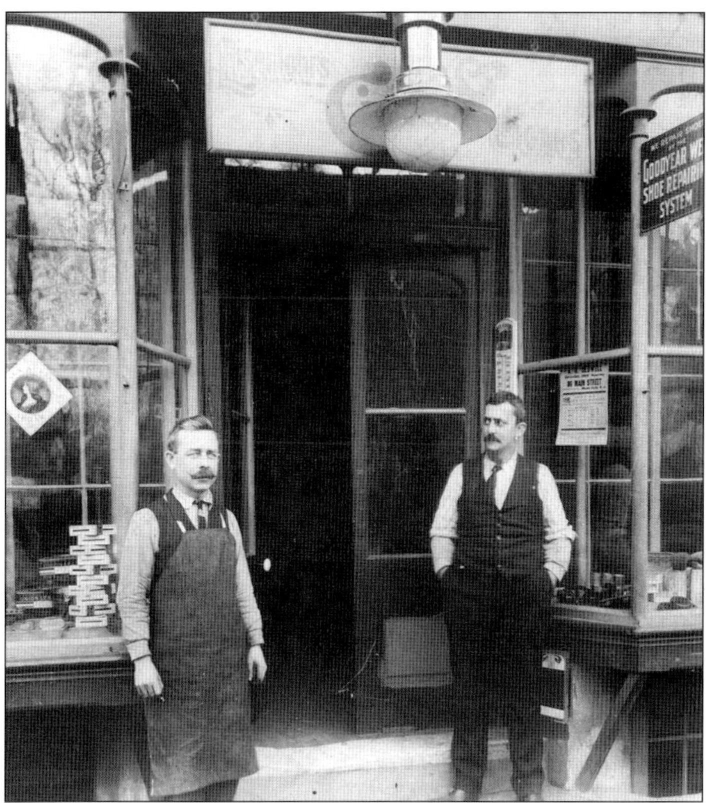

Andrew Roderick Bedwell and Edward McKenna stand in front of 86 Main Street. Here, McKenna operated a shoe repair shop on the right side and Bedwell sold cigars on the left. This building was owned by Bedwell from 1901 to 1928. It was sold to Roland Warrick in 1928 and then to Albert Leverich. Although this building still stands today, it has lost some of its original character.

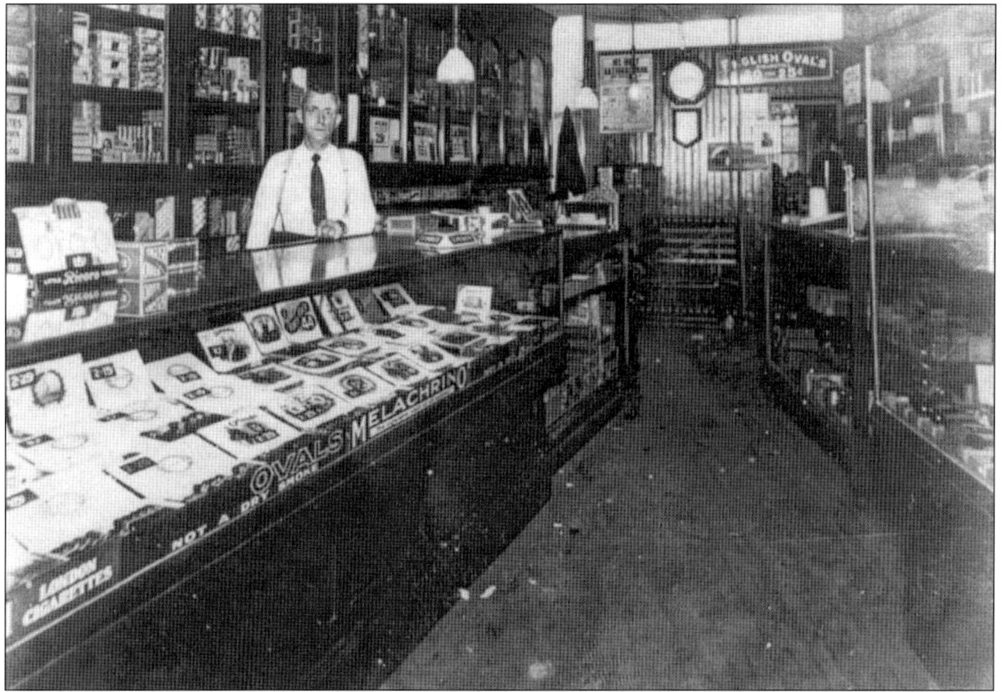

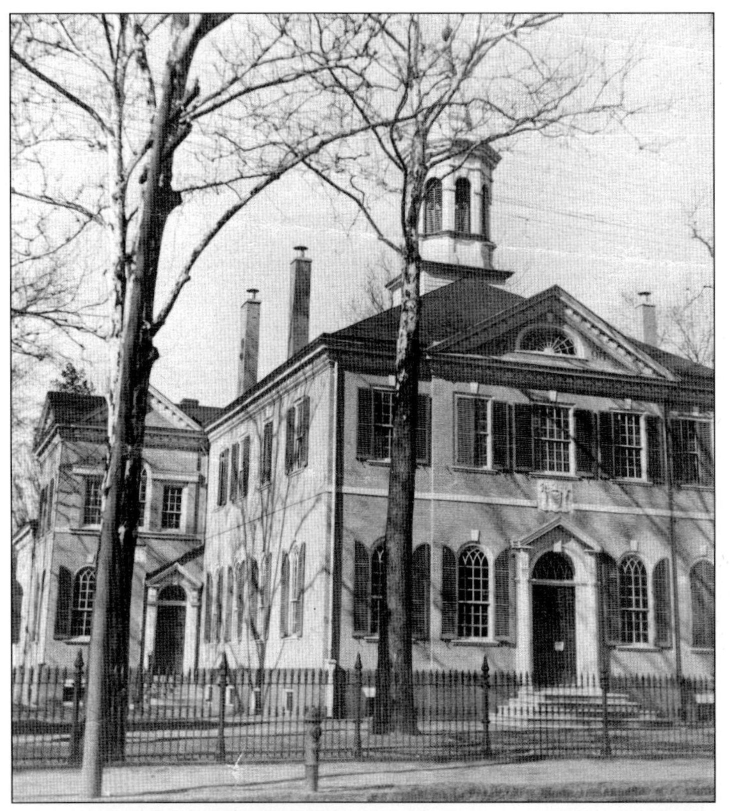

The Burlington County Court House was erected in 1796 on Main Street. Samuel Lewis, a prominent architect from Philadelphia, designed this building, noted as one of the finest examples of Colonial architecture in existence. The marble coat of arms of New Jersey over the entrance was a gift from Isaac Hazelhurst. This building has been beautifully preserved (although the wrought-iron fencing is no longer there) and is still actively used as a courthouse today.

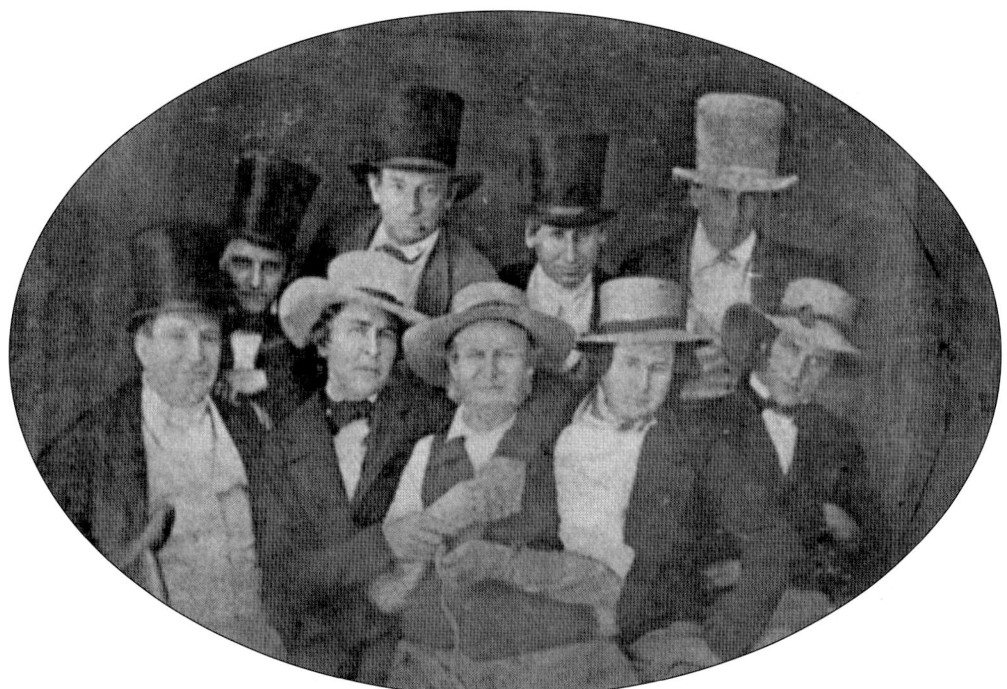

Shown in 1848 or 1849 are members of the Committee of Arrangements of the Burlington County Agricultural Society. They are, from left to right, as follows: (front row) Benjamin Buckman, Samuel A. Dobbins, Thomas J. Sutter, James Lippincott, and Barclay White; (back row) Charles H. Hollingshead, Samuel Bullock, Shreve Shinn, and Thomas Hancock.

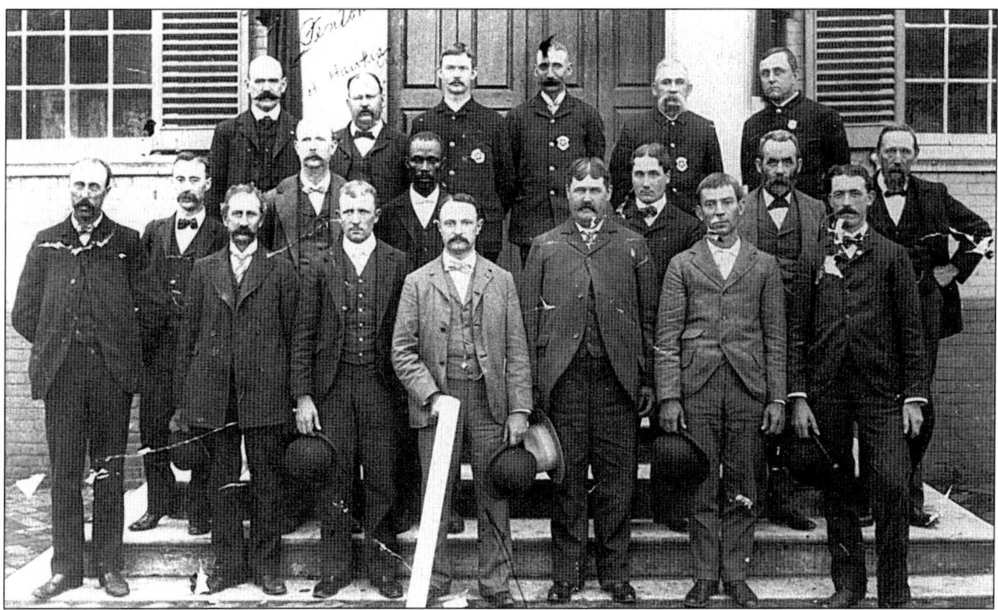

The Board of Chosen Freeholders operated Burlington County in the past as they do today. This photograph shows an early group of freeholders and possibly the sheriff's officers. The man on the far left in the back row is Sheriff Fenton. They are standing on the steps of the Burlington County Court House.

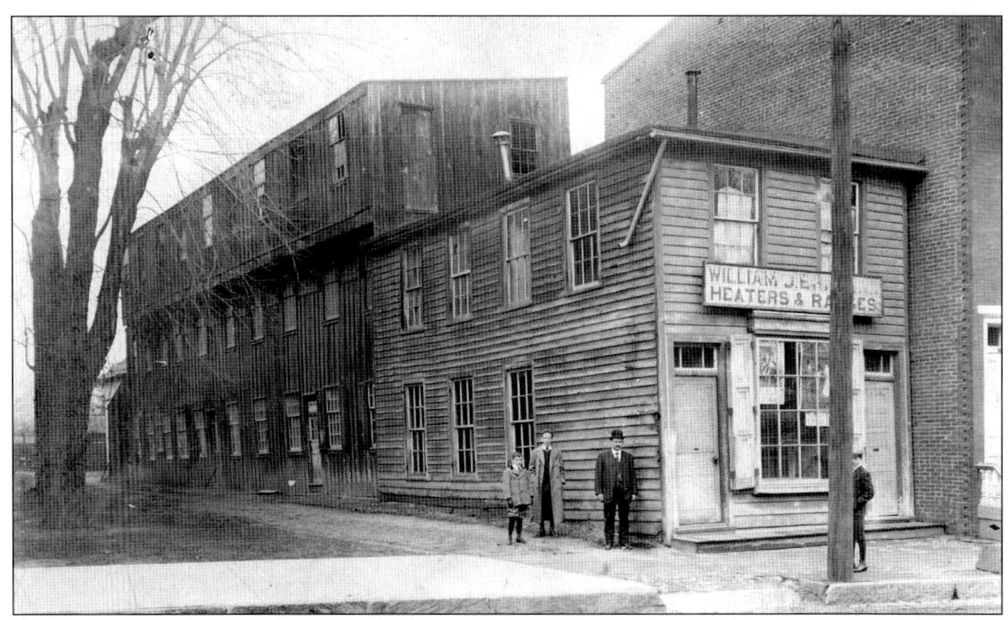

This building was located on Main Street on a narrow lot just to the east side of the current St. Andrew's Church. The lot was owned by Samuel J. Read and connected to his home on Garden Street at the rear. A blacksmith shop kept by William Fairholm, Thomas Allen, and David Hults occupied a portion. Eventually Thomas F. Keeler purchased the property, built a log frame shop, and manufactured furniture. The property became William J. Brannan's tinware and roofing store and later the site of the Zelley building. It is now the location of 117–119 High Street.

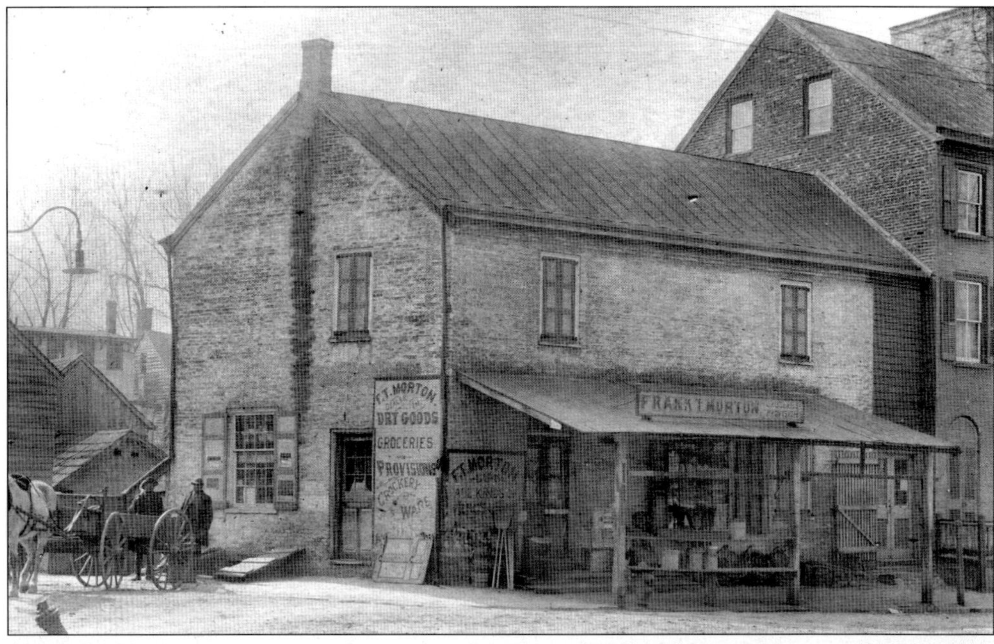

This is Frank Morton's store on the southwest corner of Mill and Pine Streets in 1892. As with many other stores, it was common to see roofs over the sidewalk to display wares outside but out of the weather.

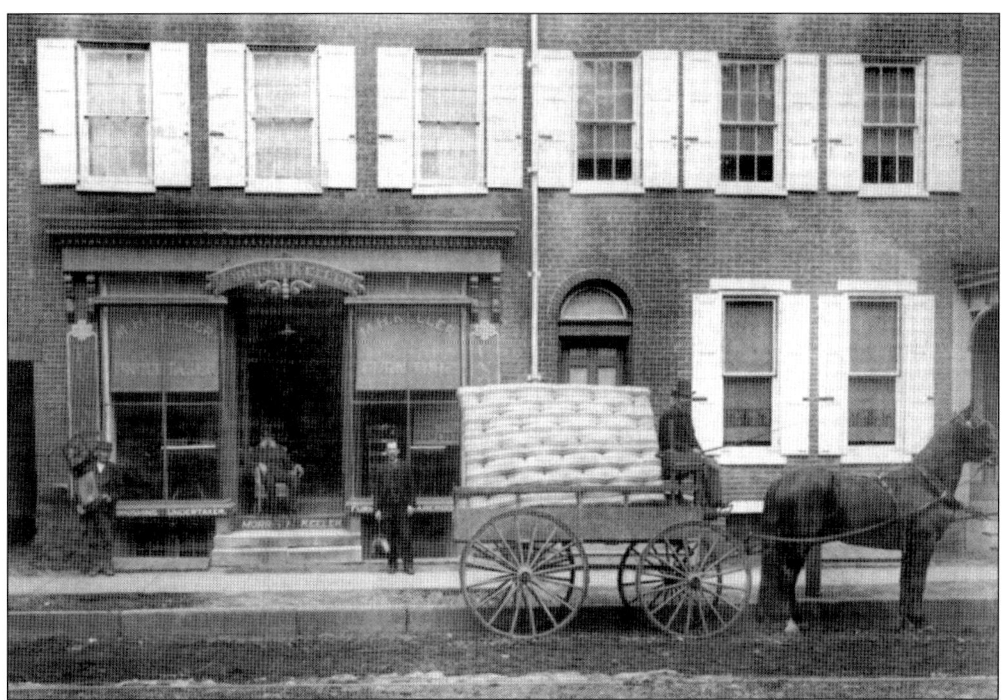

Morris Keeler was an undertaker here on Main Street. One can only assume that items being hauled away are from the estate of the deceased.

George D. Worrell operated a plumbing store and business here at the corner of Mill and Pine Streets. In addition to being a plumber, he was one of seven Bell Telephone subscribers in 1895.

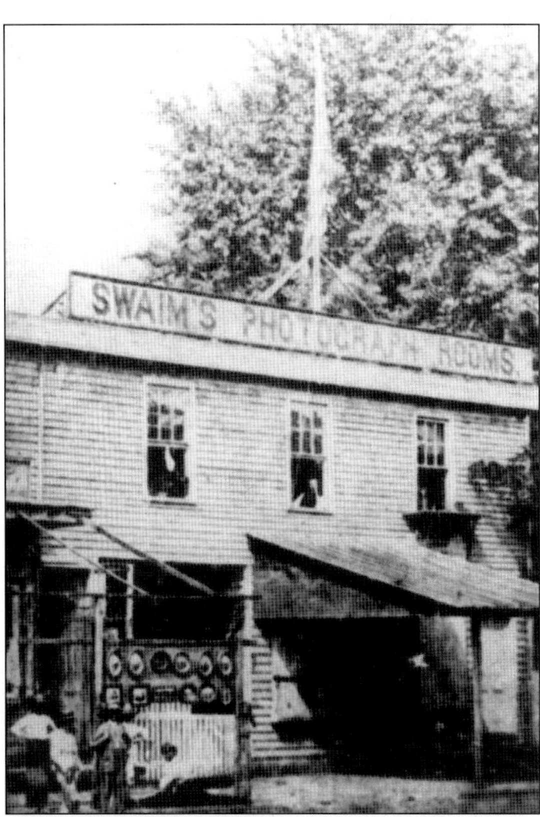

Swaim's was located on Mill Street just around the corner from the Union National Bank.

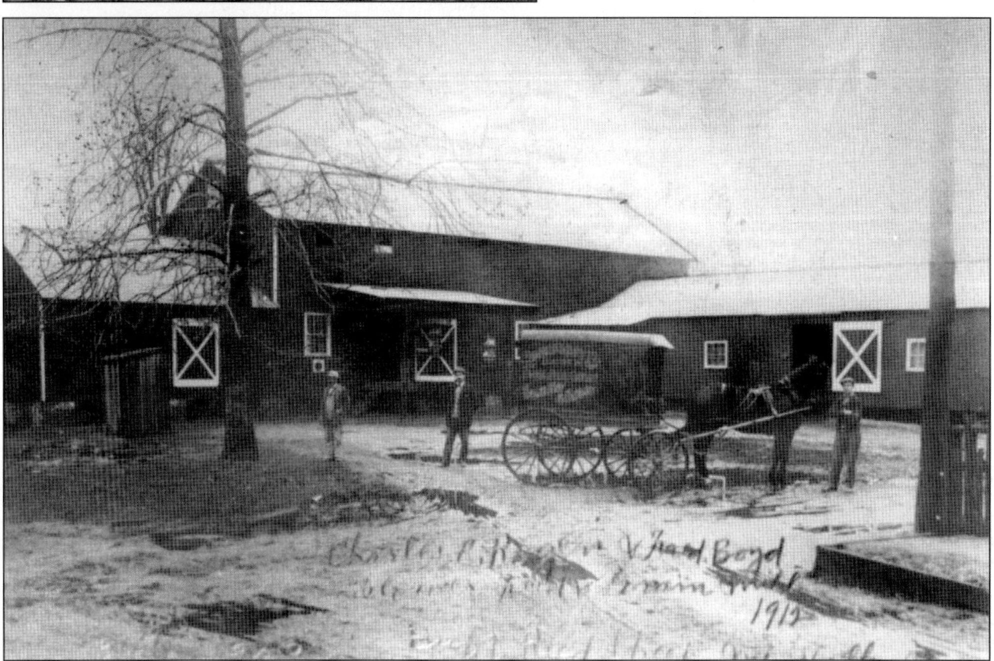

The feed mill at Budd and Reed Streets just off Bispham is seen in 1912. Charles E. Rogers and Fred Boyd operated the feed mill, selling flowers, seeds, and grain in the building built by Harry C. Allen in 1909.

This building was located on Buttonwood Street near the Buttonwood Run (waterway) on the east side. Deering Harvesting Machinery was operated out of this building, a company that also sold animal bone fertilizers at Baugh's fertilizer store. The sign outside the front door indicates that they had a telephone.

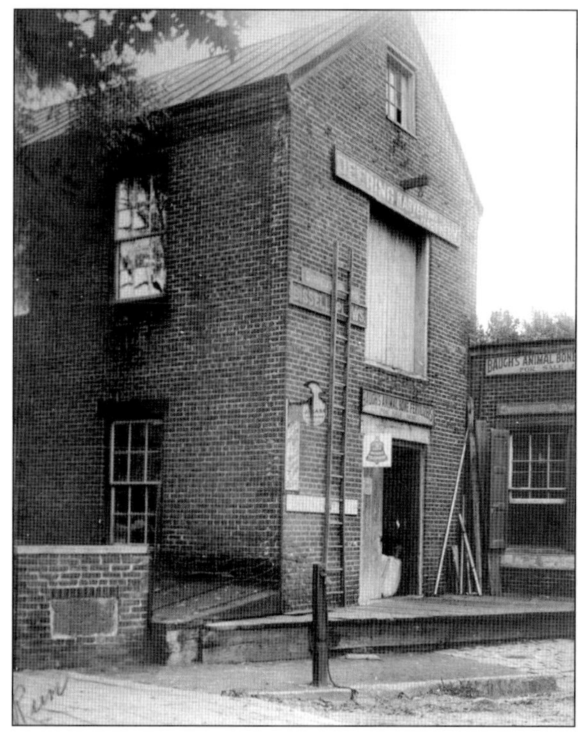

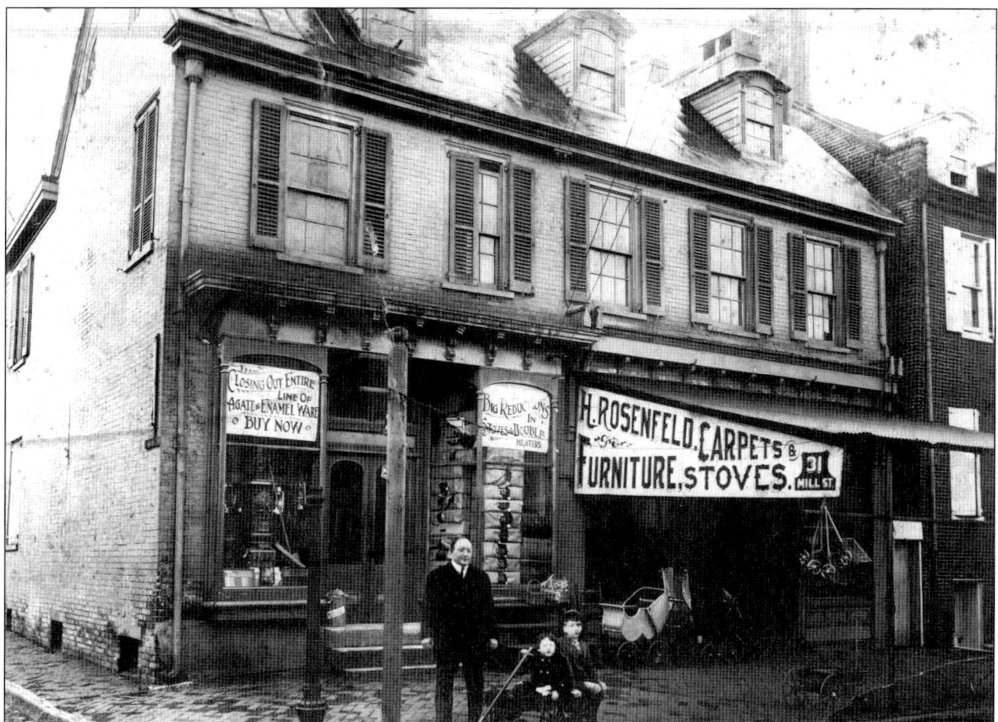

This building is located at 29 Mill Street. Ike Rosenfeld operated a store here from 1930 until 1935. Rosenfeld is standing out front. Notice the old sale signs in the window for Agate enamelware, stoves, and double heaters.

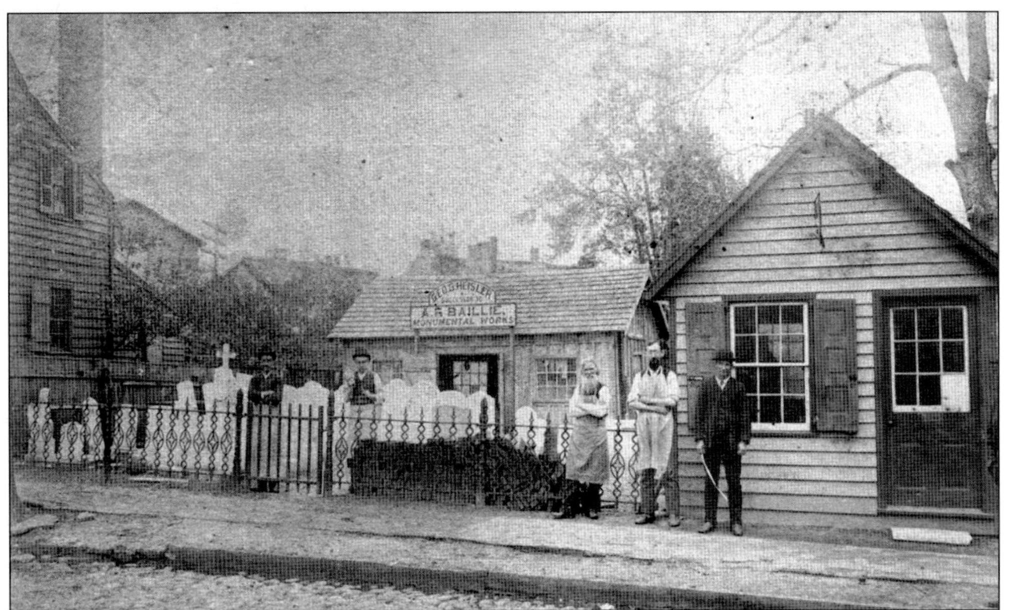

Located on Water Street, the marble works of Joseph Shaffer, Alexander F. Baillie, and George Heisler manufactured gravestones. Thomas D. Neal established the marble yard. He later sold it to a Mr. Reeder from Lambertville, who was succeeded by Shaffer, Baillie, and Heisler in 1870. The marble works is long gone and there is now a bank at this location (Summit/Fleet).

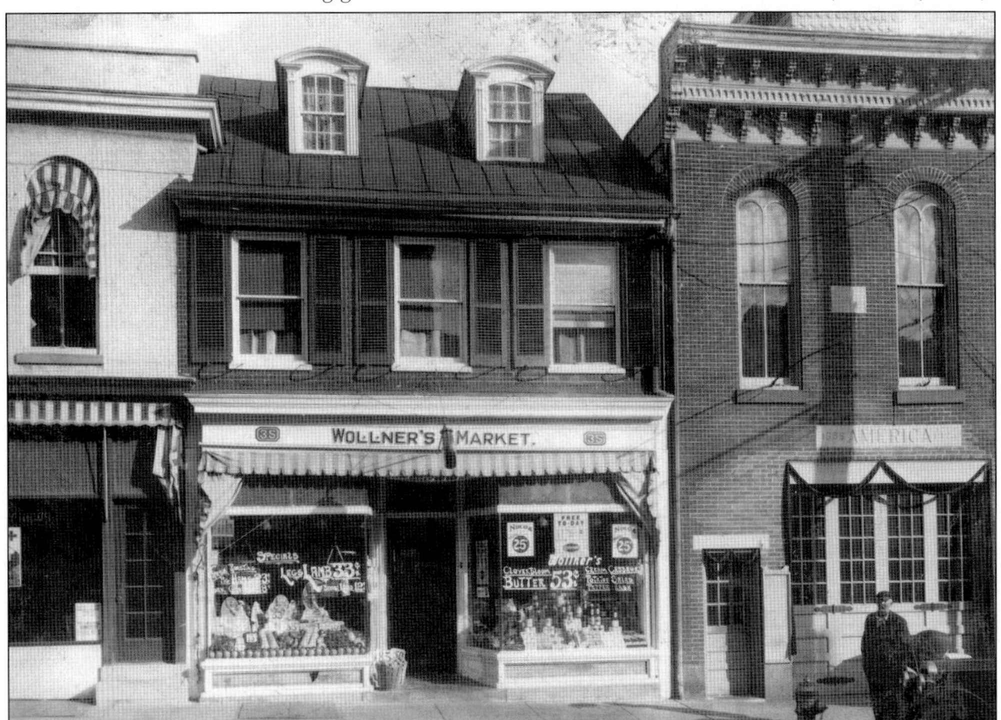

Wollner's Market was a classic main street grocery well loved by Mount Holly residents. You could get just about anything you might need to cook a great meal here, such as freshly cut meats and produce. Notice the old American Firehouse next door at 33 Main Street.

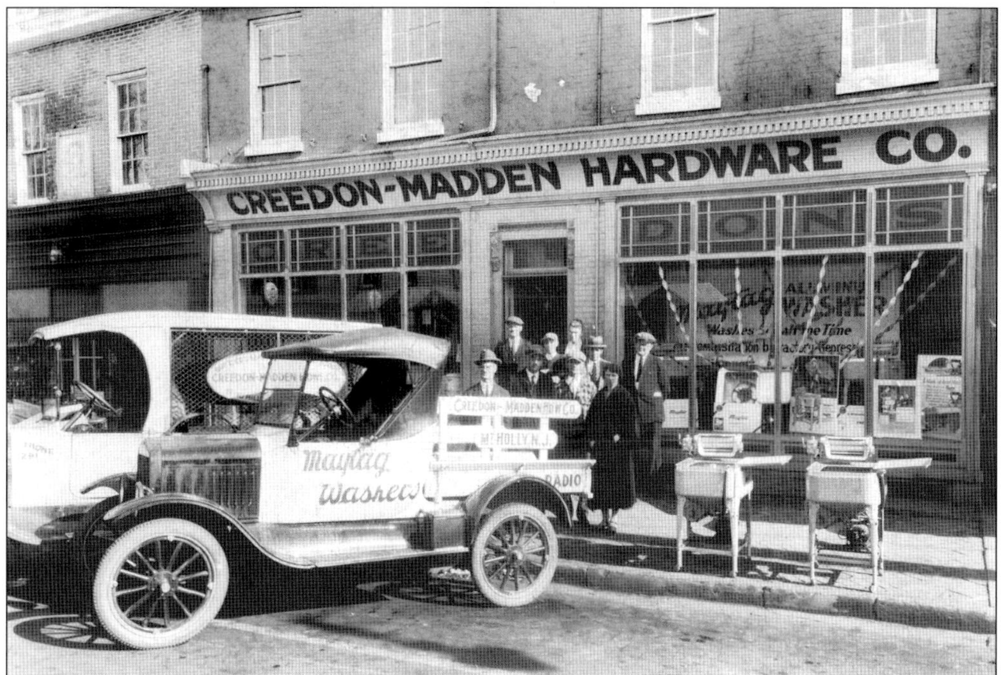

The Creedon-Madden Hardware Company has been a mainstay in Mount Holly for a lifetime. This photograph was taken in the 1920s with the staff, washing machines, and delivery truck out front. Today, Madden's Hardware still exists; however, it is struggling to compete with the larger megastores on the outskirts of town.

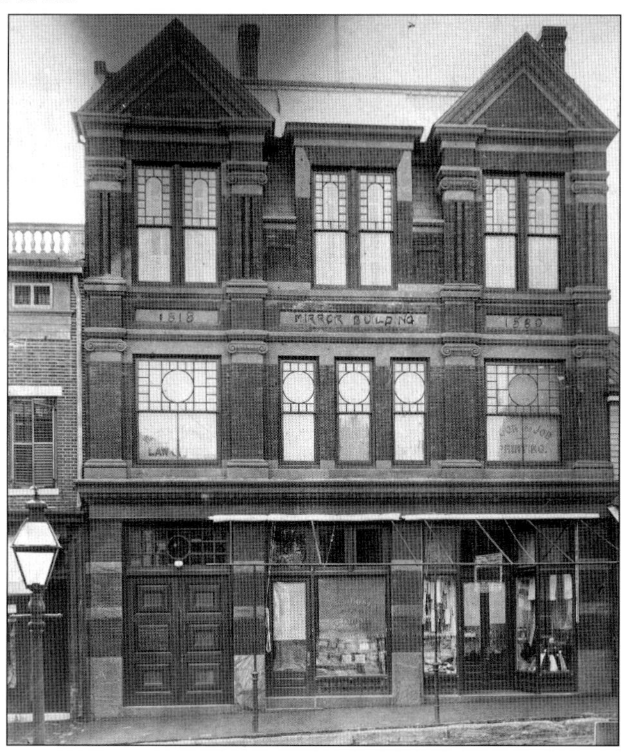

The Mirror Building was located on the west side of Main Street and housed a variety of businesses, including law offices, a print shop, and the New Jersey Mirror offices. Nathan Palmer & Sons established the *New Jersey Mirror* in September 1818 as the *Burlington Mirror* and changed its name a year later. The newspaper favored the Republican party and was one of four weekly newspapers in Mount Holly.

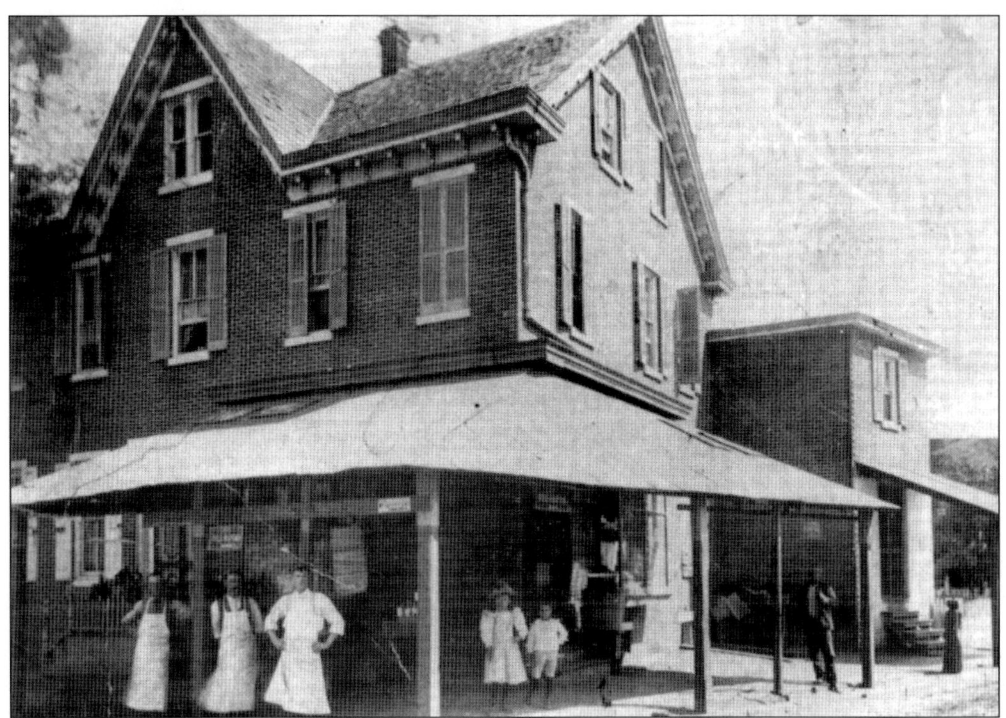

Cooney's Market was located at the southeast corner of King and Water Streets . This building was demolished, and the area became part of French's Lumberyard. It is now the Center Stage Antique Shop parking lot.

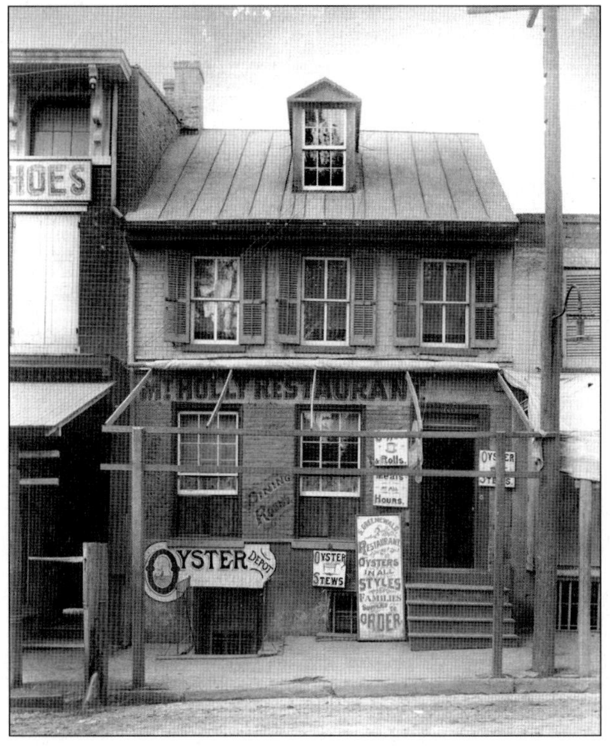

The Mount Holly Restaurant, or Samuel Greenwald Restaurant, was located opposite Brainerd Street on Main Street. Oysters were very popular and were harvested in New Jersey to supply the many Mount Holly restaurants specializing in oyster dishes.

The Fleischmann's Yeast truck is shown making a delivery to Albert Mayer, seen at the side of the truck. Mayer's Bakery was located at 2 Washington Street, at the corner of White and Washington Streets at Fountain Square. Mayer's also sold soda and ice cream while in operation during the early 20th century. Today, Mayer's Bakery is the Robin's Nest Bakery and Restaurant and has been restored very much like it was in Albert Mayer's time.

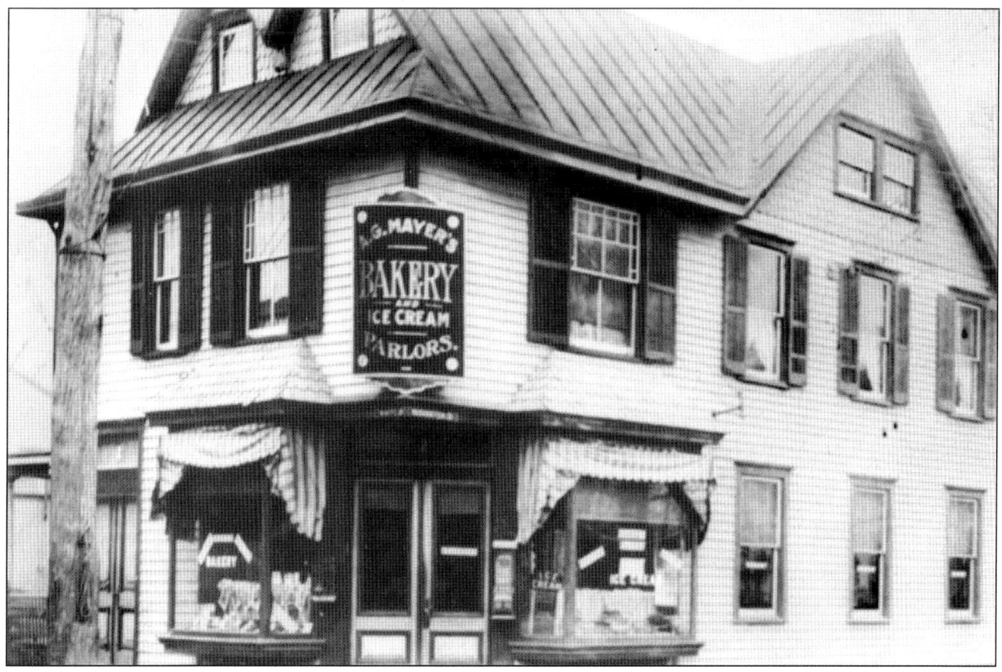

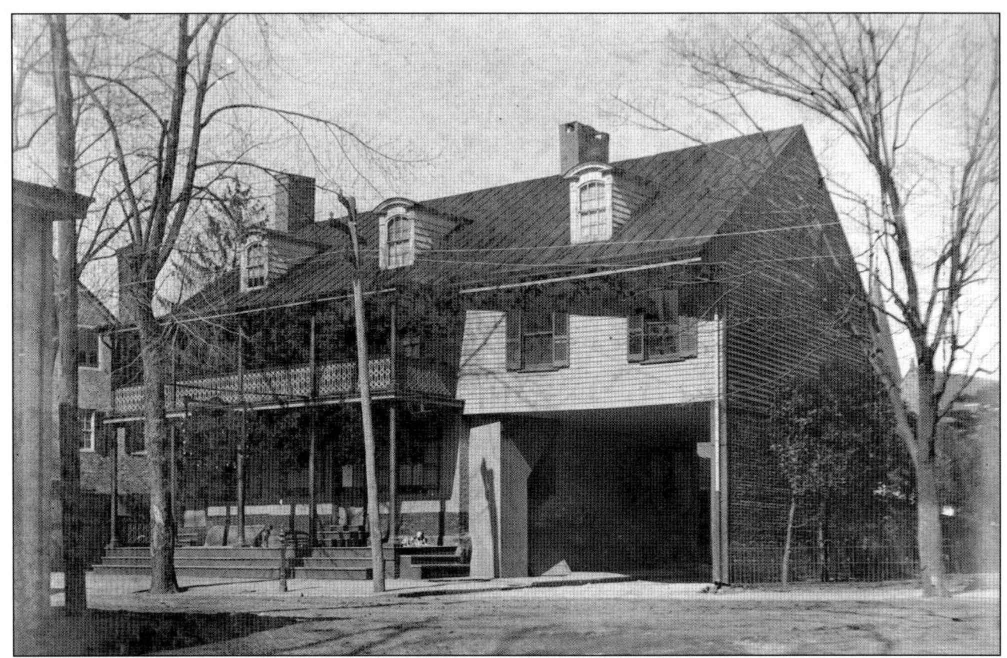

Perhaps one of the most interesting buildings in Mount Holly, the Mill Street Hotel was built c. 1723 and has been in continuous use as a hotel and tavern since the doors first opened. John Woolman visited there, and Sir Henry Clinton's Red Coats occupied the building. Handbills for runaway slaves were posted here. The hotel has known many owners over the years and is commonly called the Bucket of Blood or Three Tuns Tavern by locals.

These buildings on Main Street are now known as 19-21 High Street. The buildings are occupied by Don's Barbershop, Friants Store, and the old Heritage building (right). Notice the stone street and trolley line.

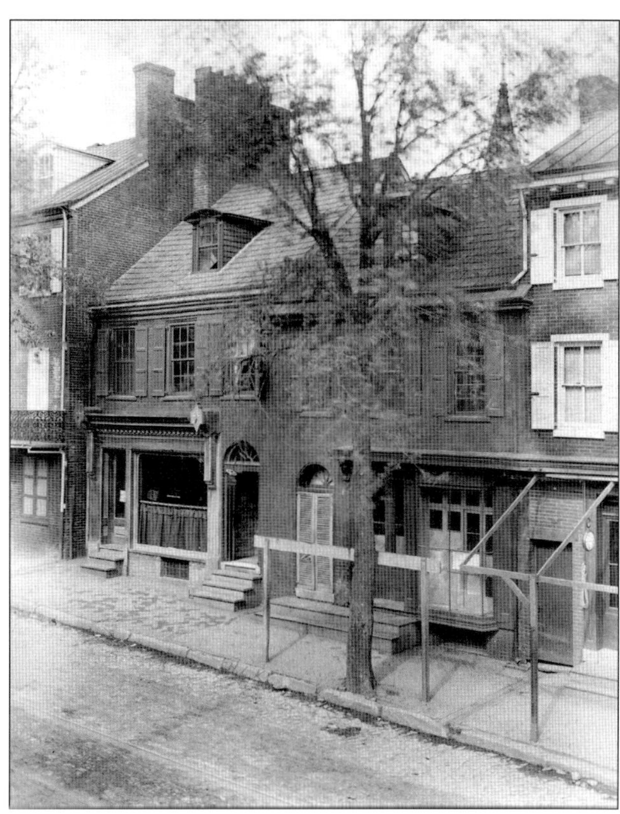

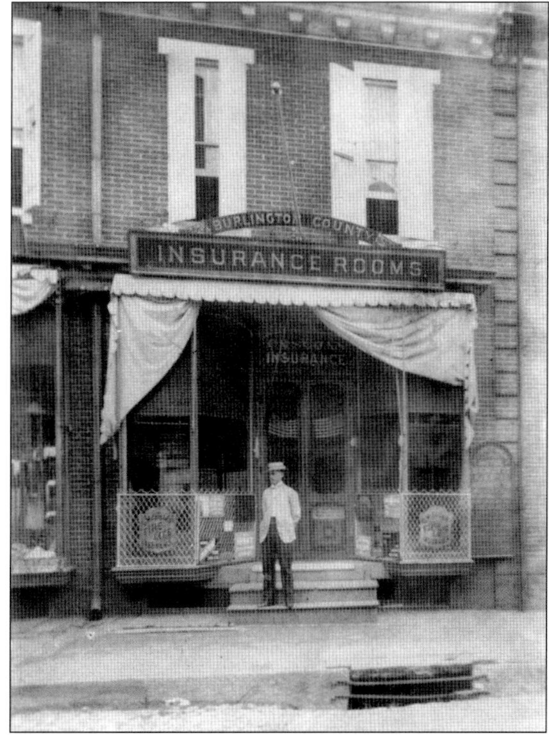

The building at 40 Main Street was occupied by the Burlington County Insurance Room business, operated by Charles M. Sloan. Sloan had formerly operated an insurance business on Arcade Row, built *c.* 1859.

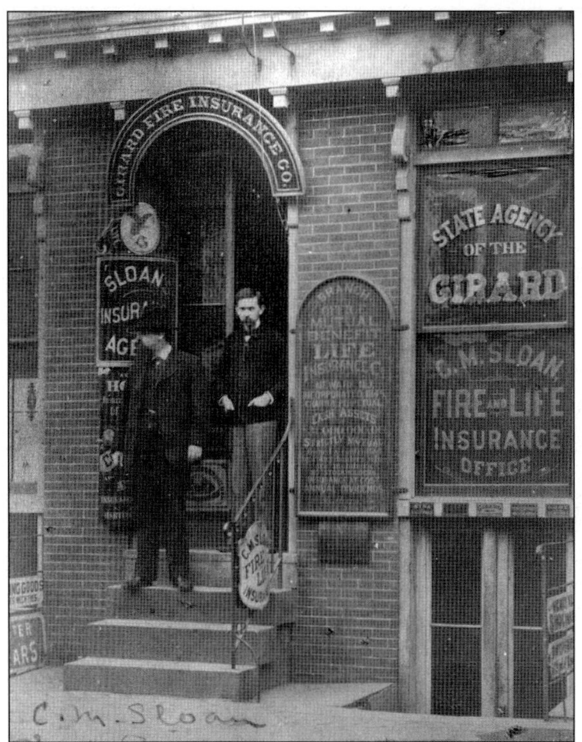

The Arcade Hotel had many businesses housed in this grand place. The Girard Fire Insurance Company, C.M. Sloan Life Insurance office, a cobbler (shoemaker), and an oyster cellar in the basement are located here. The two fellows in front are C.M. Sloan and W.C. Lawrence.

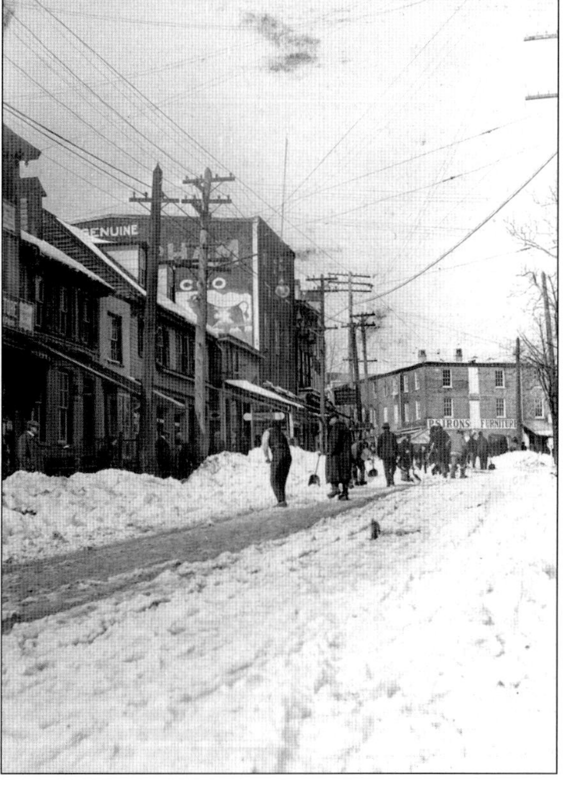

A severe snowstorm dumped lots of white stuff on Main Street on March 1, 1914. Note the teamwork required to get the snow cleared. Philip S. Irons furniture store is to the north on the corner of Garden and Main where the cobbler shop stands today. Note too the advertisements painted directly on the tall brick building on the left.

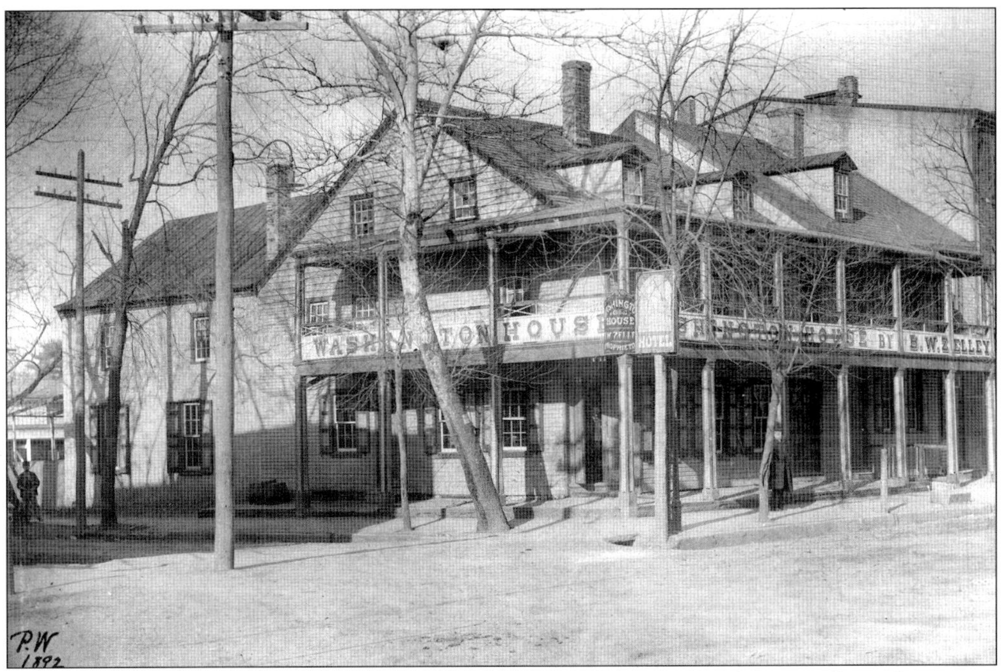

The Washington House, on the corner of Main and Water Streets, has transformed in many ways over the years. Richard Lamb purchased the tavern in 1904, demolished the landmark in 1910, and built the brick structure that still stands today. The Lamb family continued to operate the hotel as the Washington House until 1953. Since there was a Western Union Telegraph office next door and it was just down the street from the county courthouse, many reporters stayed and reported from here, including those covering the Lindbergh kidnapping trial.

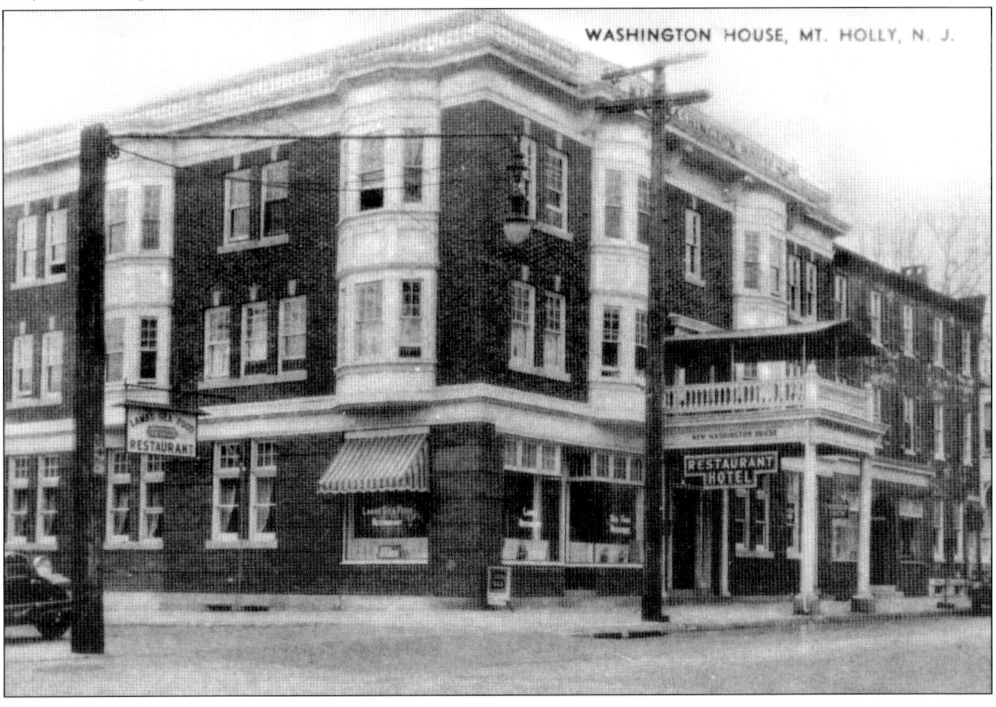

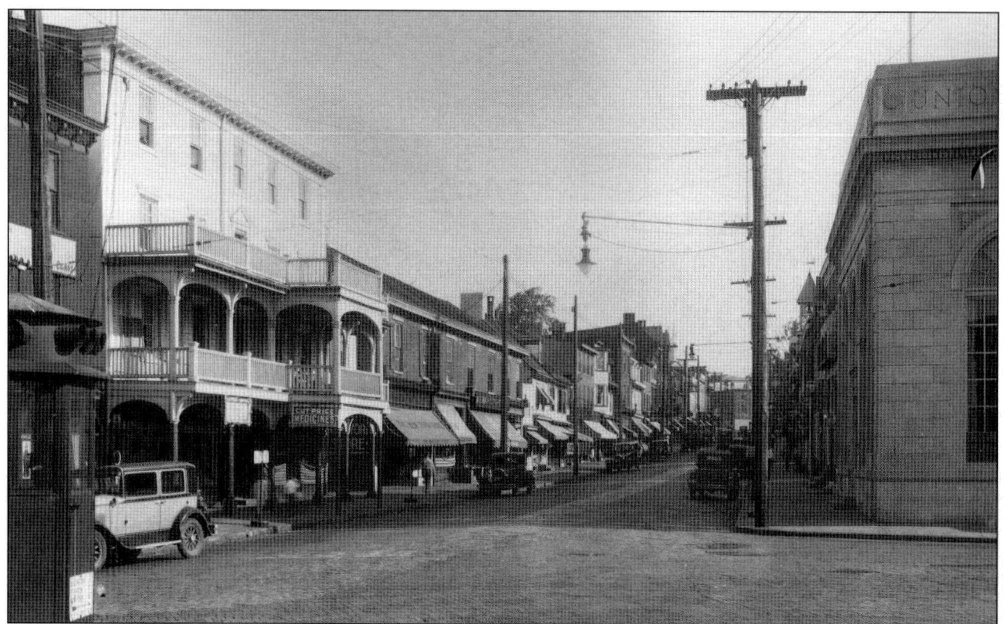

In this scene looking north up High Street are an abundance of interesting features, starting with the police box (left) in the center of Fountain Square and then the Arcade Hotel, with its large balconies over the sidewalk, where a parking lot exists today. The permanent covers over the sidewalks have turned into retractable awnings and the Union National Bank has been greatly altered from its earlier look with a corner entrance.

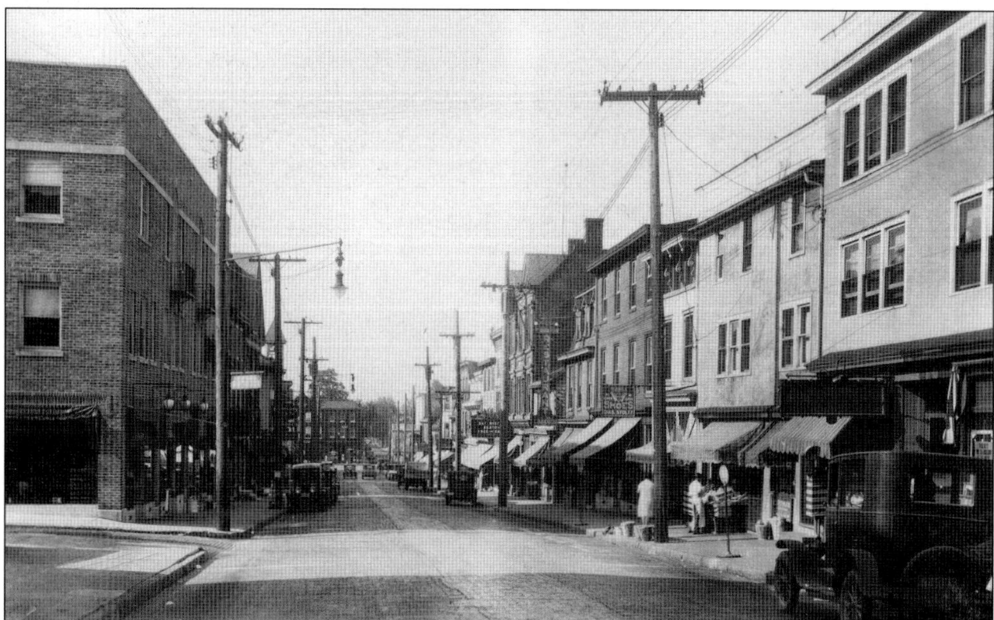

In this view looking down High Street are trolley tracks that have been paved over and plenty of vehicles lining the streets. Although the downtown facade has sometimes changed for the worse through urban renewal mistakes and building enhancements that have ruined the original character, some changes, such as the installation of underground utilities, are a true enhancement.

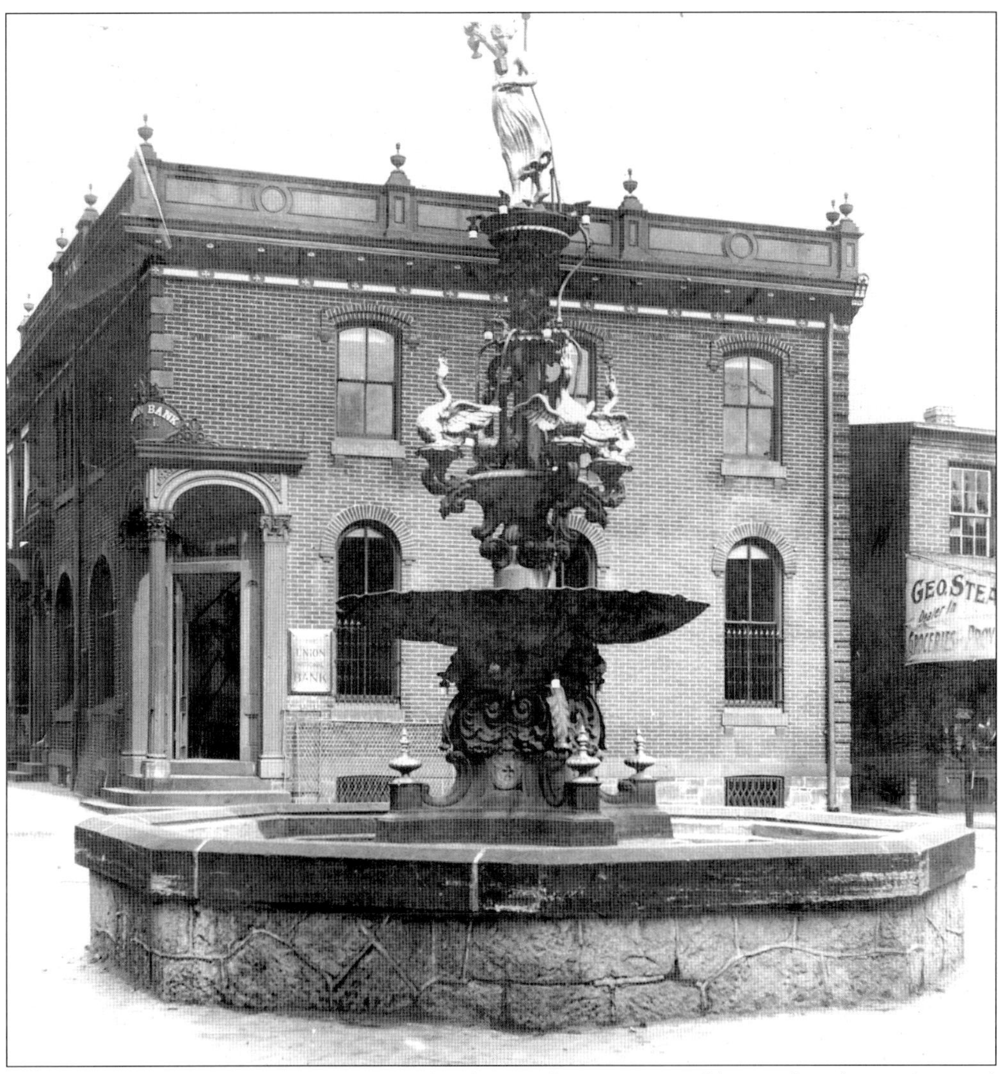

The fountain at Fountain Square was a focal point for visitors, and horses loved to grab a cool drink on hot days. Behind the fountain is the Union National Bank as it originally looked, with a fabulous corner entrance and tons of detail lost over the years to modernization. Note George Stead's grocery market to the right on Mill Street.

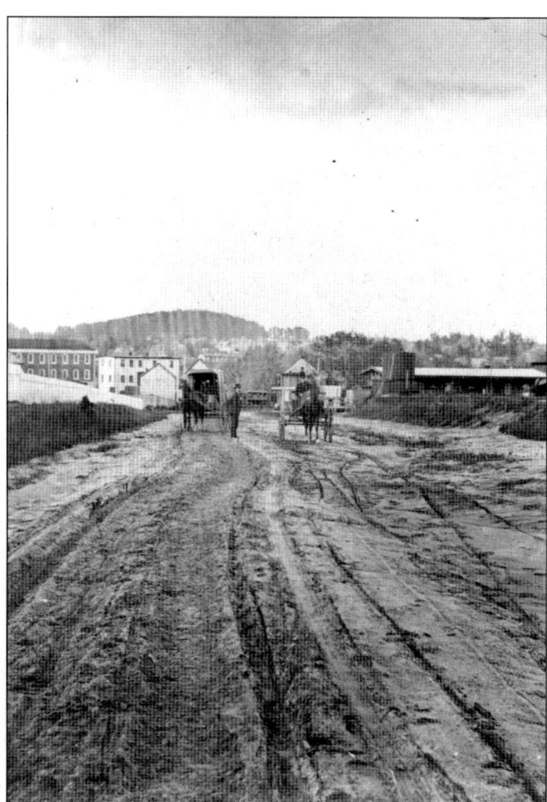

The mount is in the background and the train station is on the right in this view looking north down Madison Avenue toward town. Large grooves in the mud to catch the wagon wheels made traveling through town on this newer road to Lumberton difficult.

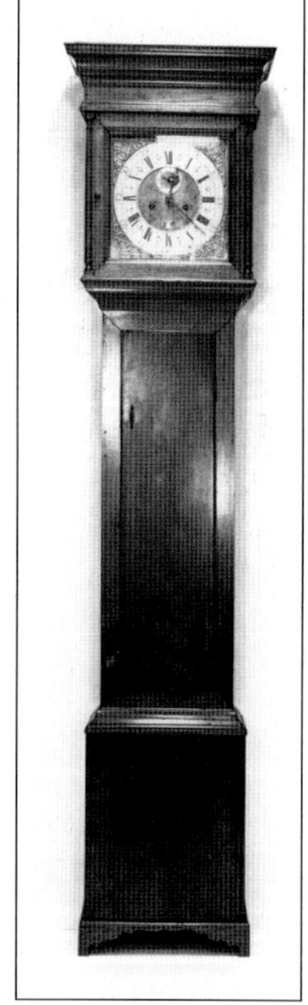

This tall case clock was made by Isaac Pearson (*c.* 1685–1749) of Burlington. Pearson was a proprietor of the Mount Holly Iron Works on the Rancocas Creek east of Pine Street. He also sold land to St. Andrew's Episcopal Church that is now part of their graveyard and home to the Dobbins Chapel.

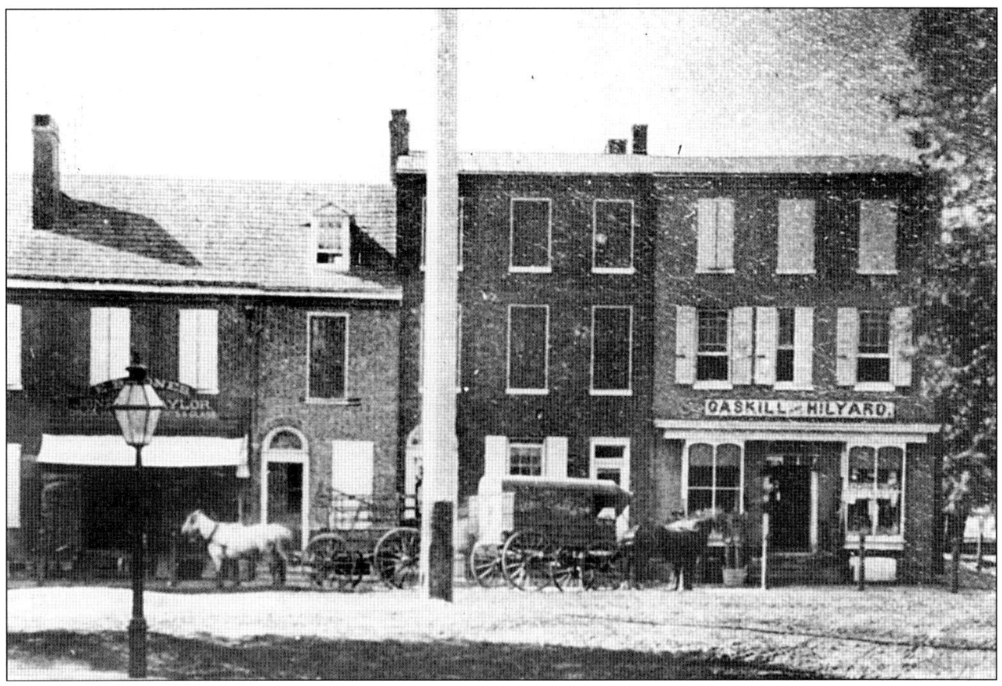

This is a very early scene of Fountain Square. Notice the absence of the fountain in the center, where the large flagpole stands. The flagpole was probably erected during the Civil War in honor of Gen. Alexander E. Shires, a nearby resident. The horses are tied to hitching posts in front of businesses along Mill Street. Some of these buildings still stand today.

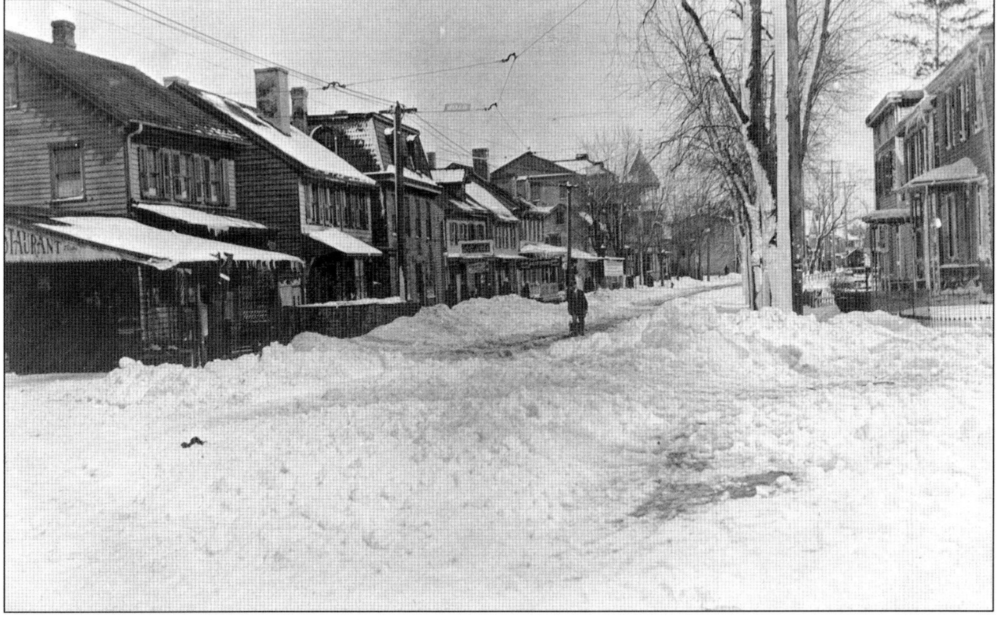

This March 1, 1914 view is aimed down Washington Street from the intersection of Madison Avenue. The tree-lined street was home to interesting houses and businesses, detailed wrought-iron fencing, and structures with shingle and metal roofs.

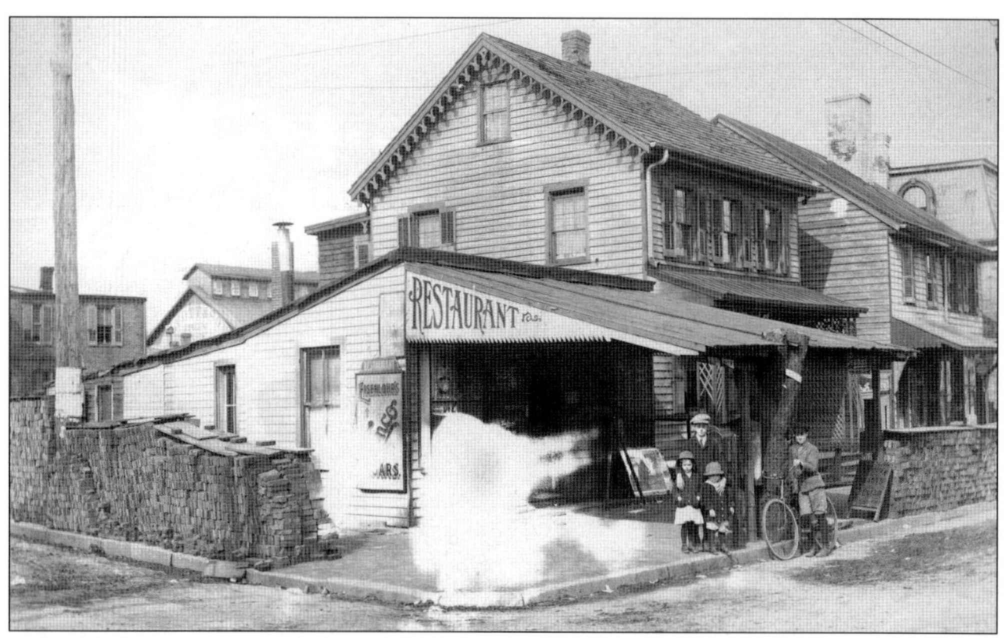

A close look at the corner of King and Washington Streets reveals a little restaurant selling ice cream, cigars, and other good things most corner stores supplied the neighbors. It may be the Alcott & Son Iron Foundry behind the restaurant in this April 5, 1914 picture. Shingle and metal roofs and well-dressed young folks are also included in the shot.

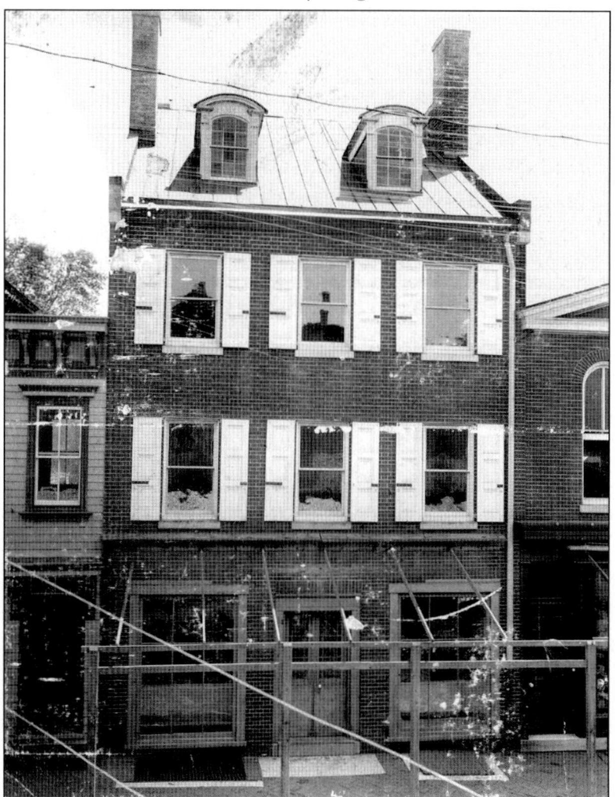

Henry C. Shinn built this building in 1871. It was used as a paint store and then as the offices of the New Jersey Mirror, one of three newspapers located in Mount Holly at the time. After the newspaper moved to the other side of the street, the building was occupied by the Mount Holly News. The building is located at 37 High Street, but there is no local newspaper today covering just Mount Holly.

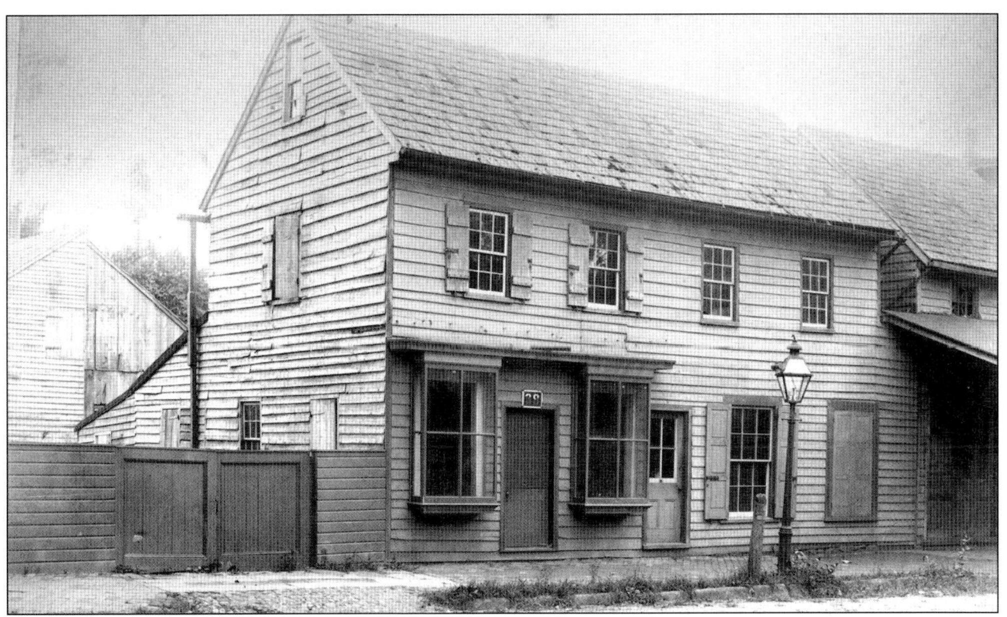

This is yet another building, on the south side of Mill Street, where the New Jersey Mirror had its offices. It was demolished in 1888, the same year Howard L. Keeler took this photograph.

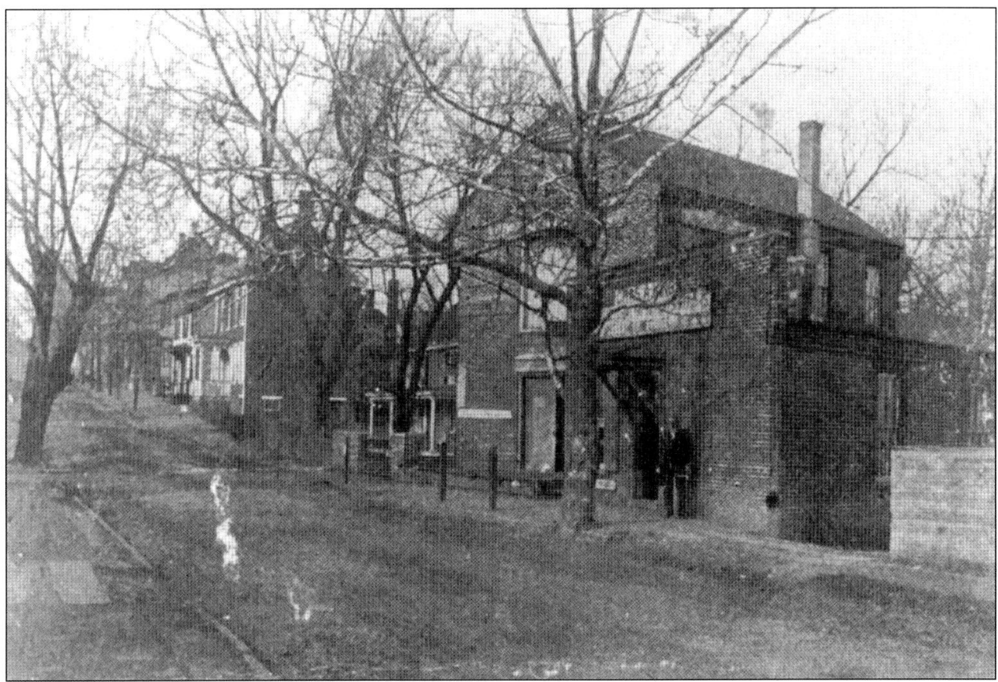

This is the Fenimore Feed Store, shown in 1910, on Buttonwood Street near Mill Street and Buttonwood Run. The feed store is no longer there, but the homes in the distance still stand. These homes have been refurbished thanks to the positive influence that the Medford Leas Retirement Community has had in this area.

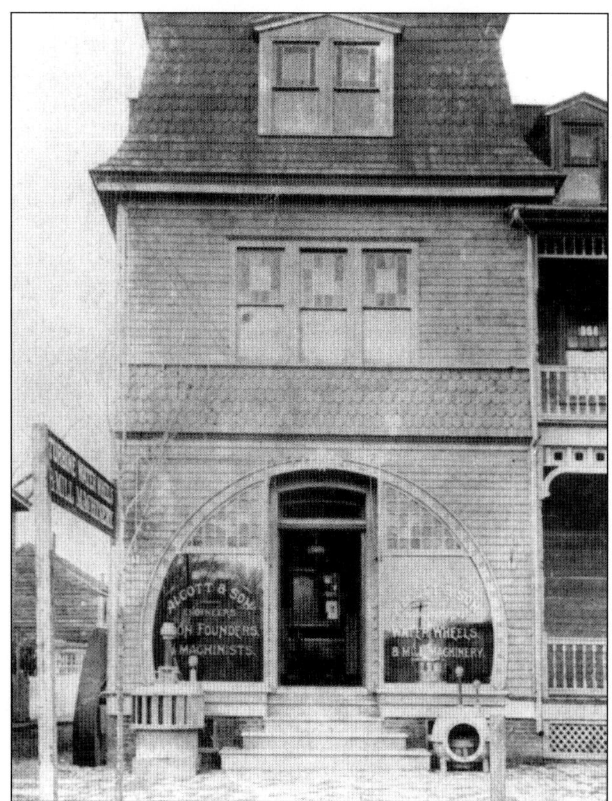

The Alcott Foundry office was located here at the rear of the West End Hotel on Washington Street. Founded in 1837, the T.C. Alcott & Sons Company made turbine wheels, widely used in South America. The business thrived until 1895.

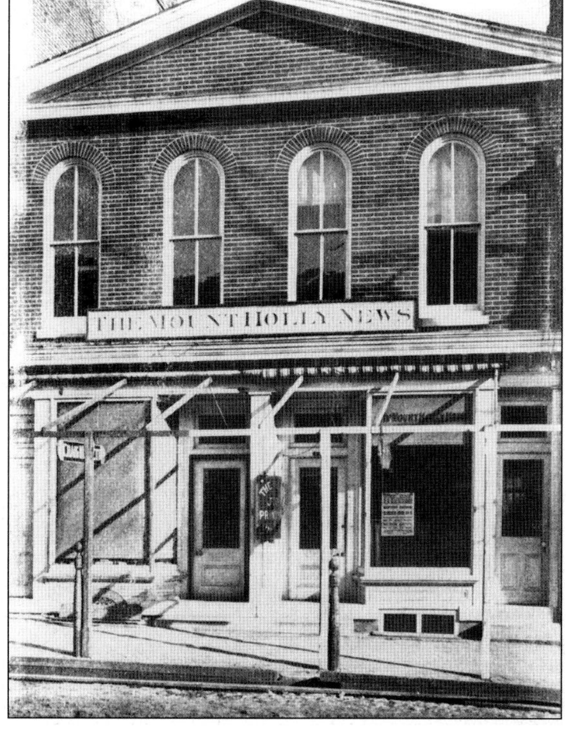

The *Mount Holly News* was one of four papers (the *New Jersey Mirror*, *Mount Holly Herald*, and *Mount Holly Dispatch*) covering activities in Mount Holly and the surrounding area. This was its office on the east side of Main Street between Mill and Murrell Streets.

A careful inspection of this photograph of the west side of Main Street reveals many buildings still standing. Notice the interesting and altering roofline, the corbels and soffits, the quaint signs, the storefront windows, and more sidewalk covers, keeping shoppers cool and dry in the summer months. Today there is a movement to turn today's High Street back to Main Street by restoring the buildings and businesses to their original charm.

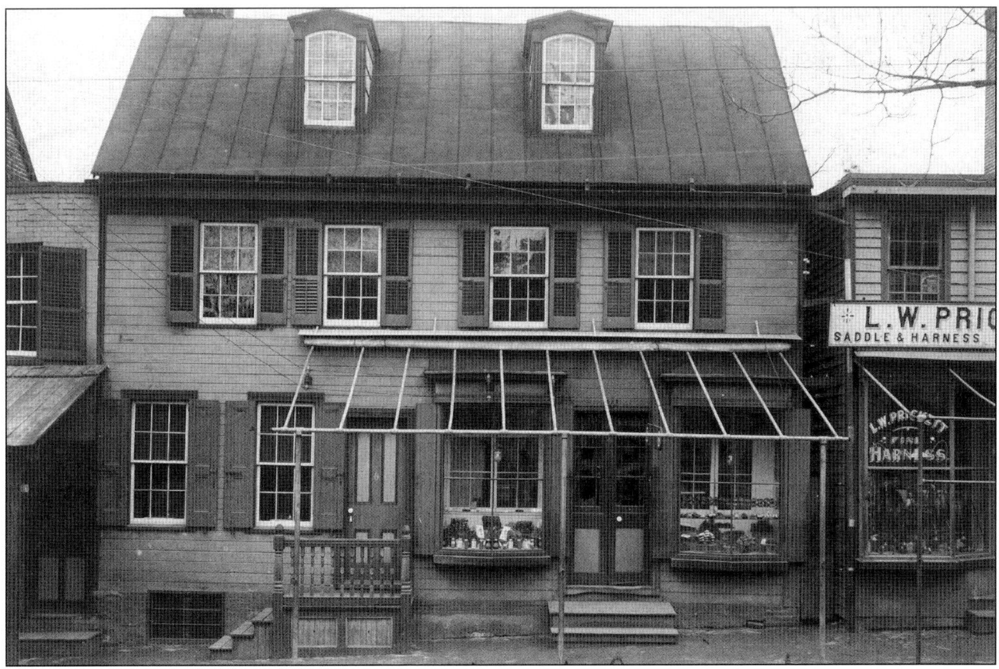

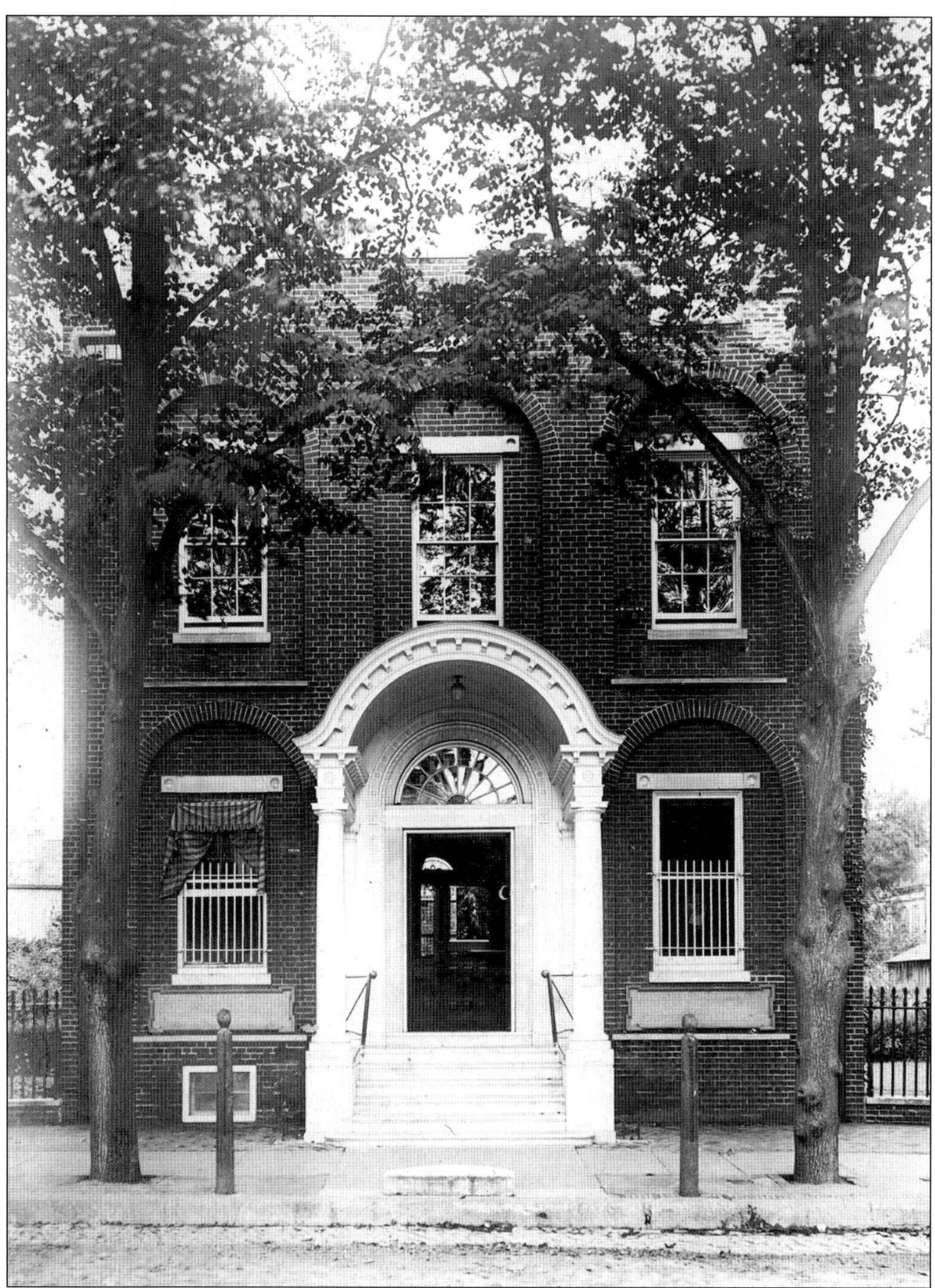

The Farmers Bank Trust Company was founded on July 9, 1814, and the building was erected in 1815 on Mill Street. The president's salary was $300 per year, the cashier $800, and the clerk $400. An attempt was made to rob the bank on January 12, 1855. The bandits forced open the vault door and used gunpowder to blast through the inner chamber. They were without success and fled with nothing. This bank still stands with some alterations to this arched entrance and the modern convenience of a drive-through to suit its modern customers.

Three

Sport and Leisure

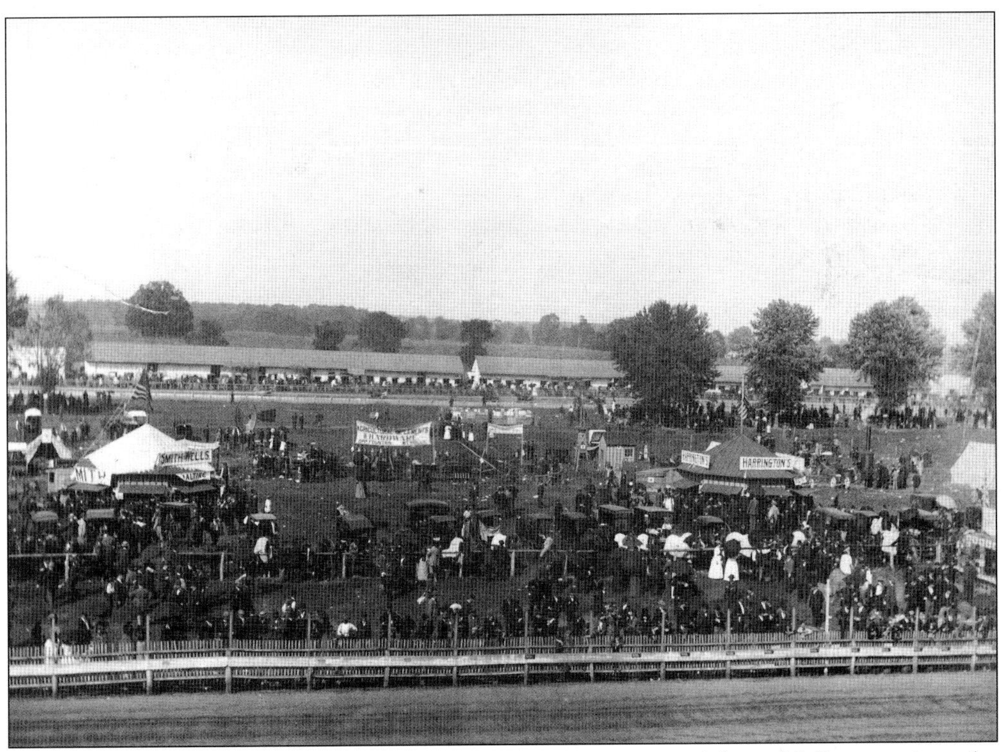

The Burlington County Fairgrounds was a premier attraction in Mount Holly ever since the first fair was held there on October 28, 1847. The 24-acre site featured horse racing and, as seen from the photograph, local business and restaurant vendors. This is the showing area and stables where visitors could stroll around and visit directly with the horses. The fair was discontinued in 1926.

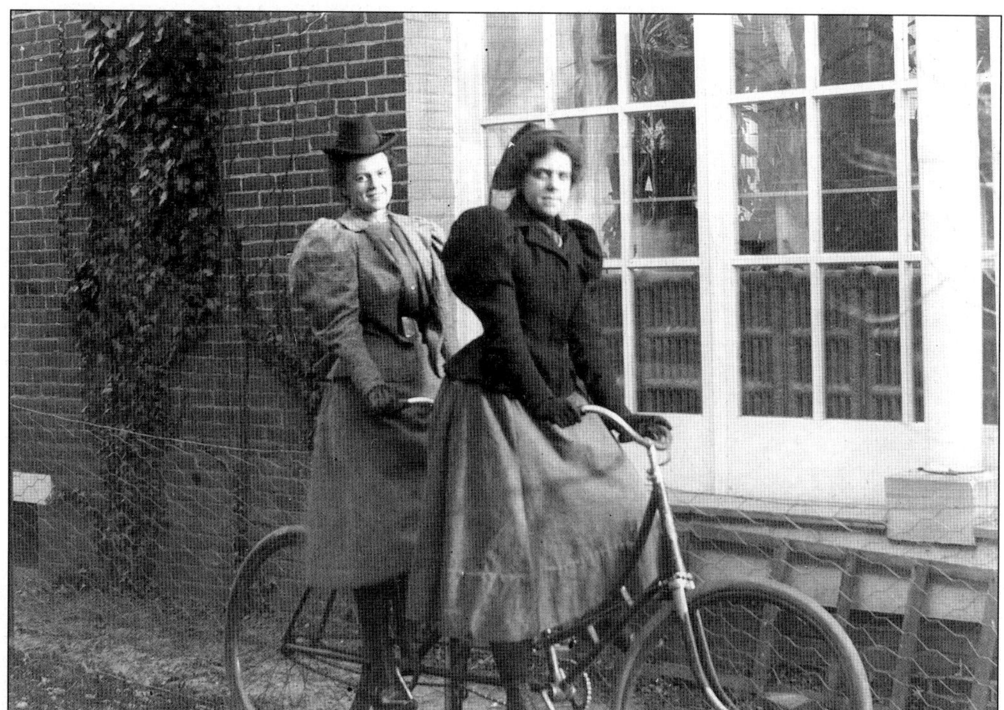

This photograph shows Edith and Mabel Kelly of Smithville on a bicycle built for two at 218 High Street. Their father was connected with the Kelly-Springfield Tire Company, which was involved in the development of the pneumatic tire. He also held a position with the H.B. Smith Machine Company at Smithville.

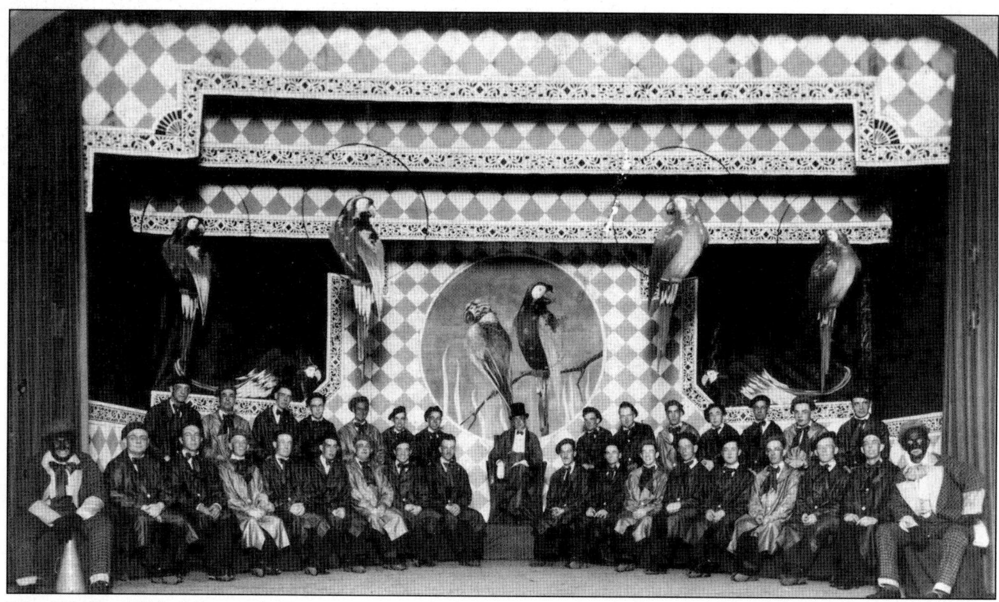

The Holly Club Minstrels put on an annual show for the public in the theater on Main Street. This theater also continued to be known as the Opera House in later years. From *c.* 1915 through 1940, everyone in town looked forward to the songs and skits the volunteers performed.

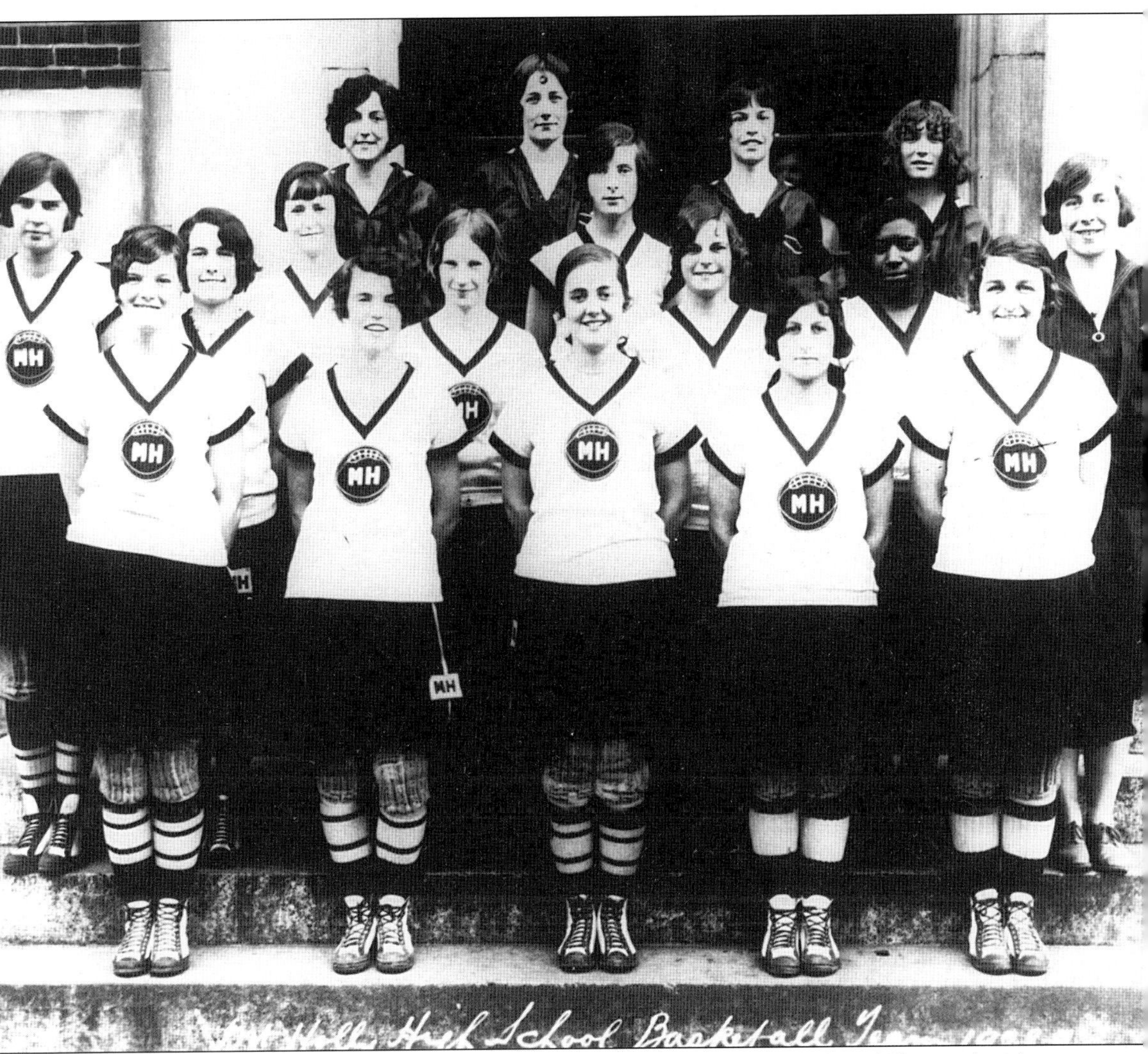

The Mount Holly High School girls basketball team in 1928 included, from left to right, the following: (front row) Margaret Reamer, Dot Cahill, Betty Marren, Eleanor Kaelin, and Peg Gauntt; (second row) Elizabeth Jennings, Dot Pierce, Ellen McLoughlin, Alice Myers, and Gladys Mason; (third row) Blanche Wilkins, Eleanor Flynn, and coach E. Adams; (fourth row) Bernadette Gsell, Martha Hildebrant, and two unidentified players.

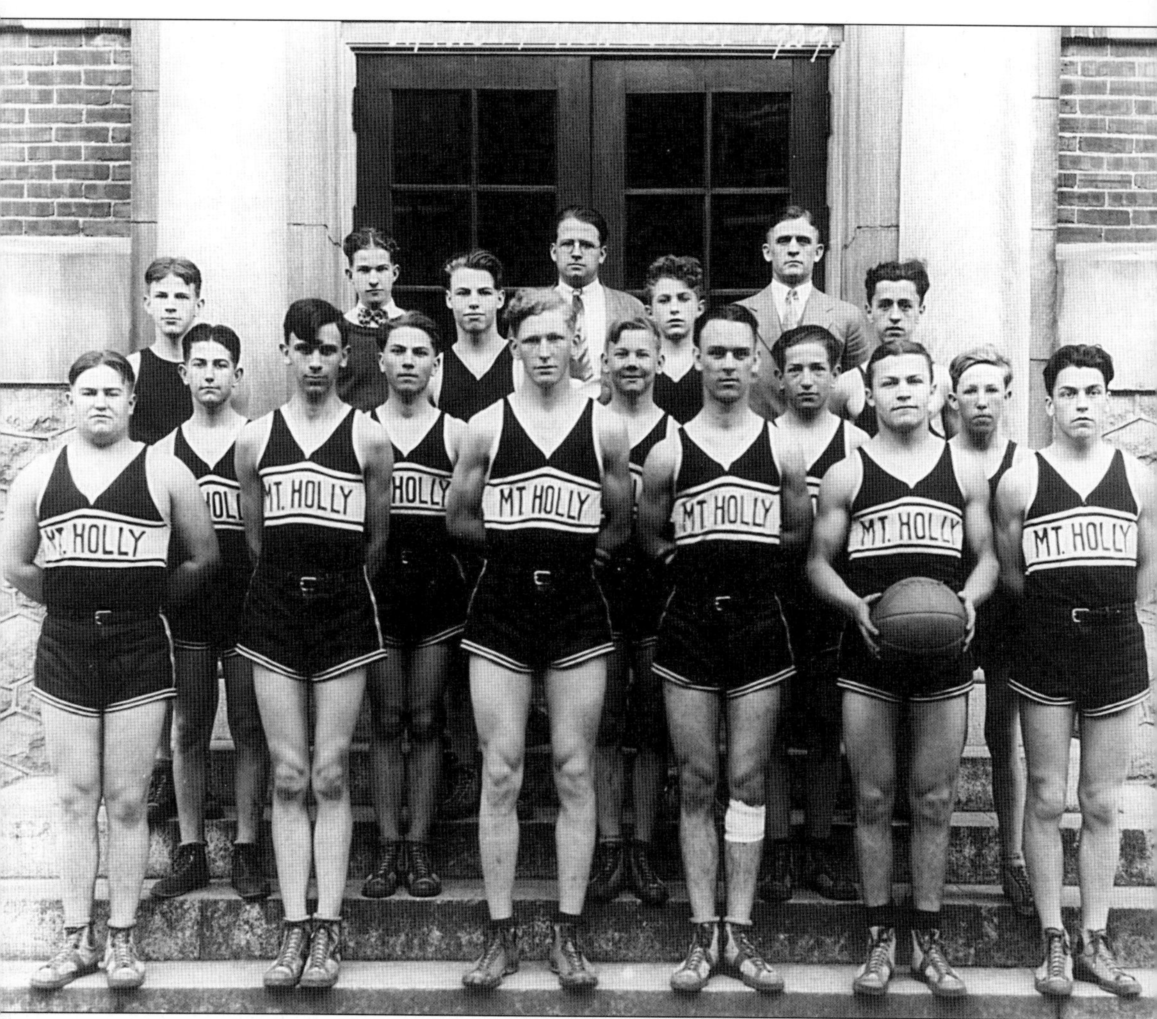

The Mount Holly boys' basketball team in 1929 included, from left to right, the following: (first row) George Smith, John Tilton, Marriott Haines, Arnold Shinn, Ellis Parker, and Ed Durand; (second row) Jack Smith, Tony Janone, Ray Hutchins, Myer Feinstein, and Orville Green; (third row) three unidentified players and Lawrence Hager; (fourth row) Fred Crozier, Ken Shinn, and Wilbur Crosley.

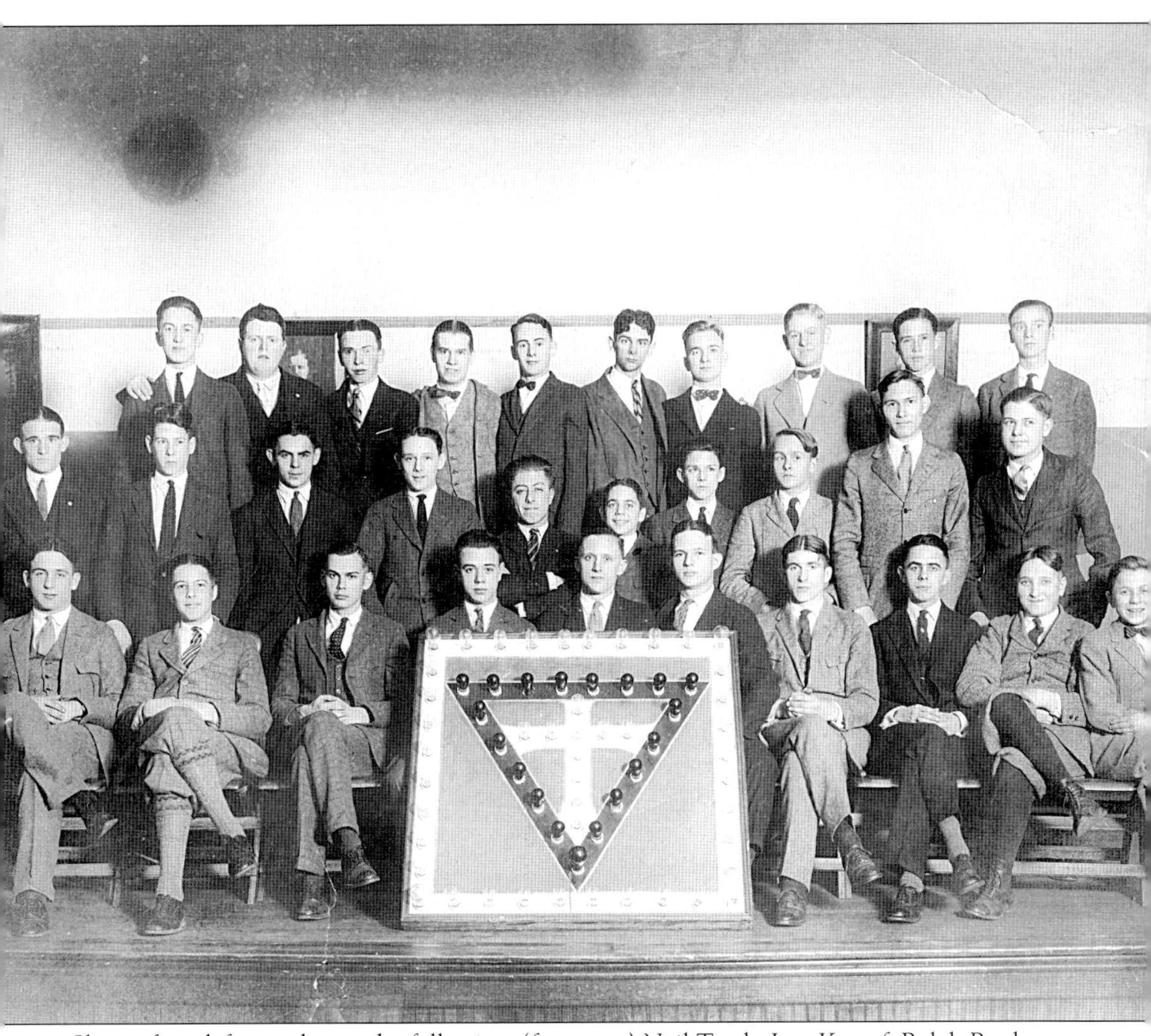

Shown from left to right are the following: (front row) Neil Troth, Lou Kumpf, Ralph Borden, Wilmer Robbins, Joe Jones, Dixon Heyer, unidentified, Robert Wills, Leon Rosenfeld, and John Volgarino; (middle row) Phillip Bauntt, Wally Eldridge, Norman Miller, unidentified, Russell "Hop" Stoddard, Frank Miller, unidentified, Bev Kingdon, Norman Newell, and Bob Jones; (back row) unidentified, Harold Russell, unidentified, Bob Semple, Granville Haines, two unidentified players, Jack Johanson, ? Bridgum, and Raymond Ewan.

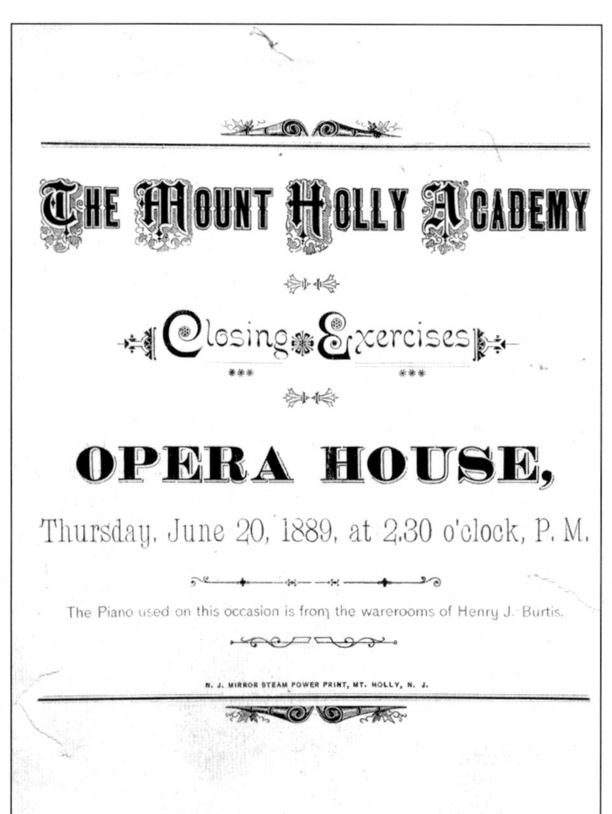

THE MOUNT HOLLY ACADEMY

Closing Exercises

OPERA HOUSE,

Thursday, June 20, 1889, at 2.30 o'clock, P. M.

The Piano used on this occasion is from the warerooms of Henry J. Burtis.

N. J. MIRROR STEAM POWER PRINT, MT. HOLLY, N. J.

The Mount Holly Academy, located on Brainerd Street, held its closing exercises in 1889 at the Opera House (also called the Concert Hall). The Opera House had been built in 1876 on the west side of Main Street opposite Murrell Street. In 1881, Charles Folwell bought the front lot, and his deed required him to provide and entrance to the concert hall through the new Mirror Building in 1882.

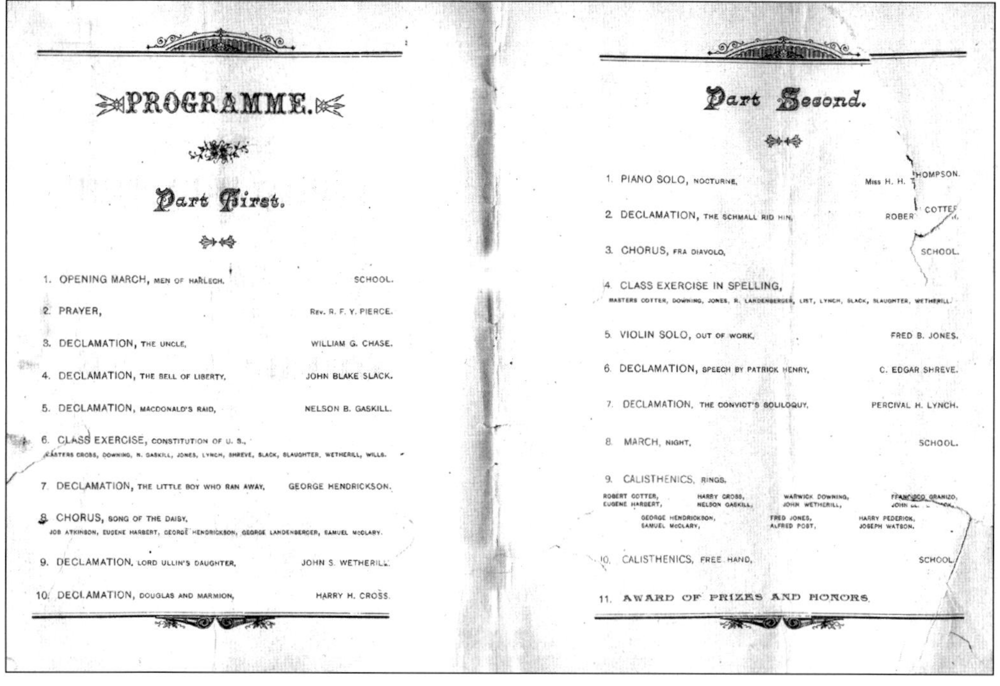

PROGRAMME.

Part First.

1. OPENING MARCH, MEN OF HARLECH. SCHOOL.
2. PRAYER, REV. R. F. Y. PIERCE.
3. DECLAMATION, THE UNCLE, WILLIAM G. CHASE.
4. DECLAMATION, THE BELL OF LIBERTY, JOHN BLAKE SLACK.
5. DECLAMATION, MACDONALD'S RAID, NELSON B. GASKILL.
6. CLASS EXERCISE, CONSTITUTION OF U. S., MASTERS CROSS, DOWNING, N. GASKILL, JONES, LYNCH, SHREVE, SLACK, SLAUGHTER, WETHERILL, WILLS.
7. DECLAMATION, THE LITTLE BOY WHO RAN AWAY, GEORGE HENDRICKSON.
8. CHORUS, SONG OF THE DAISY, JOB ATKINSON, EUGENE HARBERT, GEORGE HENDRICKSON, GEORGE LANDENBERGER, SAMUEL McCLARY.
9. DECLAMATION, LORD ULLIN'S DAUGHTER, JOHN S. WETHERILL.
10. DECLAMATION, DOUGLAS AND MARMION, HARRY H. CROSS.

Part Second.

1. PIANO SOLO, NOCTURNE, Miss H. H. THOMPSON.
2. DECLAMATION, THE SCHMALL RID HIN, ROBER COTTER.
3. CHORUS, FRA DIAVOLO, SCHOOL.
4. CLASS EXERCISE IN SPELLING, MASTERS COTTER, DOWNING, JONES, R. LANDENBERGER, LIST, LYNCH, SLACK, SLAUGHTER, WETHERILL.
5. VIOLIN SOLO, OUT OF WORK, FRED B. JONES.
6. DECLAMATION, SPEECH BY PATRICK HENRY, C. EDGAR SHREVE.
7. DECLAMATION, THE CONVICT'S SOLILOQUY, PERCIVAL H. LYNCH.
8. MARCH, NIGHT, SCHOOL.
9. CALISTHENICS, RINGS. ROBERT COTTER, EUGENE HARBERT, HARRY CROSS, NELSON GASKILL, WARWICK DOWNING, JOHN WETHERILL, FRANCISCO GRANIZO, JOHN [illegible], GEORGE HENDRICKSON, SAMUEL McCLARY, FRED JONES, ALFRED POST, HARRY PEDERICK, JOSEPH WATSON.
10. CALISTHENICS, FREE HAND, SCHOOL.
11. AWARD OF PRIZES AND HONORS.

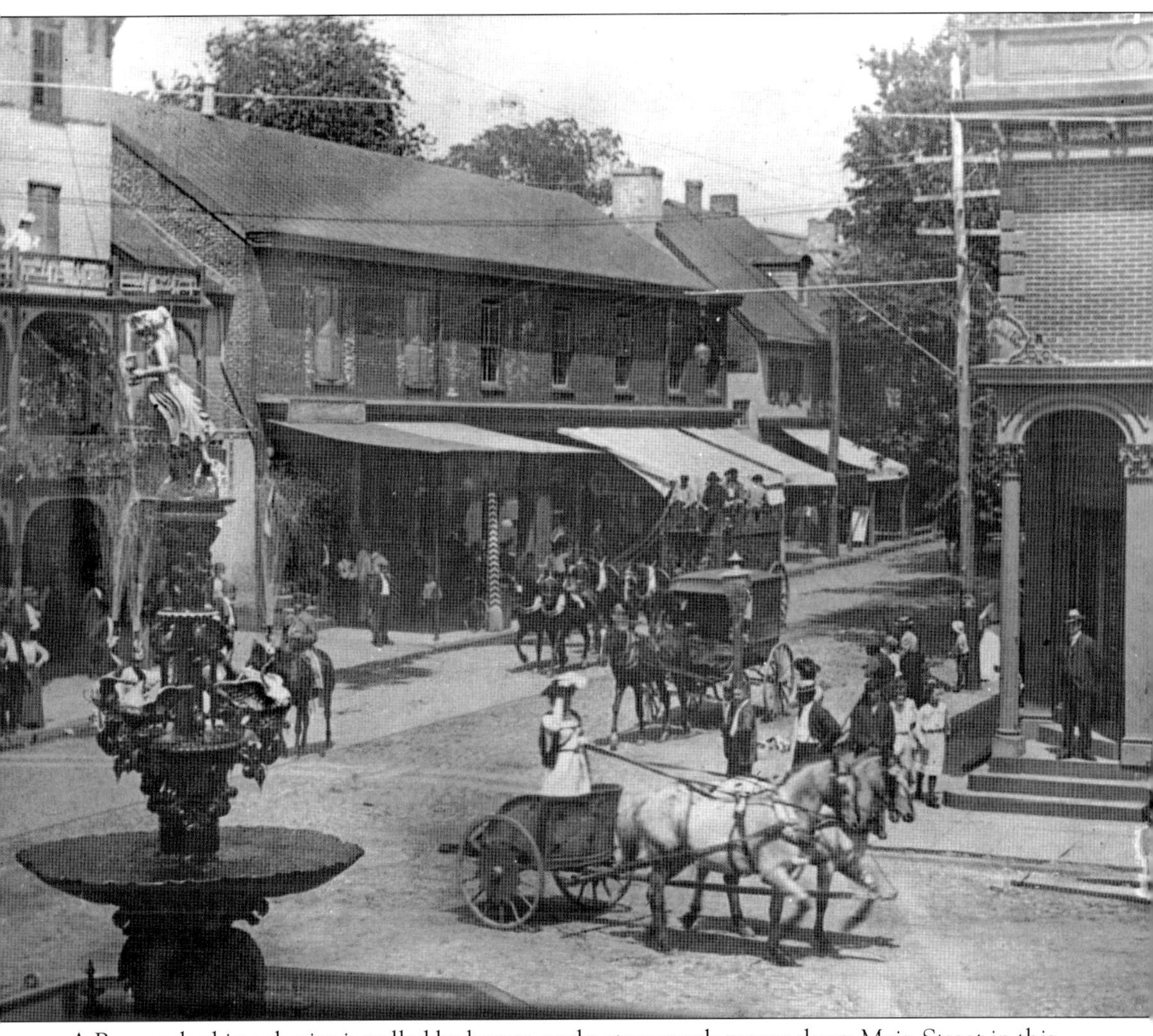

A Roman-looking chariot is pulled by horses, and a stagecoach moves down Main Street in this parade. Notice the beautiful fountain and the folks on the balcony of the old Arcade Hotel, making this a lovely scene.

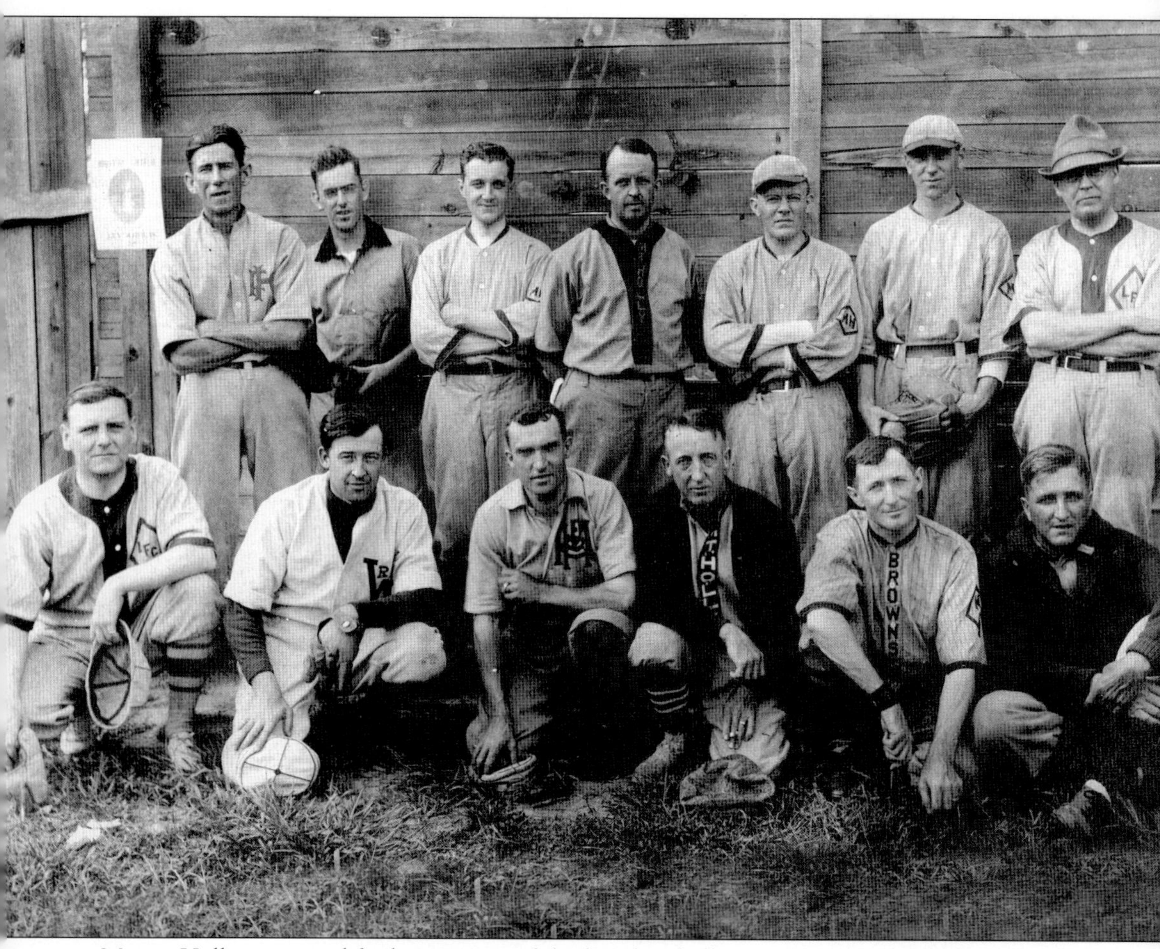

Mount Holly was noted for having one of the best baseball teams around. Talk to anyone who lived when there was a big baseball diamond in the center of town and they will say how great a pastime it was to root for a hometown team. The players were from all over the region and played for no money, just the love of the game. Now the baseball field is a township parking lot, but the memories of the great Mount Holly baseball games will live on forever.

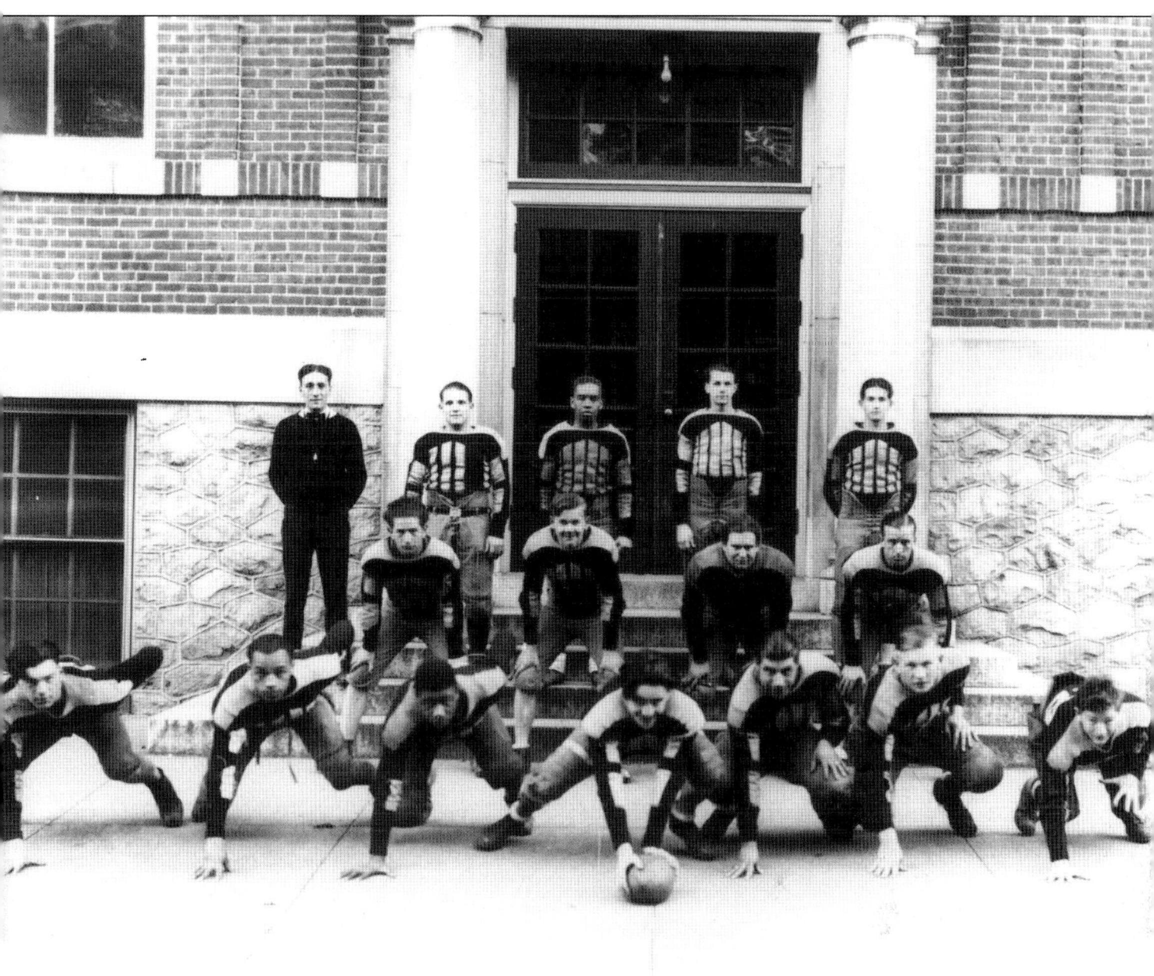

The Mount Holly High School football team from 1930 or 1931 included, from left to right, the following: (front row) unidentified, Warren Moore, Ezekial Stafford, Lester Lewis, Nate Wilson, George Pew, and Jimmy Lamb; (middle row) Meyer Feinstein, Ray Hutchins, George Smith, and unidentified; (back row) coach Pete Dileo, Alfred Morgan, unidentified, Joe Adams, and Jack Smith.

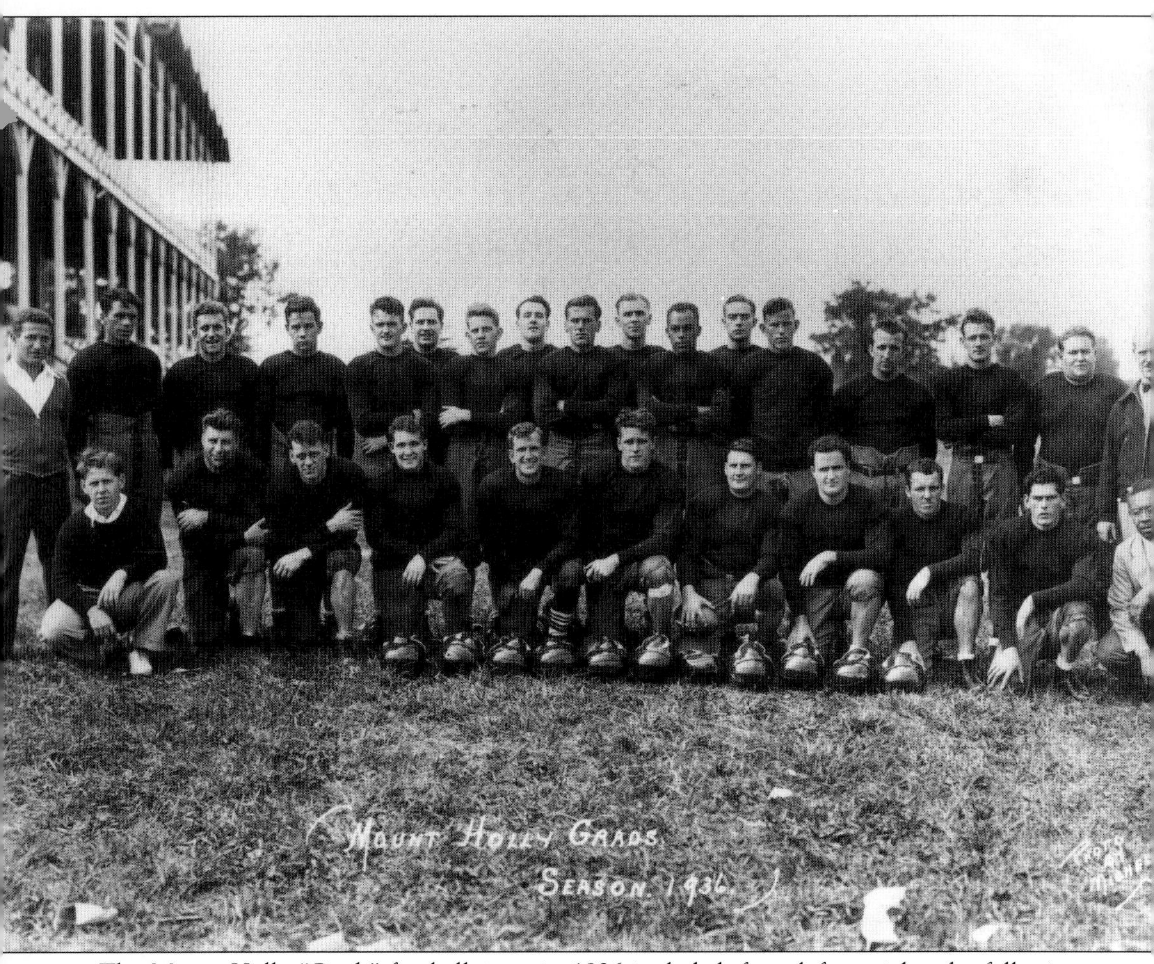

The Mount Holly "Grads" football team in 1936 included, from left to right, the following: (front row) Charles Lott, Nate Wilson, unidentified, Al Morgan, Doug Ritter, ? Rossell, two unidentified players, Ed Pennock, Alfred Gillison, and unidentified; (middle row) Meyer Feinstein, unidentified, Ed Haines, two unidentified players, Cliff Boxer, two unidentified players, Russ Saxton, Joe Moore, unidentified, and George Smith; (back row) Les Lewis, Bill Bedwell, unidentified, and John Ford.

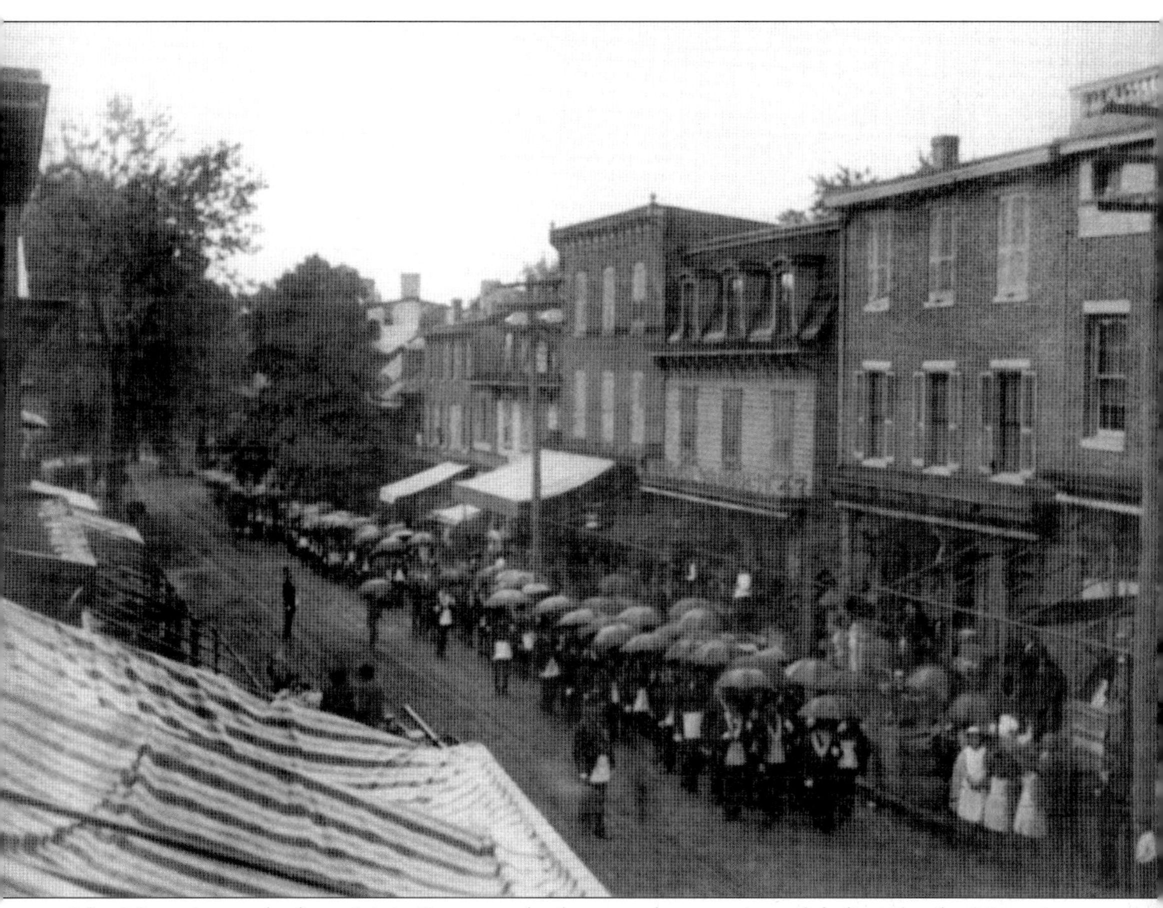

The Mason's parade down Main Street took place on the occasion of dedicating the Masonic Temple on the corner of Main and Brainerd Streets in 1891. Although it was a dismal rainy day, it did not impede the Mason's from their mission. It could be said that the sea of black umbrellas actually added to the occasion.

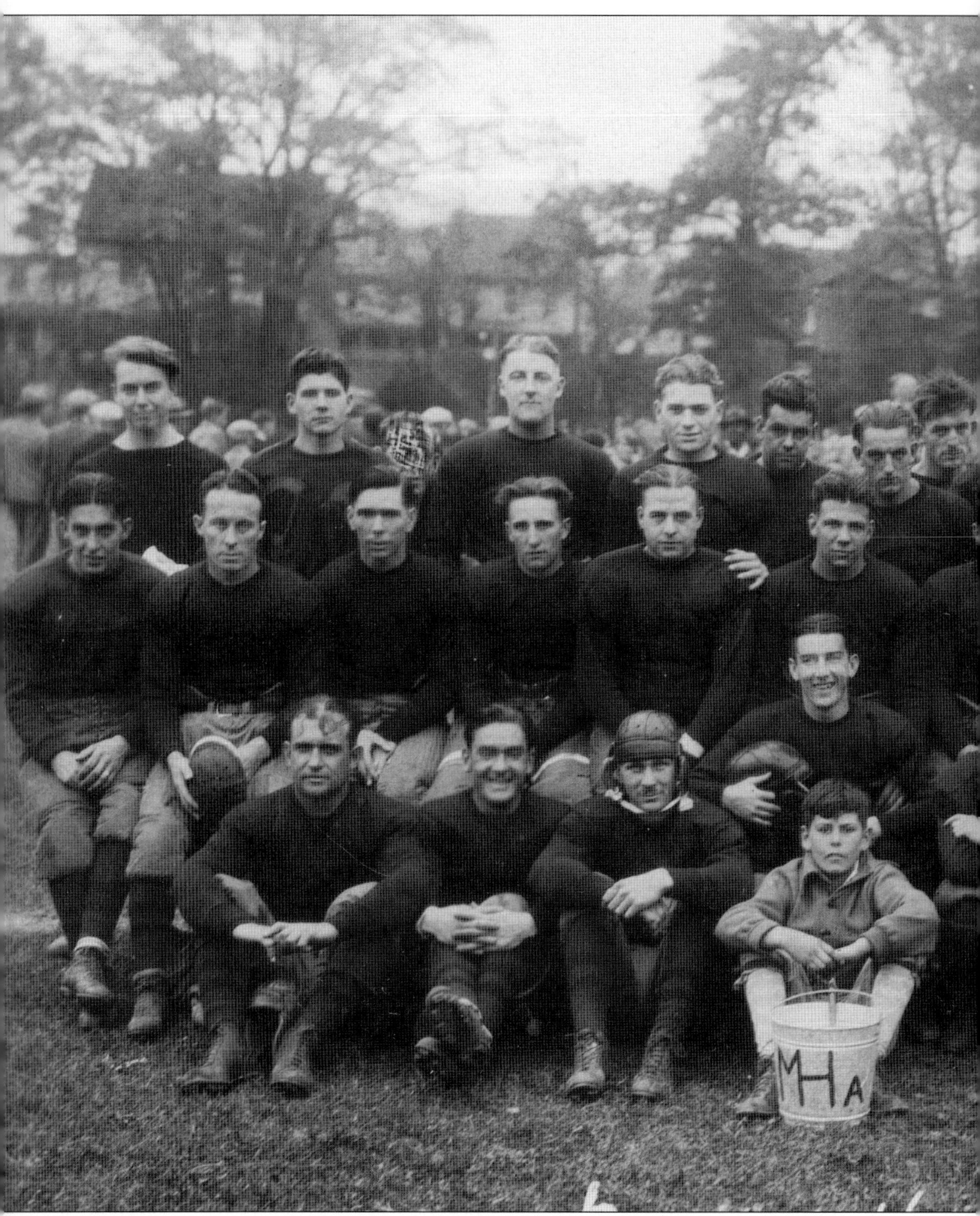

The Mount Holly football team of 1928 poses at R&P Field off Washington Street. From left to right are the following: (front row) unidentified, Charles Bradley, unidentified, Herb McGuigan, Scobey Albertson, Warren Moore, unidentified, Wallace Eldridge, and James French (of French's Lumber); (middle row) unidentified, Edward Miller, unidentified, Ernie

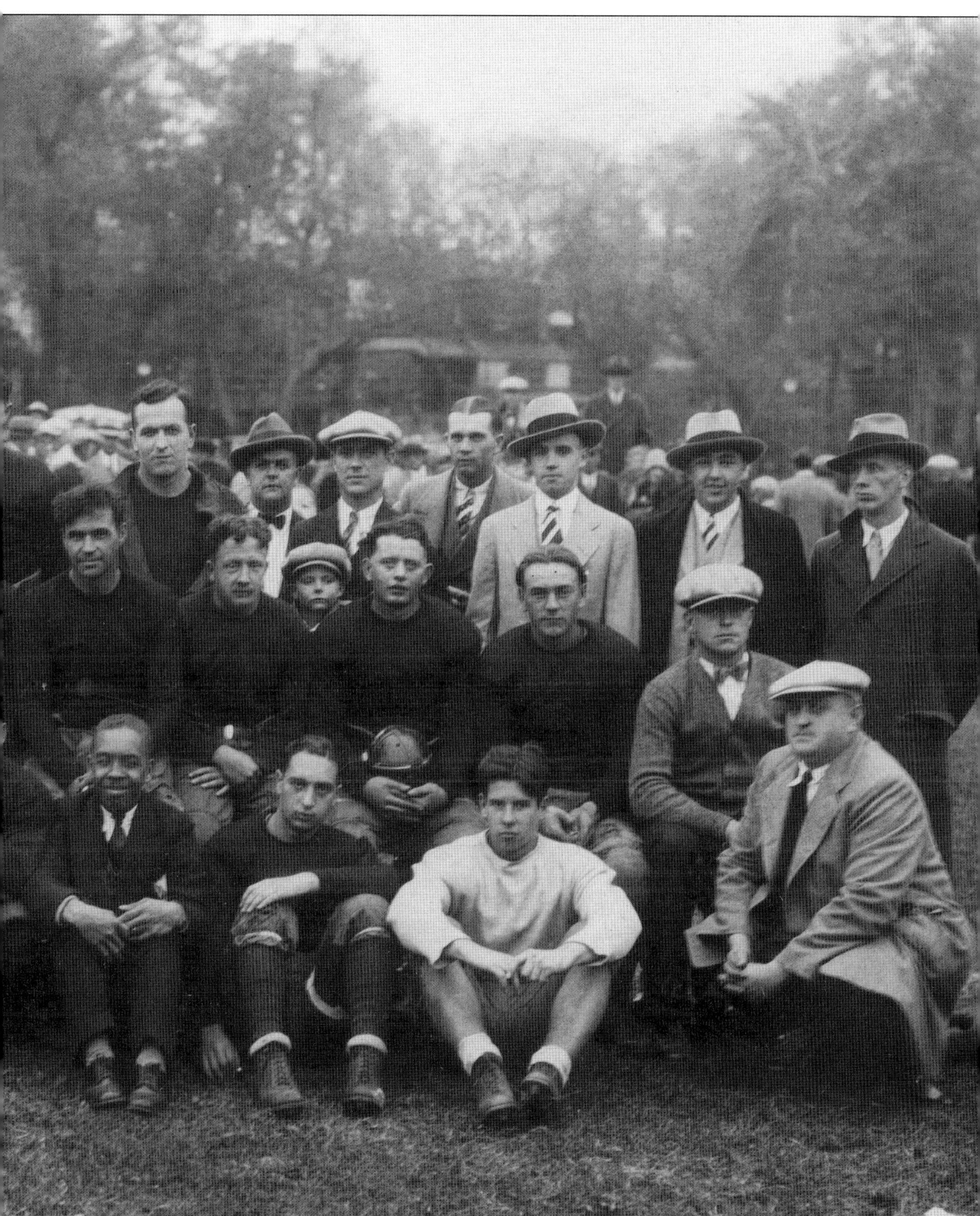

Mellon, Earl Donnelly, Lloyd Fryer, unidentified, Ralph Austin, and Elmer Durand; (back row) unidentified, Jack Eldridge, unidentified, Russell Atkinson, Tug Worrell, unidentified, Vinton Easlick, unidentified, Francis Garbarino, three unidentified players, William Mellon, and James Bedwell.

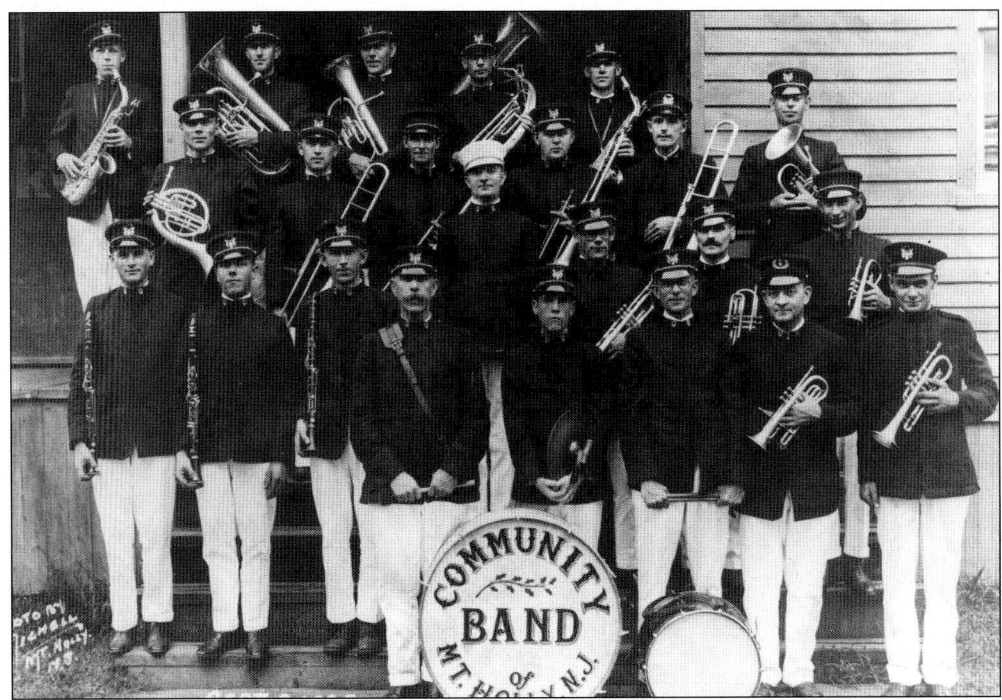

Mount Holly used to have a thriving community band entertaining the town during special events, parades, and holidays. Unfortunately, it has not been possible to uncover all of the names of these handsome gentlemen who gave their time to provide Mount Holly with music through the early and mid-1900s. Three people are identified below: (front row, drum, left) Charles Griffith, (second row, trombone, fourth from the left) Richard Holeman, and (third row, trombone, third from the left) Oscar Sprow.

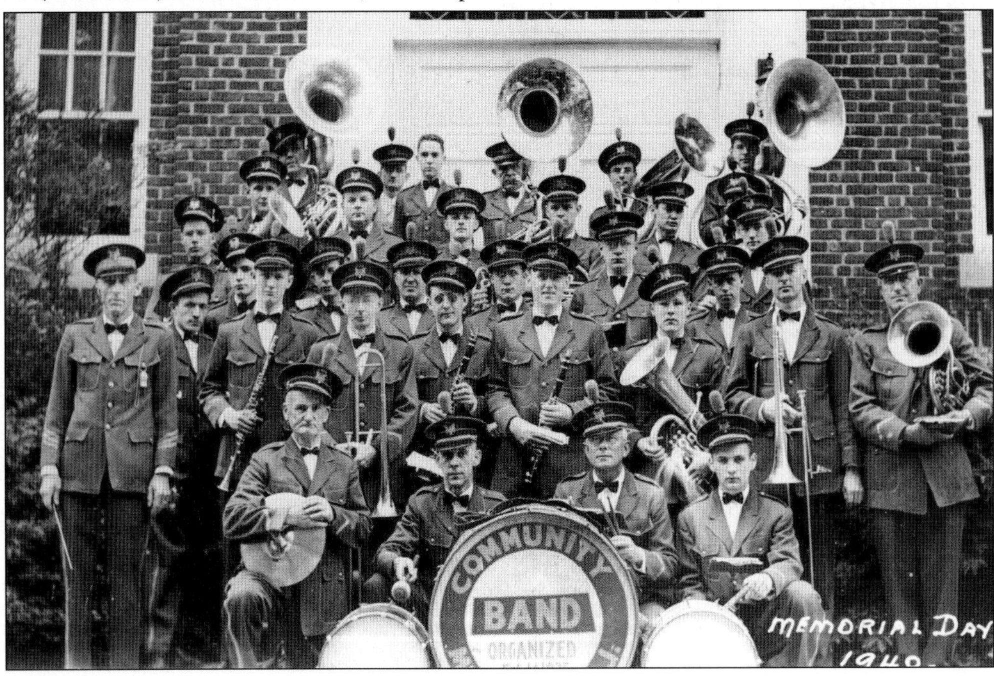

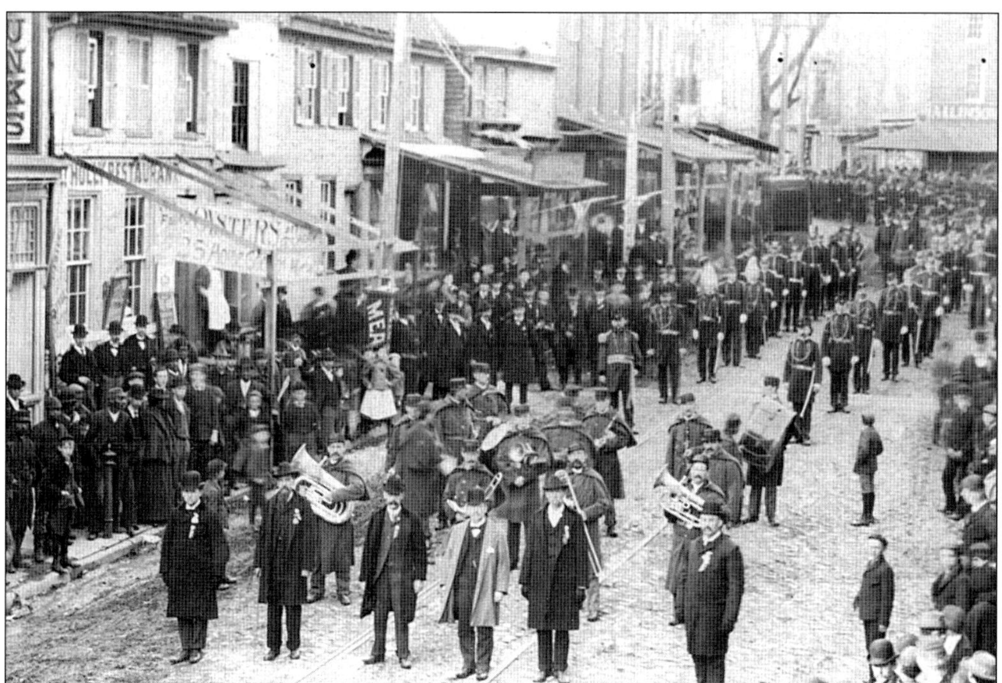

Another early parade included a small band up front (possibly the county or township officials in front of the band) and firemen in neat rows behind.

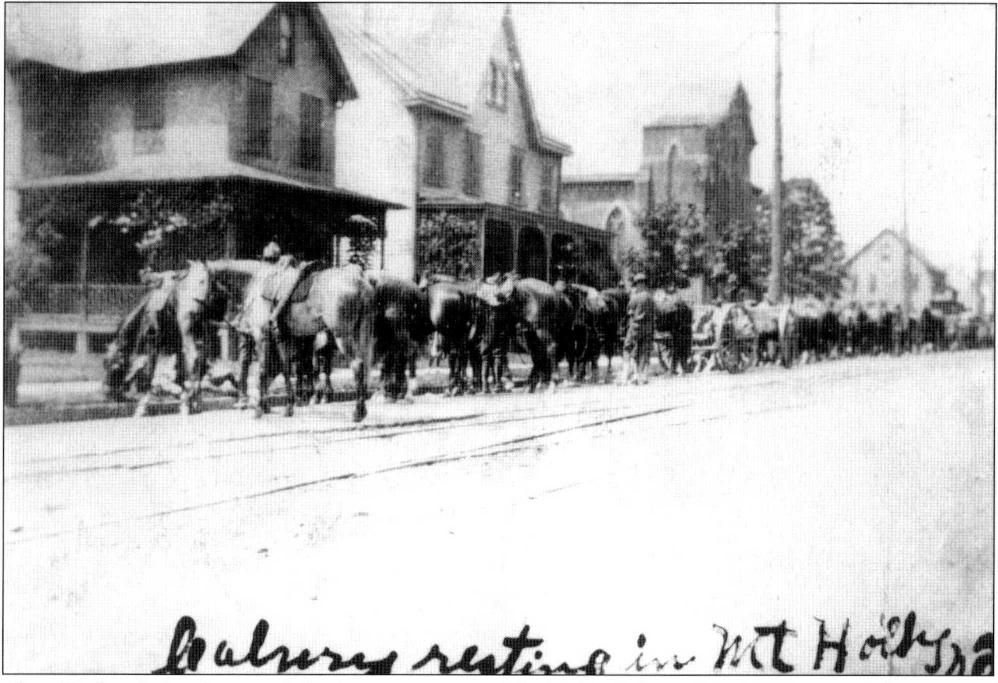

Identified only by the words "calvary resting in Mt. Holly," this calvary was presumably part of a reenactment. It certainly would have been a sight to see all those horses, men, and wagons resting here on Washington Street with the old Sacred Heart Church behind them.

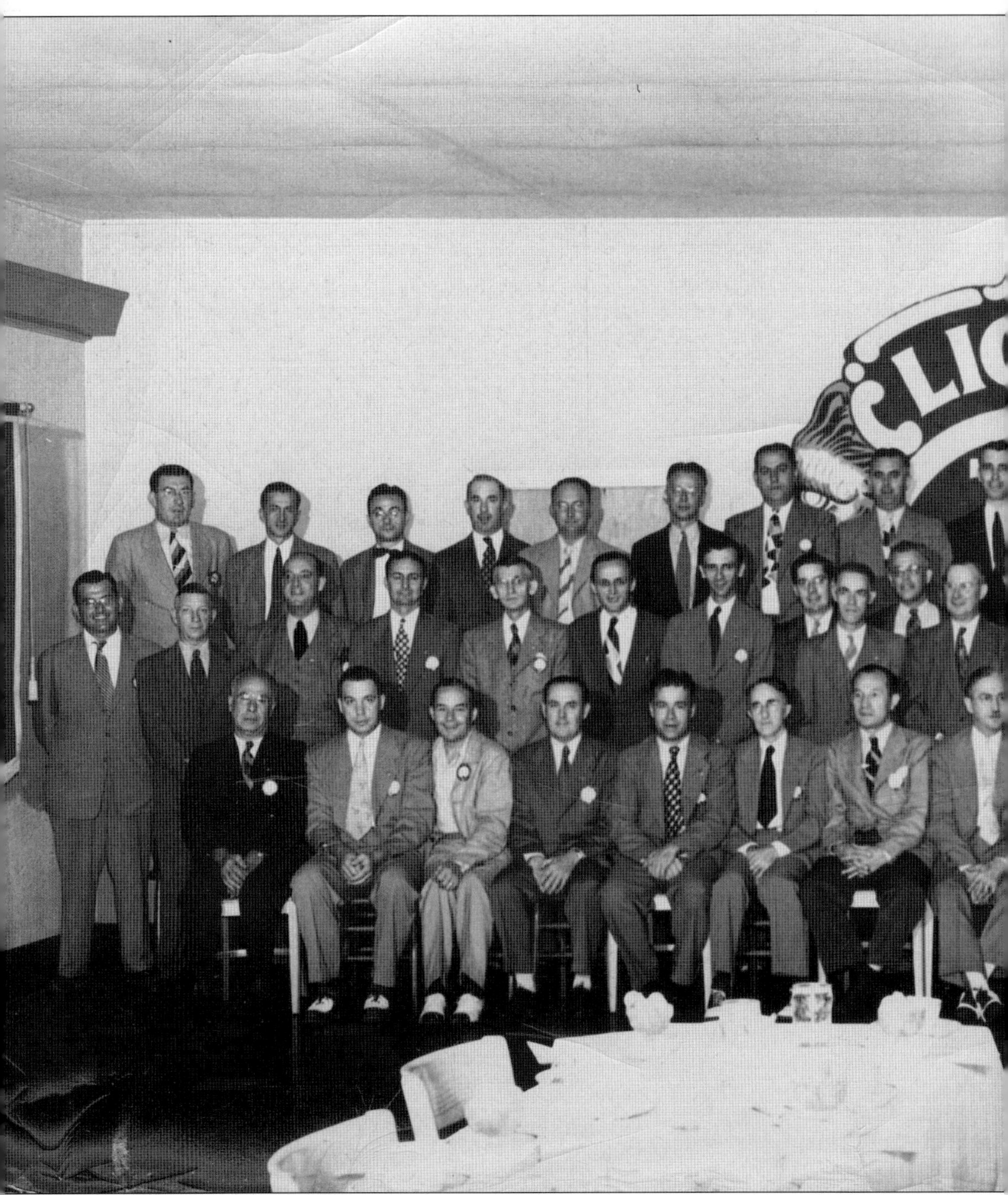

The Mount Holly Lions Club is shown in 1948. From left to right are the following: (front row) Bate Sleeper, Doc Summers, Bill Ford, Theodore Quay, Justus Deacon, Nelson Myers, Norman Zelley, Arnold Morgan, Harry Johnson, Courtney Woodside, George McDowell, Russell "Hop" Stoddard, Stacy Stockton, Charles Claus, and Clarence Price; (middle row) Lloyd Fryer, Edward Johnson, unidentified, Ward Gsell, Oscar Anderson, unidentified, John Tilton, five unidentified members, Ralph Smith, unidentified, Ernie Cook, Robert Shinn, Elmer Miller,

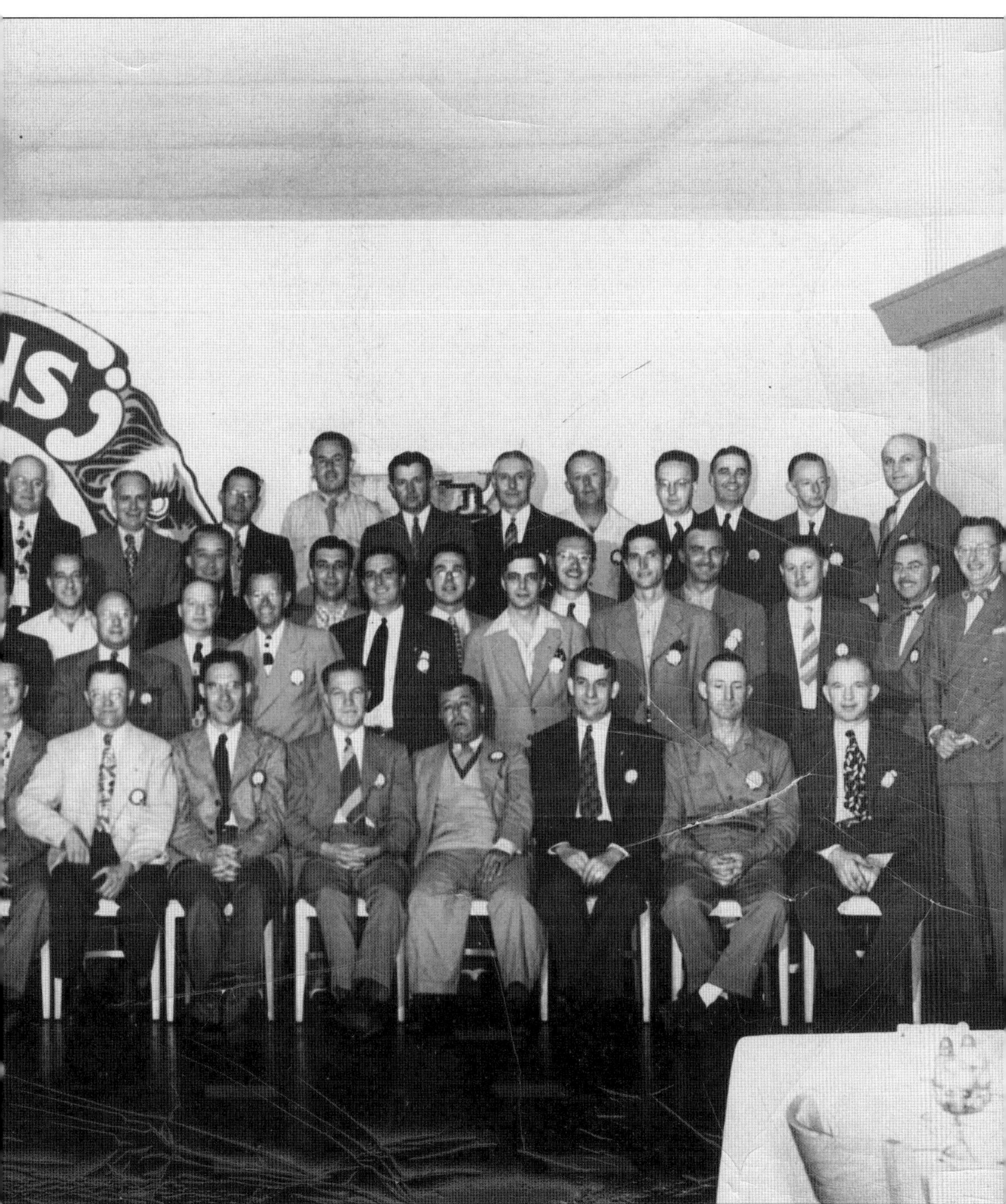

three unidentified members, Jerry White, unidentified, Bud Luckenbill, two unidentified members, Jack Johansen, Cal Barber, and Warren Leary; (back row) Edward Hunt, unidentified, Victor LaVolpe, Hank Budd, Charles Odus, Bayard Allen, Edward Hawkins, Charles Miller, Elliot Hussey, Edward De Bow, Dyer Fernwalt, Charles Cooper, Bill Jackson, unidentified, Samuel Van Sant, Ted Schival, John McGrath, Brooke Tidswell Jr., Dick Holman, and Ellis Parker.

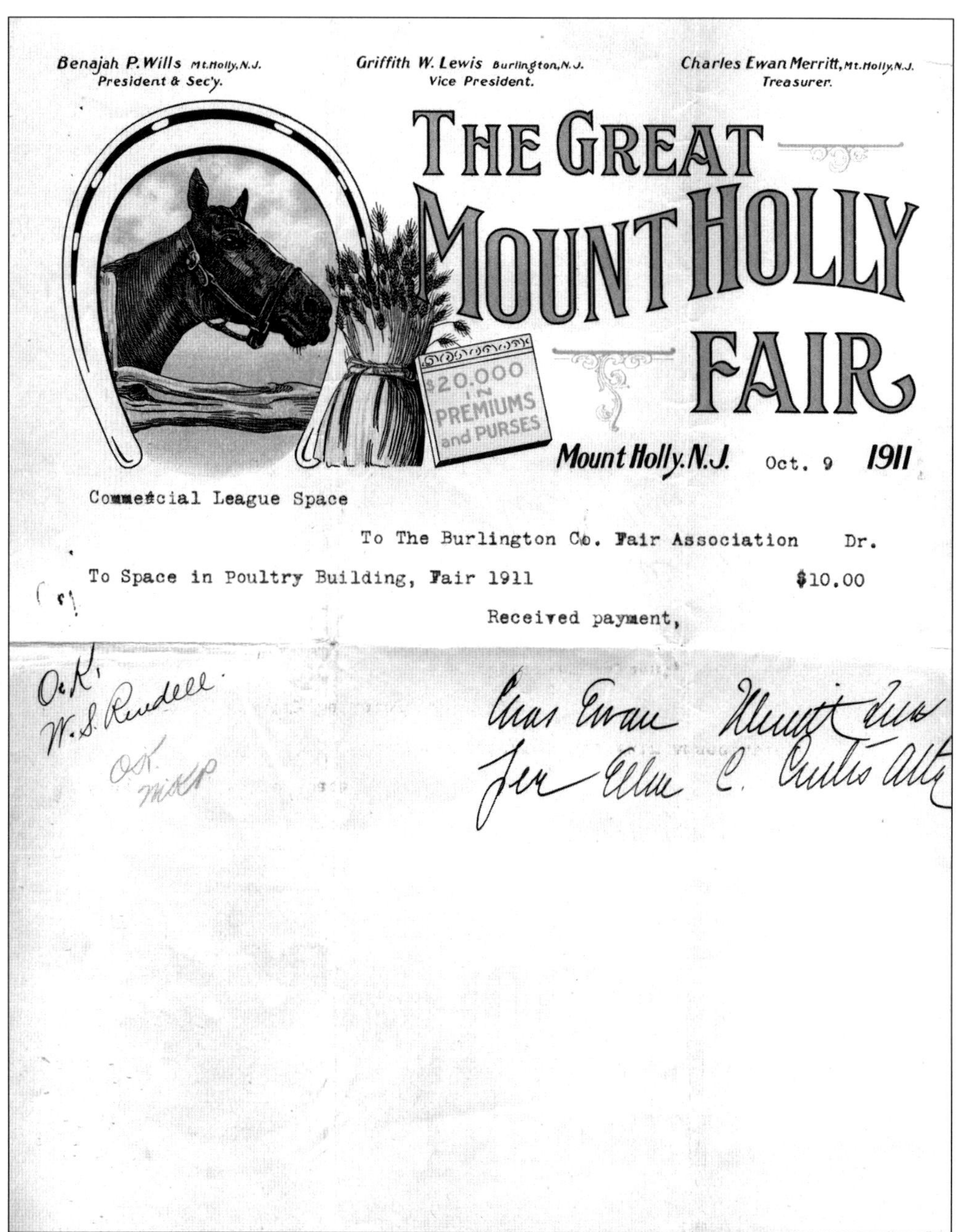

Benajah P. Wills Mt.Holly,N.J. President & Sec'y. — Griffith W. Lewis Burlington,N.J. Vice President. — Charles Ewan Merritt, Mt.Holly,N.J. Treasurer.

THE GREAT MOUNT HOLLY FAIR

Mount Holly. N.J. Oct. 9 1911

Commercial League Space

To The Burlington Co. Fair Association Dr.

To Space in Poultry Building, Fair 1911 $10.00

Received payment,

As mentioned earlier, the Great Mount Holly Fair was an enormous attraction, providing leisure activities for folks from miles around. It was also very lucrative for some in the horse business and for those who sold goods at the fair. Here is a receipt for $10 to rent a space in the poultry building for the 1911 fair. At that time, Benajah P. Wills, Griffith W. Lewis, and Charles Ewan Merritt headed up the fair's operations.

Four
EDUCATION AND CHURCHES

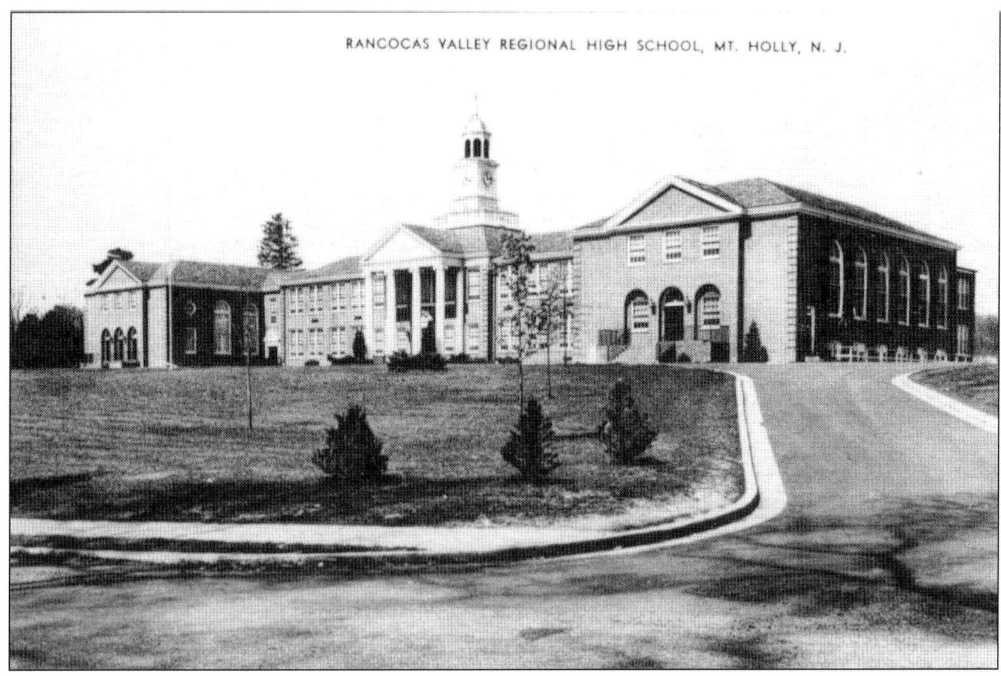

The Rancocas Valley Regional High School was built in 1936–1937 when the old high school on Brainerd Street was outgrown. Today the front of this school shows little change. However, it is expanding to meet the demand of increasing population in the Mount Holly area.

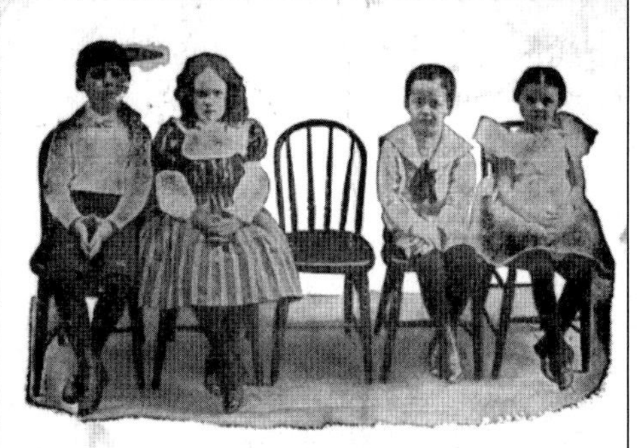

WE MISS YOU.

Feb 23rd 1919

Dear Dorothy

There was a little empty chair in your class last Sunday, and your bright happy face was missing. If you are sick will you not send us word, that we may visit you? If not, we shall expect you back in your place next Sunday.

Lovingly yours,

In 1919, so many things seemed to have more meaning and class. It was a time when formalities, note cards, and personalization was prominent. A card like this would be sent home to students when absent from class. This is the card the teacher Mrs. Kates sent home after missing Dorothy McGrath at the St. Andrew's Sunday school on February 23, 1919.

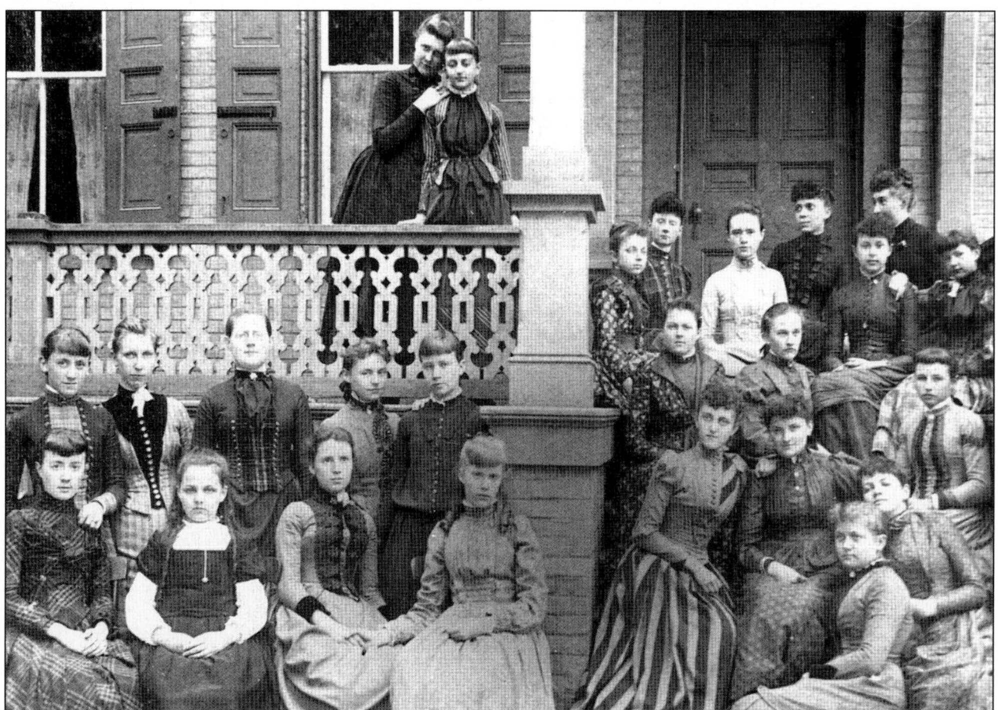

There was once a college preparatory school at 242 and 244 High Street (opposite Ridgway Street). The room over the driveway was used as a schoolroom then. Today, homeowners lovingly maintain the buildings. The five women on the top step are Avarene Budd (principal); ? Lord (teacher); and the first graduating class—Sarah Budd, Cora Hulme, and Gertrude Deacon.

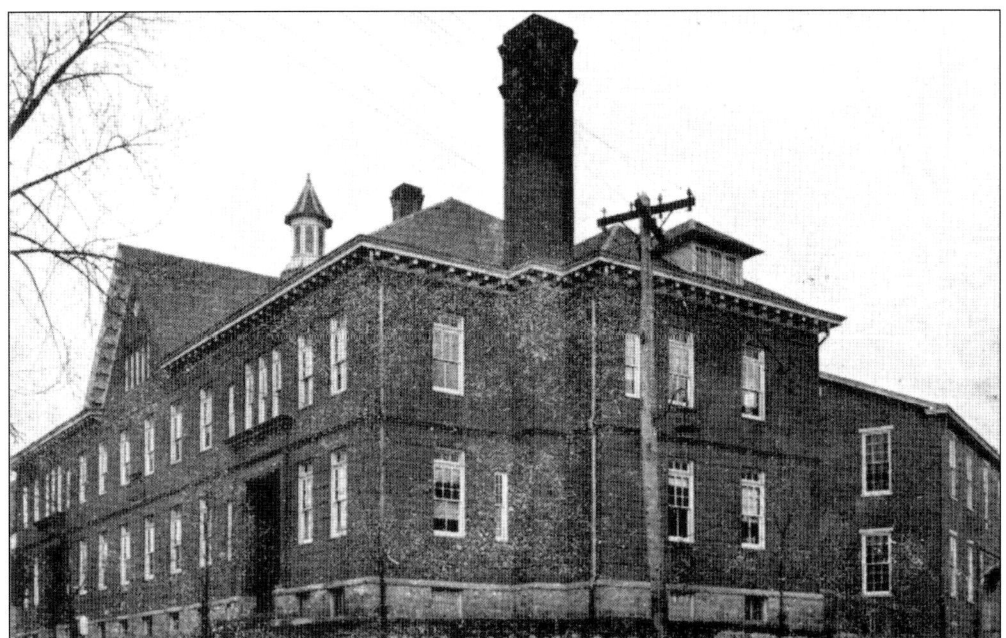

This public school was built in 1893 on the corner of Brainerd and Buttonwood Streets (where the Medford Leas Retirement Community is now). The building on the right is the Four Room School House, erected on Buttonwood Street in 1888. When the public school was demolished, its bell was removed and now resides at the Holbein School on Levis Drive.

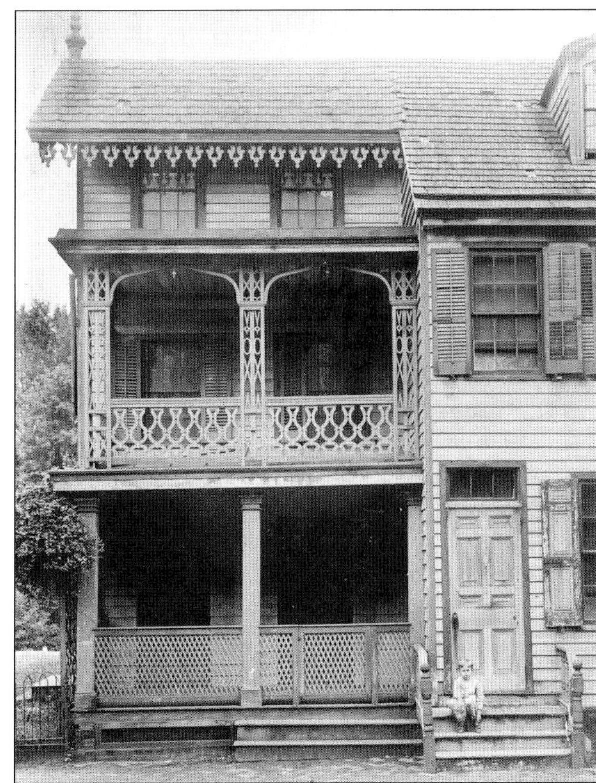

Thomas A. Heard operated a small school in his home, shown here. Gertrude Folwell taught in the Heard School and was a teacher in the Mount Holly school system for more than 50 years. This property was located where the Woolman Commons is located now and is known as the Quaker House.

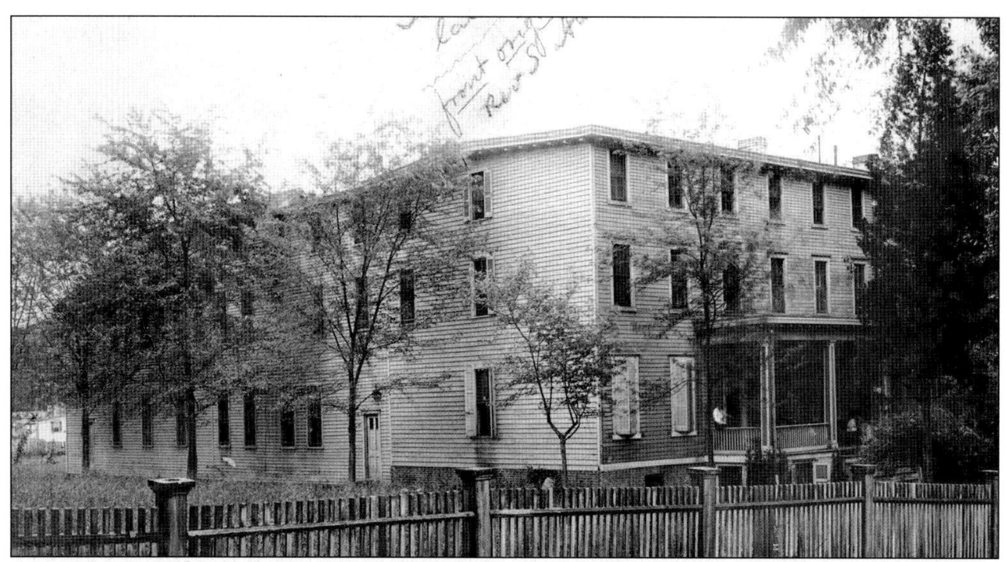

Rev. Samuel Aaron built a large boarding school at the corner of Ridgway Street and Mount Holly Avenue in 1860. After his death, Aaron's son Charles continued the school until J. Wardell Brown purchased the property. Two classes of the public school were held here in 1879. It was also used as a chicken hatchery until it was returned to a boys' school in the 1880s. It then became a boys' military academy until the doors were closed in 1898. After this string of schools, the building became a summer boardinghouse until it was demolished *c.* 1907; the scrap lumber was used to build homes in the area.

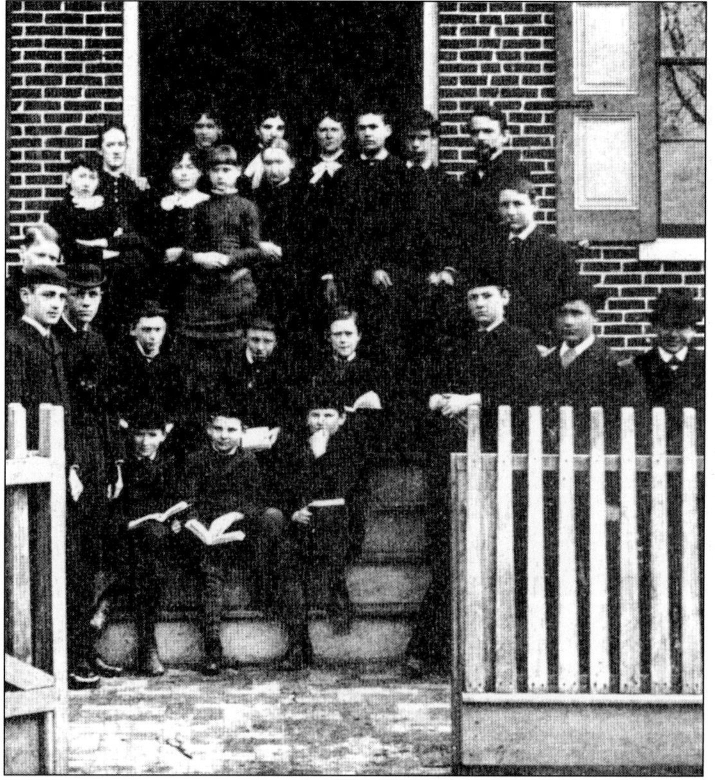

Spetheman Academy was formerly the Pfouts Academy (*c.* 1876) and was located on Mount Holly Avenue between Union and Broad Streets. Before this brick building was built, Pfouts had a school at the corner of Garden and Main Streets.

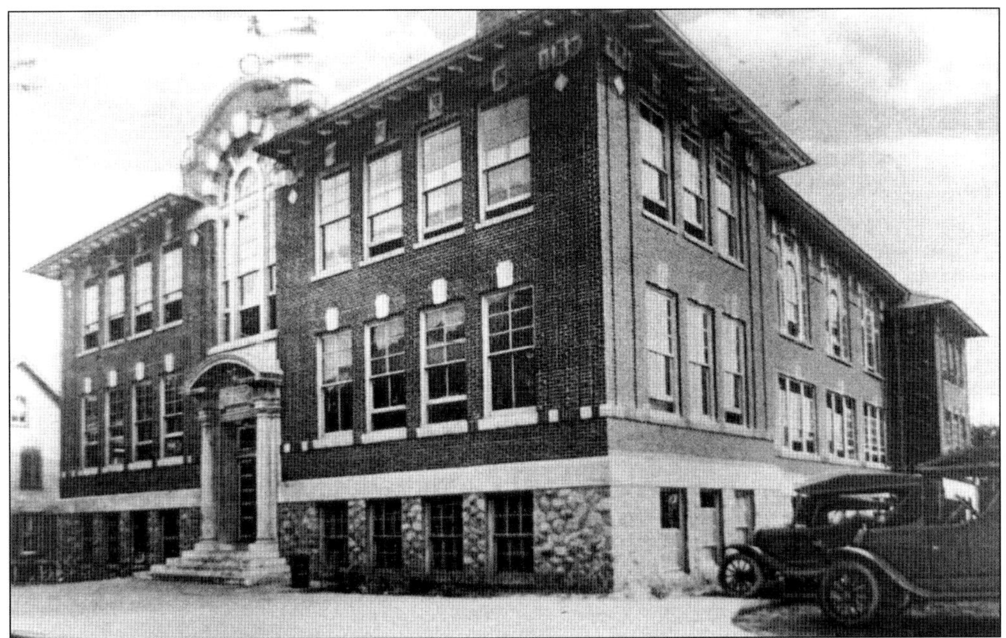

The Mount Holly High School (later used as the junior high school) was built in 1912 on Brainerd Street. This area used to be John Dobbins' apple orchard and was the location of several houses built by Thomas A. Heard, Jonathan Tuley, and Joseph Forker. Those houses were demolished to make way for the high school. The double-frame building at 36 and 38 Brainerd Street was moved to its present location east of the brick house built by John L. Stratton on Branch Street.

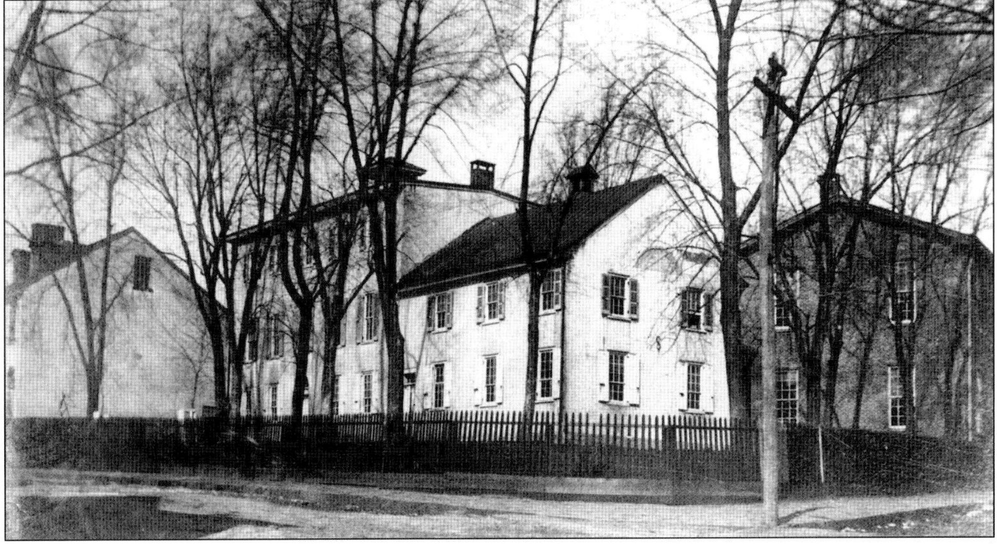

The Mount Holly Academy was located on Brainerd Street after a stock company was organized in 1810 and purchased the property from Joseph Reed to build this large boarding school. In 1830, the property (described as "a certain brick building known as the Mt. Holly Academy") was sold to John Dobbins Jr., who sold it to John Plotts for $1,400. In 1864, the Burlington County Children's Home rented a portion of the building and stayed until 1878, when it moved to Garden Street.

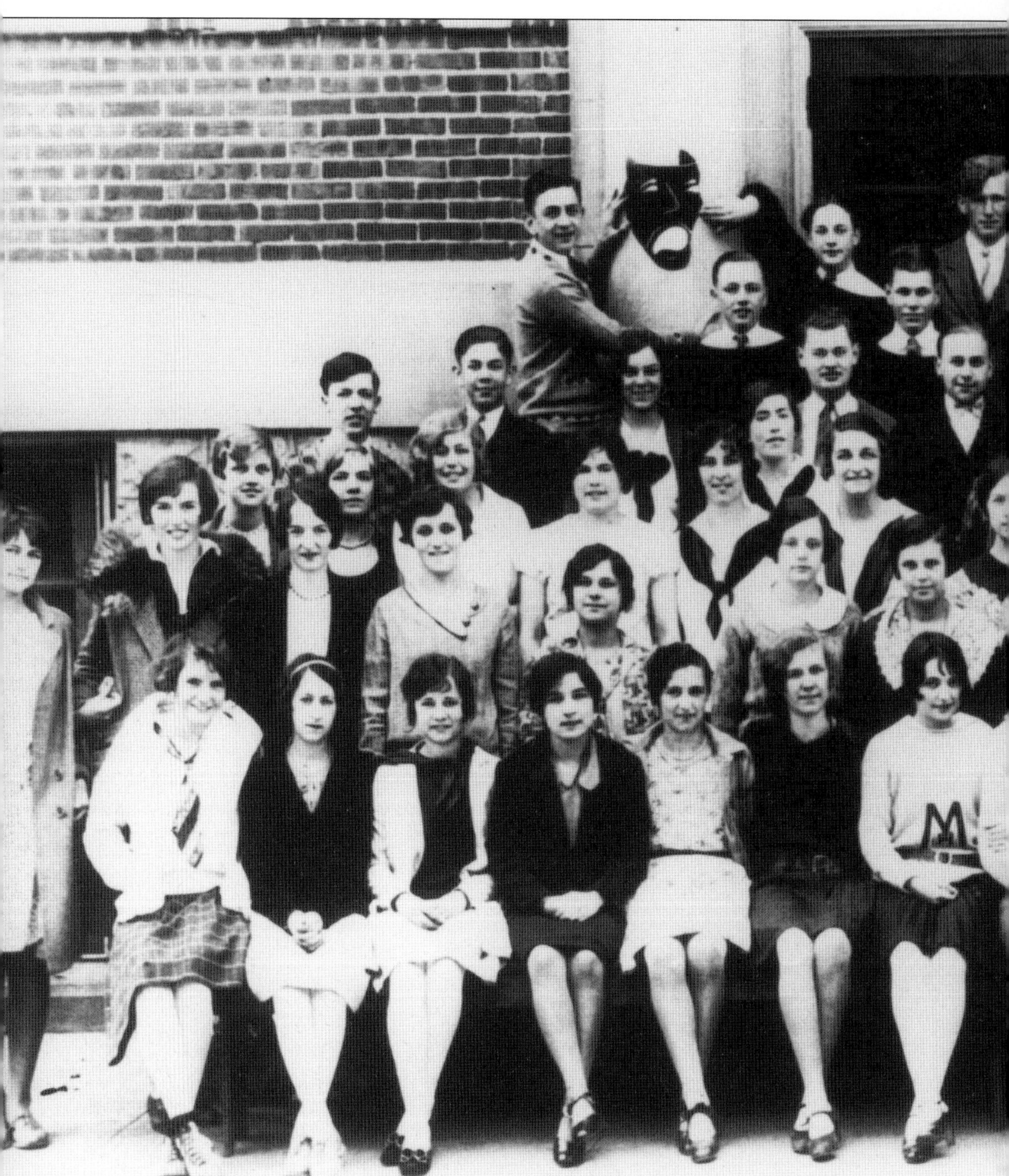

The Mount Holly High School Dramatic Club is shown in 1929. From left to right are the following: (first row) unidentified, Gladys Mason, unidentified, Hilda Ackerman, Elsie Ward, Eleanor Kaelin, Frances Gregory, Ellis Parker, Beatrice Tidswell, Samuel Fryer, two unidentified members, Betty La Tour, May Ballinger, and unidentified; (second row) unidentified, Helen Folwell, Agnes Spencer, Ruth Rosenfeld, Helen Lucas, Jane Morris, unidentified, Kathryn Gerber, unidentified, Gladys Paul, Martha Hildebrandt, Blanche Wilkins, two unidentified members, and Alice Myers; (third row) Virginia Kaser, Ruth

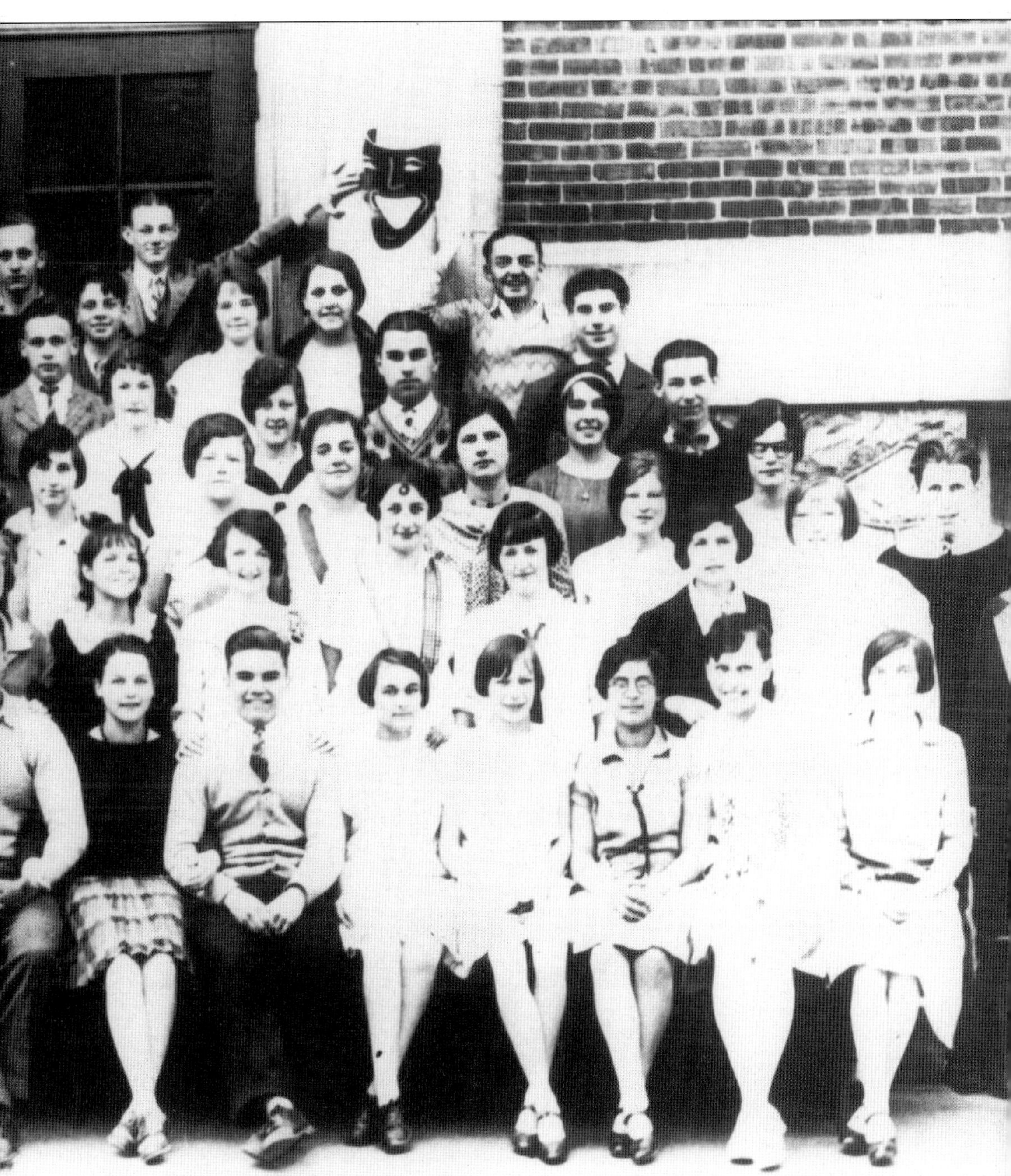

Stradling, Betty Stradling, Rae Gaskill, Norma House, Serena Gillison, Peg Gauntt, Mildred Feminore, Ellen Mcloughlin, Helen Rauser, Morrison, Folwell, Katherine Mendenhall, Evelyn Akins, Betty Marren, Marion Kirby, Dot Pierce, unidentified, Bernice Gaines, and Art Cross; (fourth row) Judson Doran, Harold Gilbert, unidentified, Norman Brown, Chase Phares, Justus Brick, Flora Walters, unidentified, Ernie Reamer, Bob Latham, and Nate Wilson; (fifth row) Earl Howe, Alvin Nitchman, Ed Hulse, Art Lord, Marriott Haines, Albert Atkinson, unidentified, and Franlkin Kates.

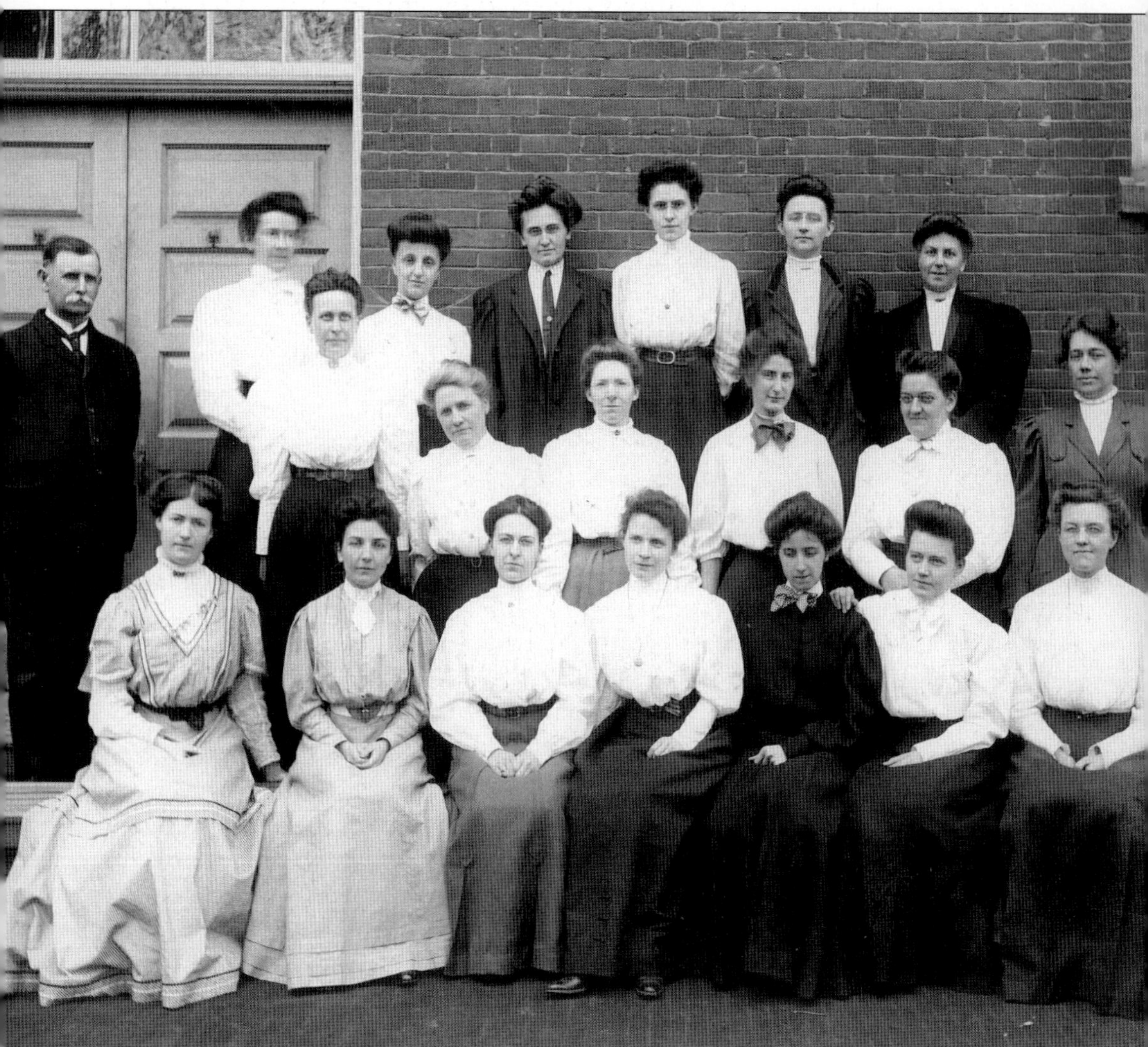

Mount Holly public school teachers are shown with Prof. William C. Cook. From left to right are the following: (front row) Josephine Kenny (Mrs. Henry Shinn), Edna Bacon, Sarah Keeler, ? Ettinger, Gertrude Folwell, Adeline Atkinson, and Myrtle Smith; (middle row) Kempte, ? Lewis, Marion Risdon, Josephine Hendrickson, Lilla J. Branson, and Cecilia Bluste; (back row) ? Mackintosh, Gertrude Kellogg, Nellie Carty, Elsie Hughes (secretary), ? Farrell, and Sarah Randall.

We do not have the names of these children, but the looks on their faces and the girls' bows and dresses made us fall in love with this photograph. We know it was Mrs. McIntosh's class at the Brainerd School in Mount Holly and are sure she had her hands full.

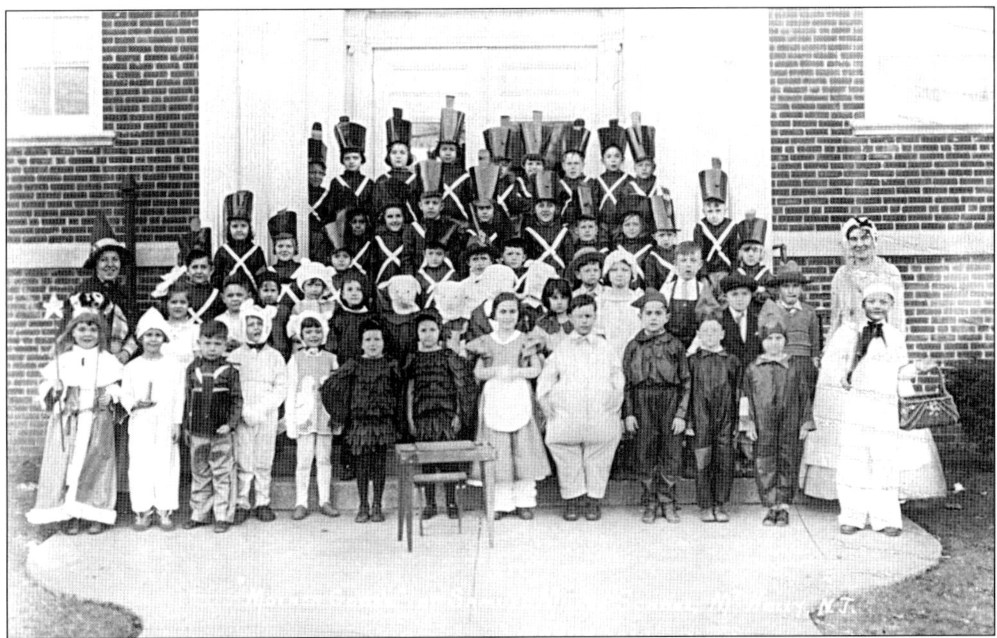

Children pose in their costumes for the production of *Mother Goose* at the Samuel Mill School in 1934. This building has now been converted into a lovely retirement community on Clifton Avenue

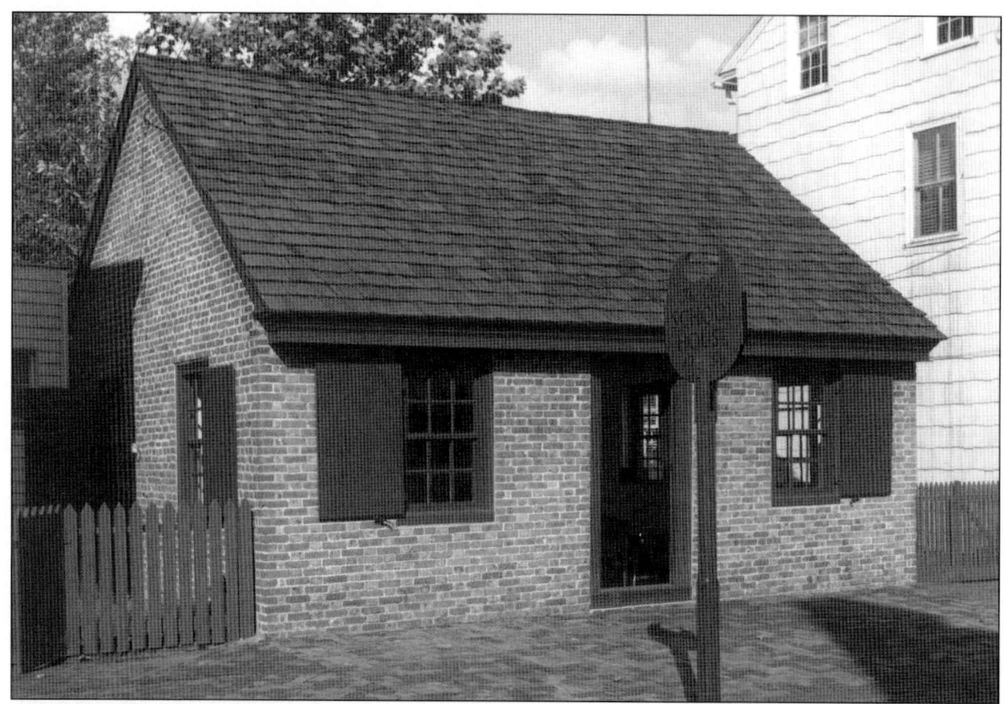

On September 21, 1759, trustees who felt the need to educate the youth purchased a lot on New Street (now Brainerd Street) and erected a school. This schoolhouse is still located at 35 Brainerd Street and is thought to be the oldest schoolhouse in New Jersey (certainly the oldest standing on its original site). It is believed John Woolman taught in this building; in 1765, he refers to the school, and his ledger record notes charges for teaching the children of several owners of the schoolhouse. In 1814, the heirs of the original owners conveyed it to the Female Benevolent Association, which continued its operation until 1847, when the public school opened. On June 28, 1951, the New Jersey Society of Colonial Dames became the owners.

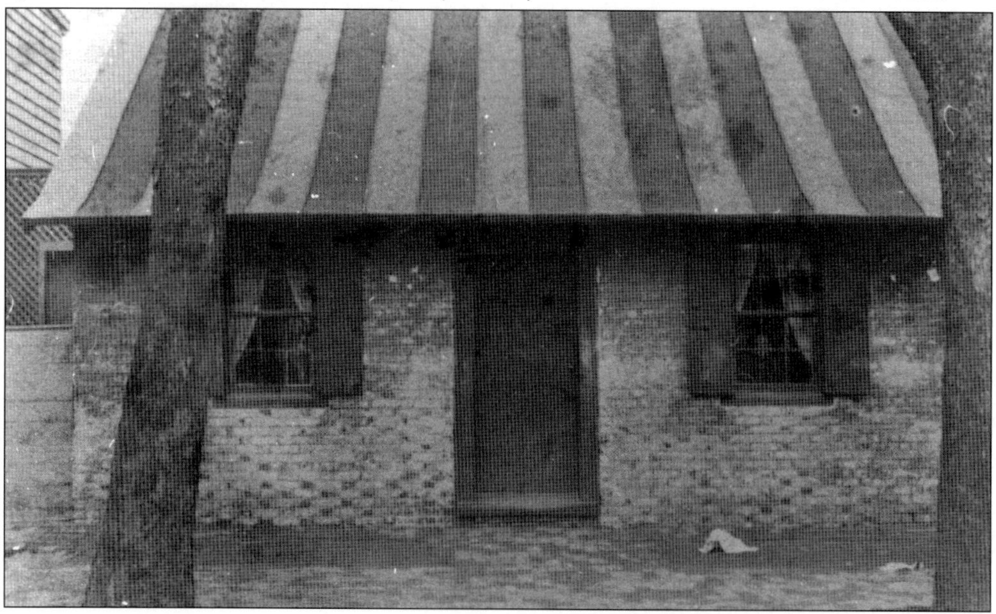

The Mount Holly First Baptist Church, located on Buttonwood Street, was organized in 1800. This Baptist church was built on Garden Street in 1881 and is now used as the Presbyterian church extension. The local Baptist church is located on North Pemberton Road outside of town. The Baptist church once baptized members in the Rancocas Creek, east of the Washington Street railroad bridge.

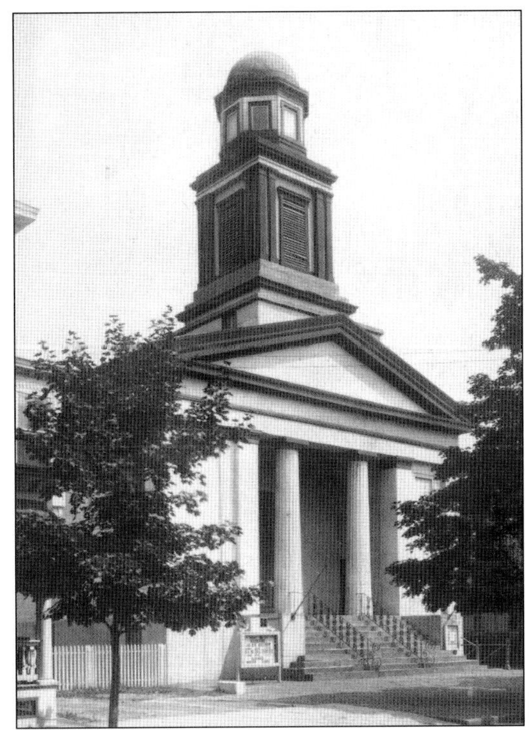

The first Mount Moriah Church was built on the north end of their burial lot c. 1826. A church was then built at its present location on West Washington Street in 1861. It was destroyed by a tornado in 1863. The new (and present) church was built on the same site in 1875.

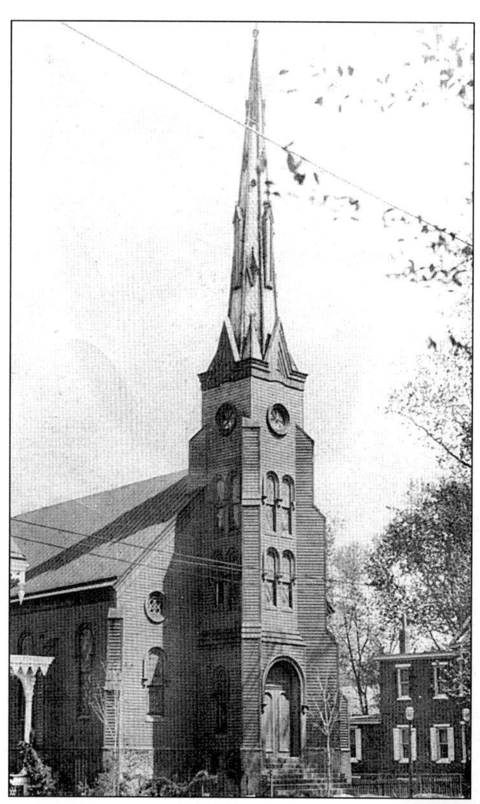

In 1859, a dispute arose in the St. Andrew's Episcopal Church over a question of ritual, and a new parish was formed the same year to accommodate those who wanted to leave St. Andrew's. Charles Bispham donated a lot on the north side of Washington Street, and the Trinity Church was built. Its first service was held on July 3, 1859. A rectory for this church was built at 11 Ridgway Street, and the Bispham homestead on the opposite side of Washington Street was purchased for a parish house. In 1904, the last service was held at the Trinity Church, and the remaining congregation rejoined St. Andrew's. Sadly, this church was demolished.

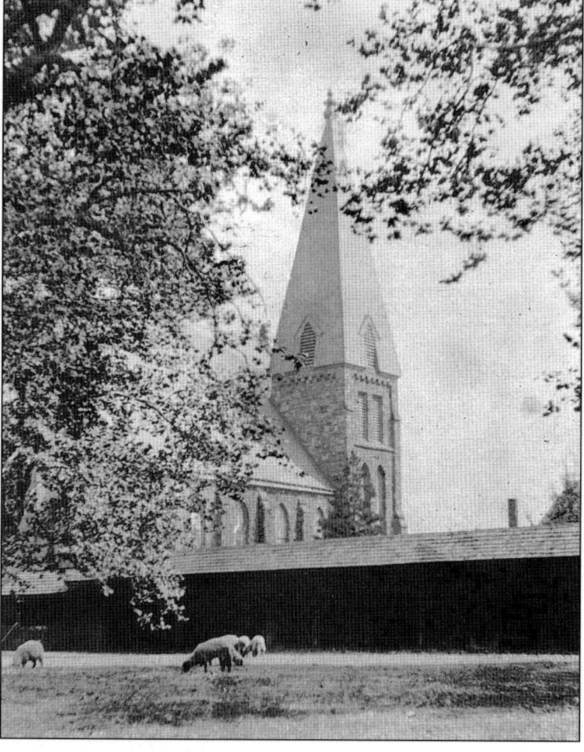

The Friends Meetinghouse rear lawn and graveyard was really no trouble to keep with the help of a few friendly sheep. Here is the stable along the rear of the property, with the Methodist church on Brainerd Street in the background.

The Friends Meetinghouse, on the corner of Main and Garden Streets, was built in 1775. At first it was a one-story building and then, in 1850, a gallery was added. Inside are cleaver marks from Hessian troops who occupied the place and used it as a commissary during the Battle of Iron Works Hill. Today the Quakers are very active, with meetings held every week and the meetinghouse open for tours on the fourth weekend of each month, from April to October.

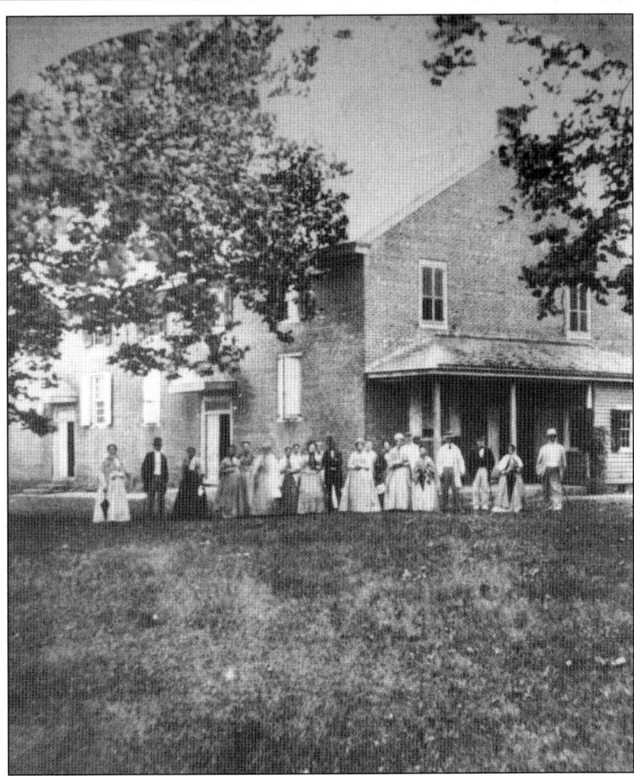

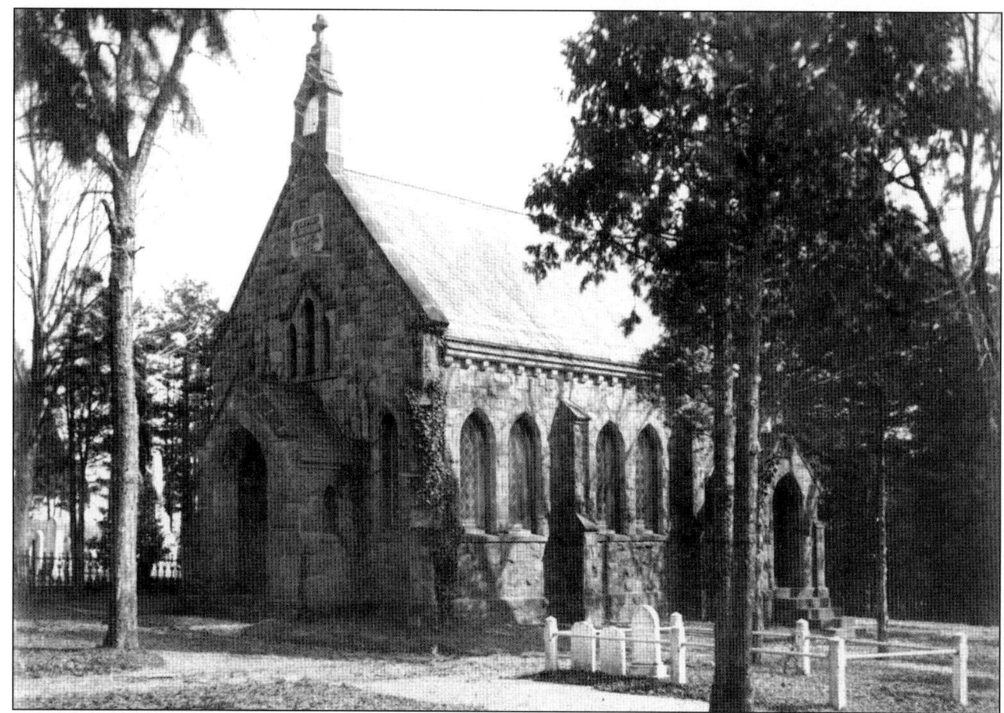

The Dobbins Memorial Chapel was consecrated in 1879. It was a beautiful addition to the graveyard just off Pine Street on Irons Works Hill. The vestry of St. Andrew's changed the entrance to the cemetery in order to make the passage to the chapel and grounds more direct.

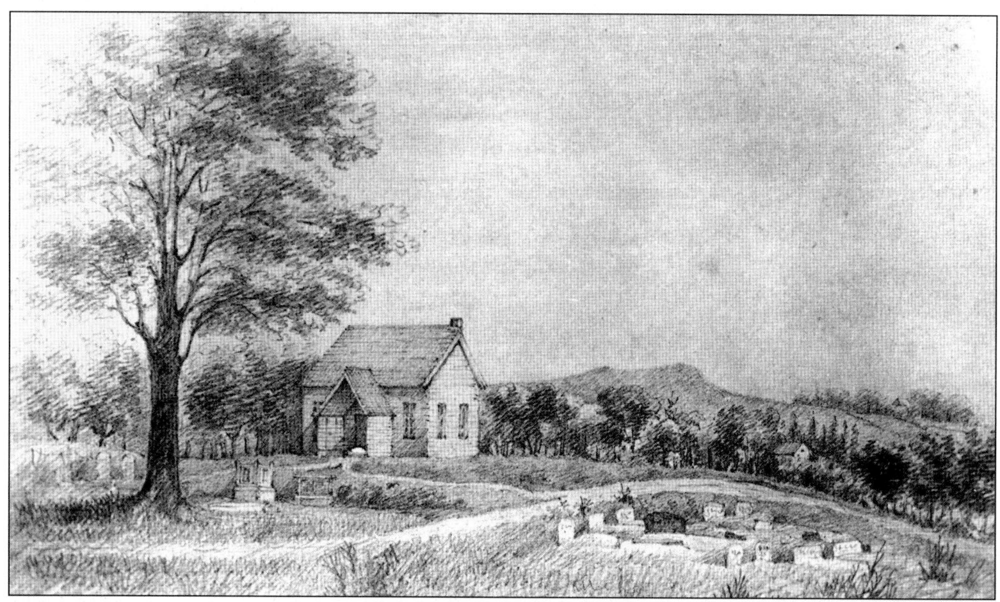

The first St. Andrew's was built in 1742 in the graveyard on Pine Street. The drawing shows the small church on the future Iron Works Hill, with the mount in the background. After this, a new church was built on Church Street (then White Street) in 1786 until the newest church was built on High Street, where it remains today.

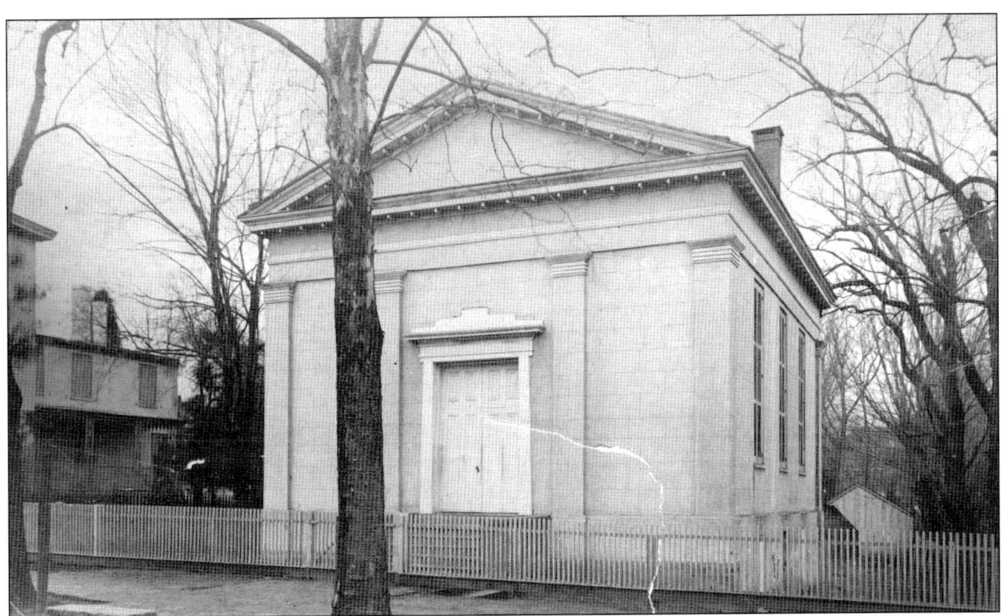

The photograph above shows the Presbyterian church as it was originally built in 1844 on Garden Street. This building was demolished to make way for the current church (below), built in 1887 on the same site. Sometime in 1761, Rev. John Brainerd purchased land on New Street and erected the first Presbyterian church in Burlington County, east of the Methodist church.

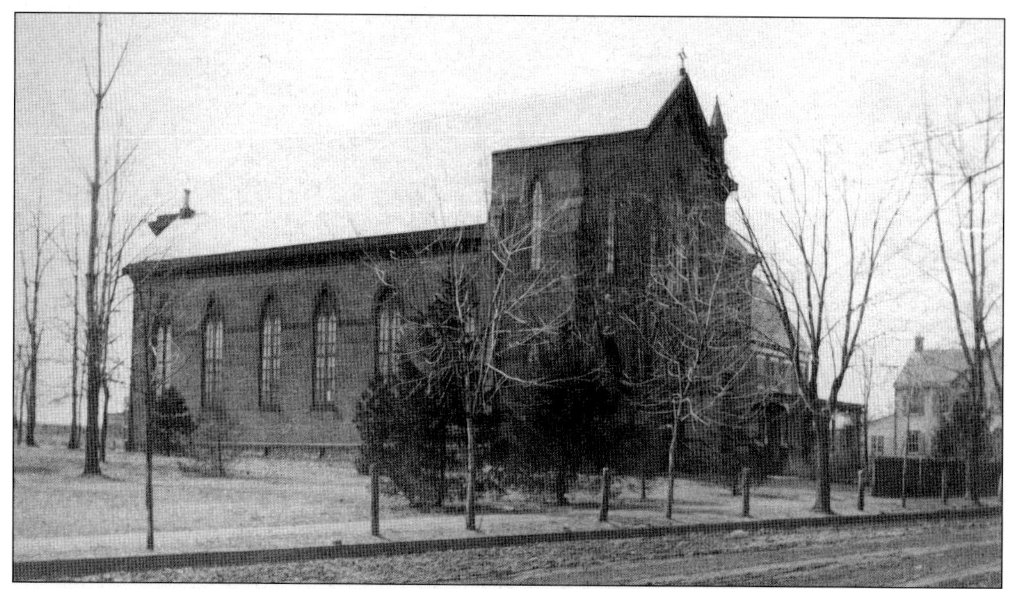

In 1852, a frame church was built on Mount Holly Avenue. Land for the Sacred Heart Cemetery was bought in 1857 on West Washington Street, and a lot was purchased for the erection of a new church on West Washington Street. That church was built in 1879. The original church was moved to its current location and is still standing, although the congregation abandoned this structure to build a church on High Street next to the Sacred Heart School in the middle of the historic district.

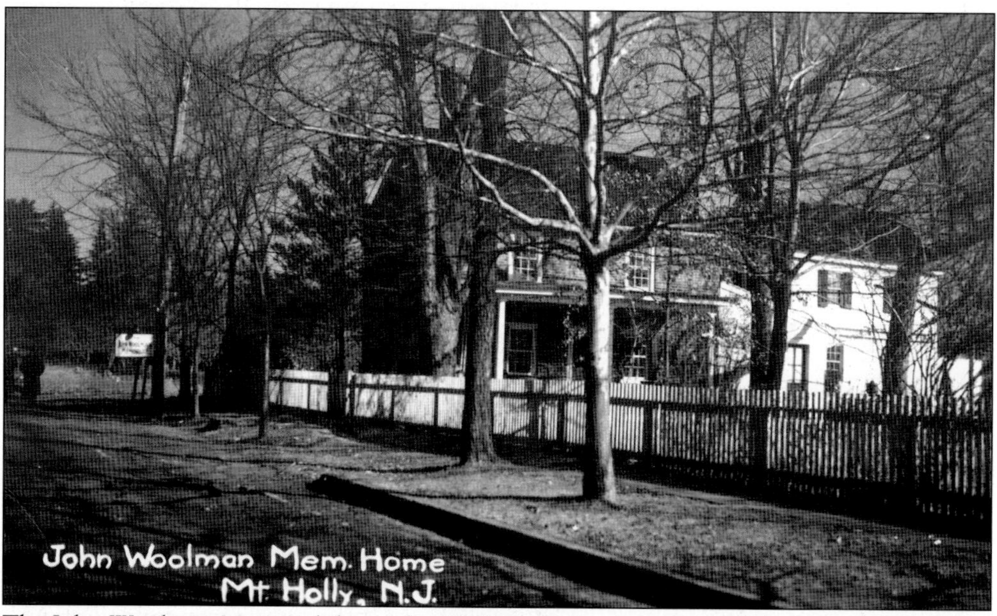

The John Woolman Memorial, located at 90 Branch Street, was established to perpetuate the memory of John Woolman (1721–1772). The memorial was built in 1783 and is maintained by a memorial organization. People travel from all over the world to visit and learn about John Woolman, one of Mount Holly's foremost citizens, a legendary Quaker, humanitarian, and abolitionist. Woolman died of smallpox in England and is buried there. The memorial is open to the public and for group tours.

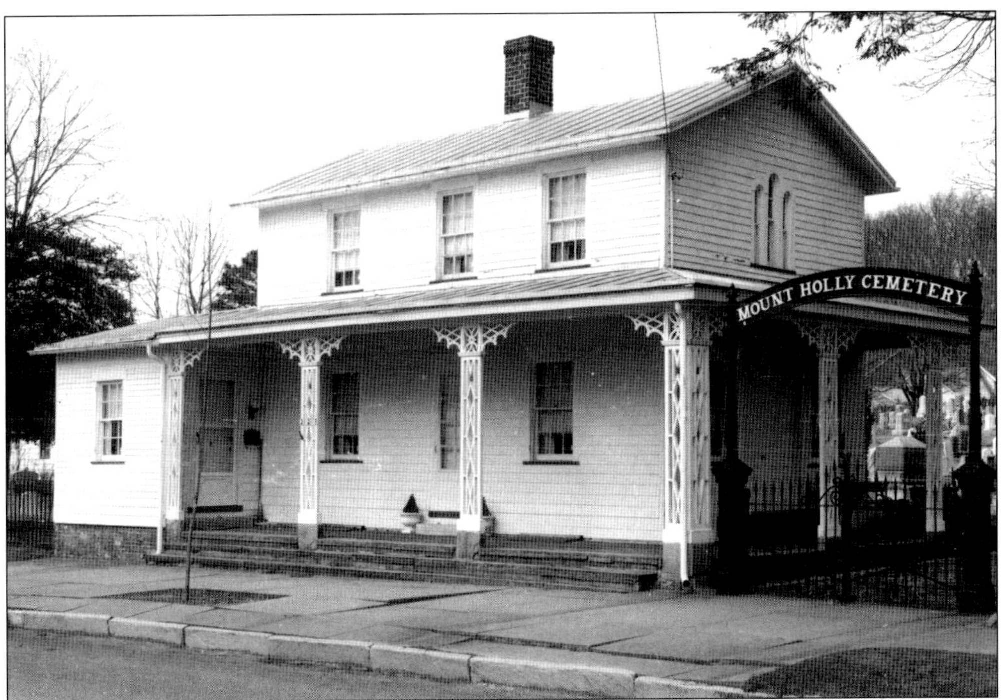

Mount Holly Cemetery Cottage on Ridgway Street was built by Isaac Risdon in 1840. Risdon also founded the Mount Holly Cemetery in the same year. The cottage was built for a caretaker's home and has a small lovely, nondenominational chapel at the east end.

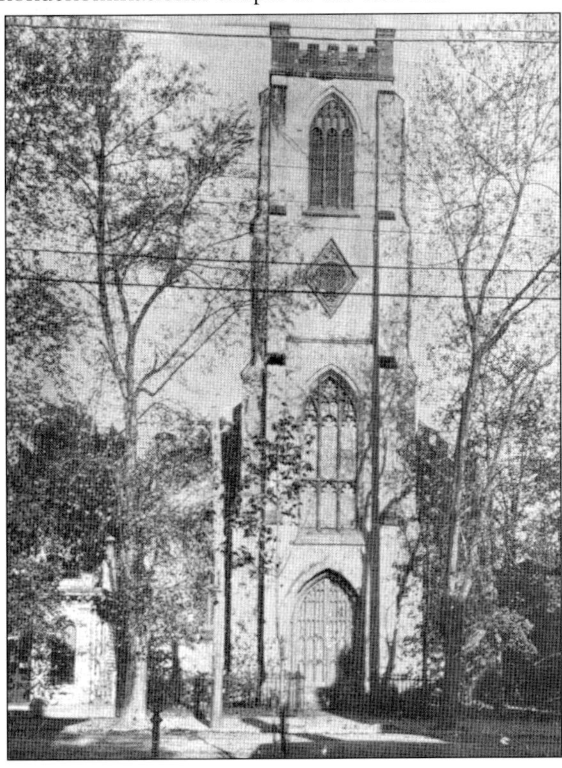

The first St. Andrew's was located north of the big oak tree, near the northwest corner of the present burying ground on Pine Street. This site is its third location in Mount Holly. The structure was completed in 1844 and was remodeled in the early 20th century, giving the church a new look. In 2001, the members of St. Andrew's worked toward another major restoration to undo some remodeling, which had ultimately become more of a problem than an asset.

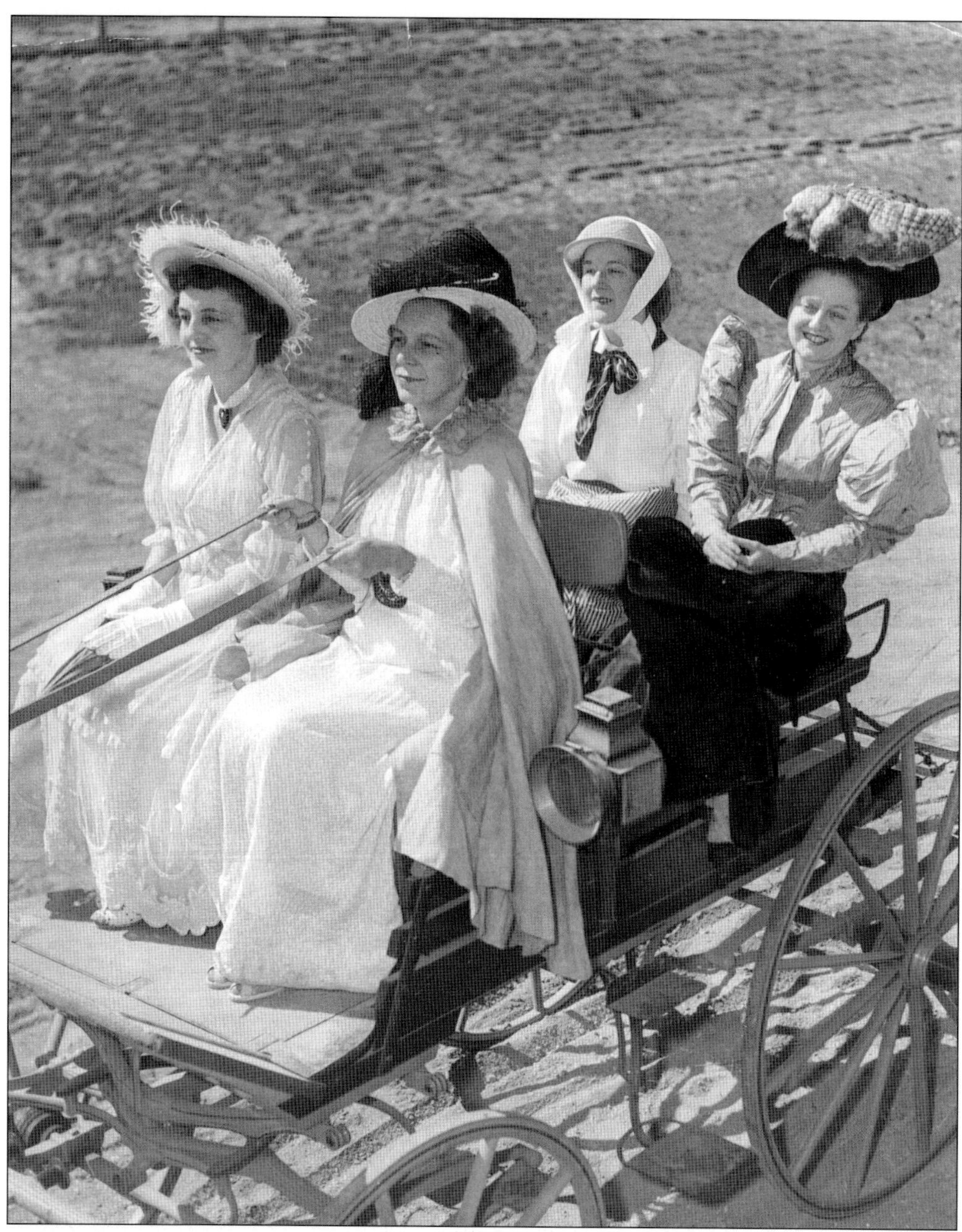

St. Andrew's held an annual antique show and sale as a fundraiser between 1950 and 1990. The event was always a big success and lots of fun for the members. Here, church members stage photograph opportunities for newspapers before the show for publicity. The church members in the photograph are, from left to right, as follows: (front row) Mary Lewis Smith and Doris Mickle Tidswell; (back row) Edith Vaughn Quay and Georgia Neveil Denton.

Five

Special Times and Places

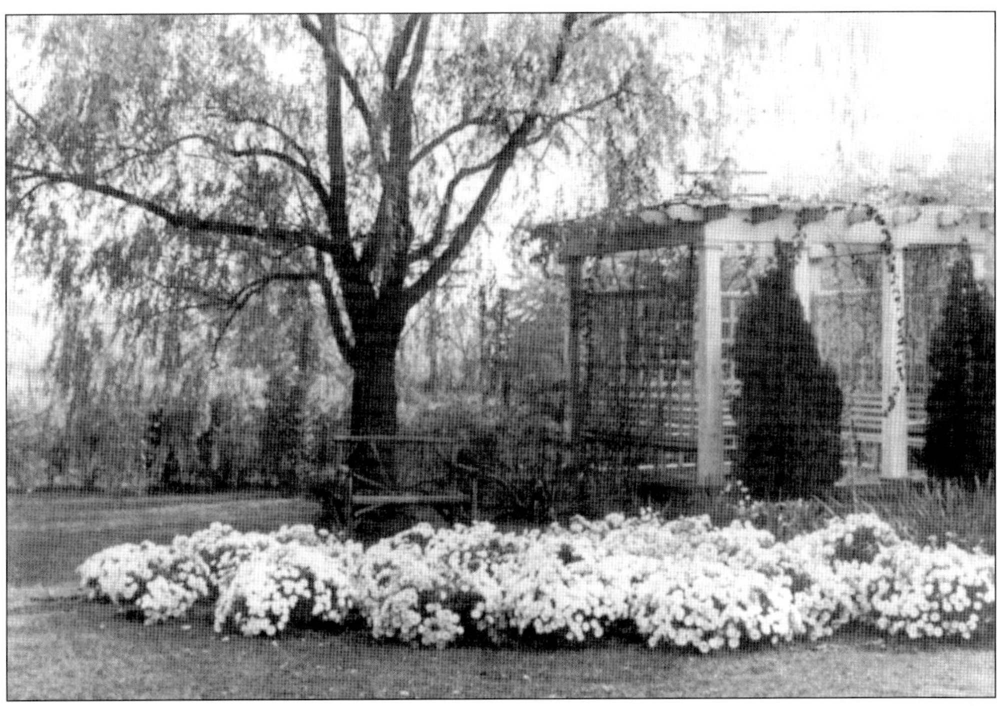

The Levis Gardens off upper Main Street were on the grounds of Edward H. Levis. This property is now the Perenchief Funeral Home, and much of the garden area and rare trees and plants were destroyed to make way for the present day Holbein School's lawn area.

The Holly Club Minstrel Production was a yearly affair and very well received. Everyone looked forward to the music, dancing, and comedy acts they would perform when volunteers put the show on in the local theater. This photograph was taken in 1926.

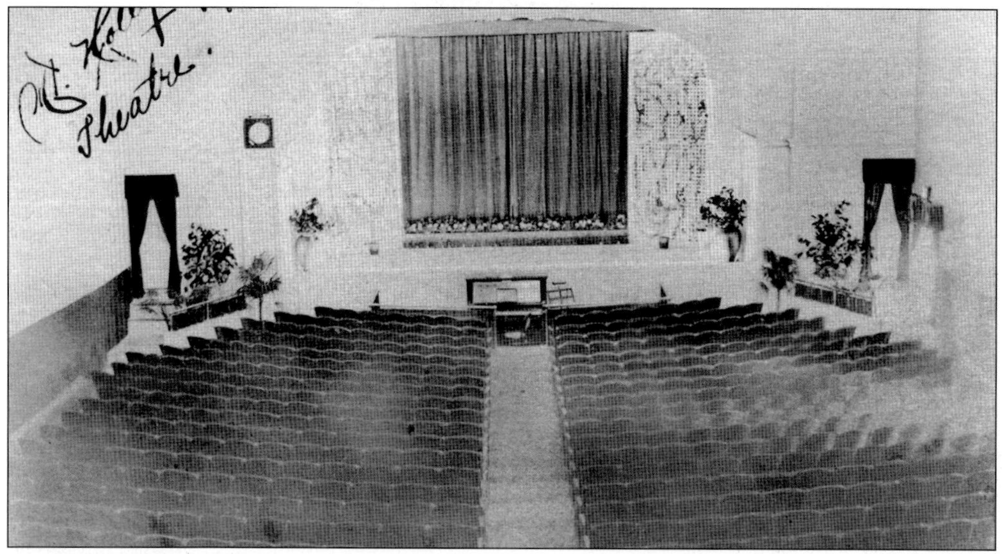

The Mount Holly Theater/Opera House was originally called the Concert Hall and was located on Main Street. It officially opened in August 1876. In 1904, William and Frank Wright purchased the hall and showed motion pictures on Saturday nights. Later, basketball games were held here until *c.* 1911. Eventually, movies were the principle entertainment until the new theater was built on Washington Street, when the old Opera House became a roller-skating rink. This building became another casualty of urban renewal.

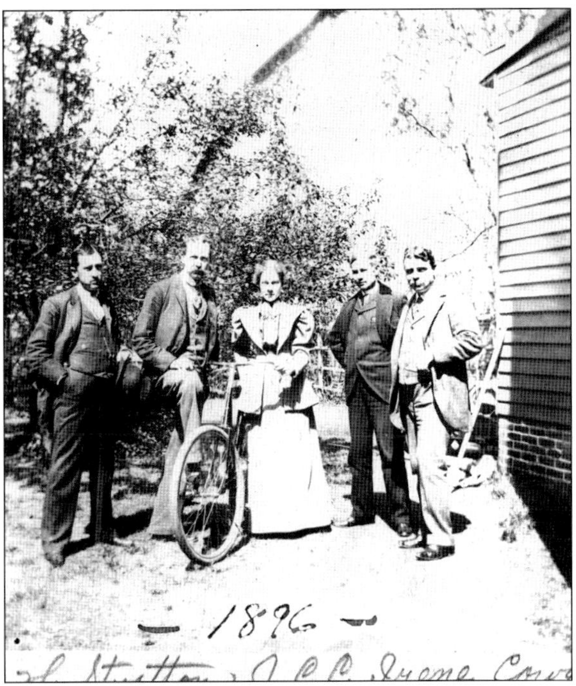

Shown in 1896 are, from left to right, H. Stratton, Joseph Cowgill, Irene Cowgill, Dr. C.R. Barrington, and H. Eder. Harry Eder owned the property on the corner of Broad and Cherry Streets. Dr. Barrington operated a drugstore on the west side of Main Street. Irene was a pianist and performed at the Mount Holly Opera House. Joseph Cowgill was considered the town historian and was an active member of the Relief Fire Company.

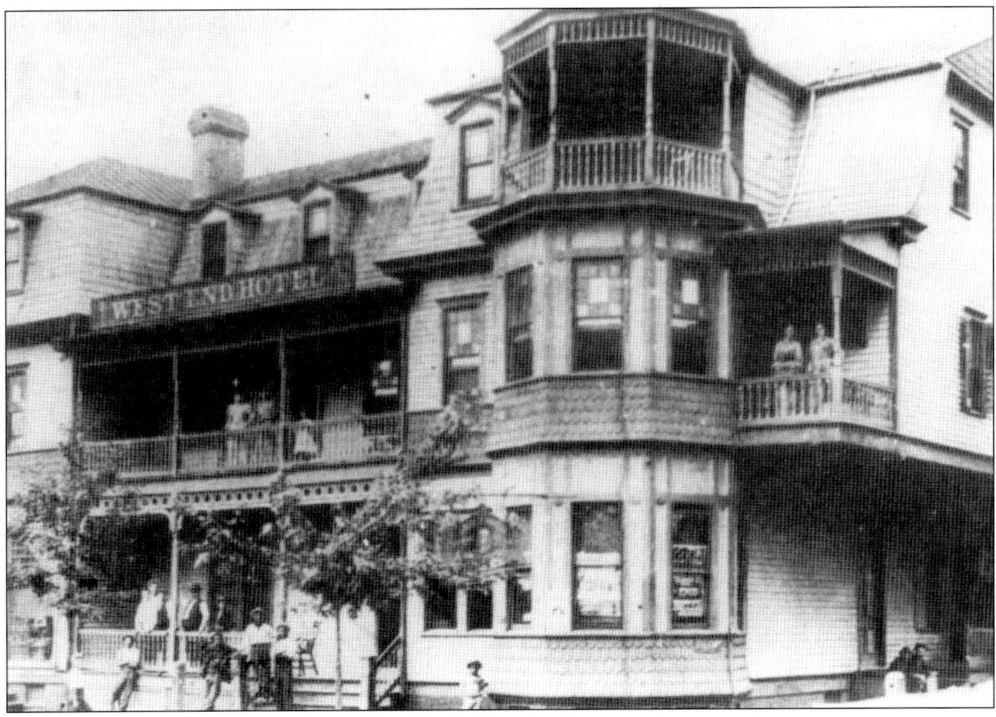

The West End (or Imperial) Hotel was built in 1889 by Alfred Wolfrom on the site of an old roller-skating rink on Washington Street. It had 32 rooms and a very unusual set of stairs, with risers half the distance of usual risers, which gave guests a thrill climbing the stairs. This building was known as ODAT (One Day At a Time) and eventually fell into a state of disrepair until it was destroyed by fire in 1994.

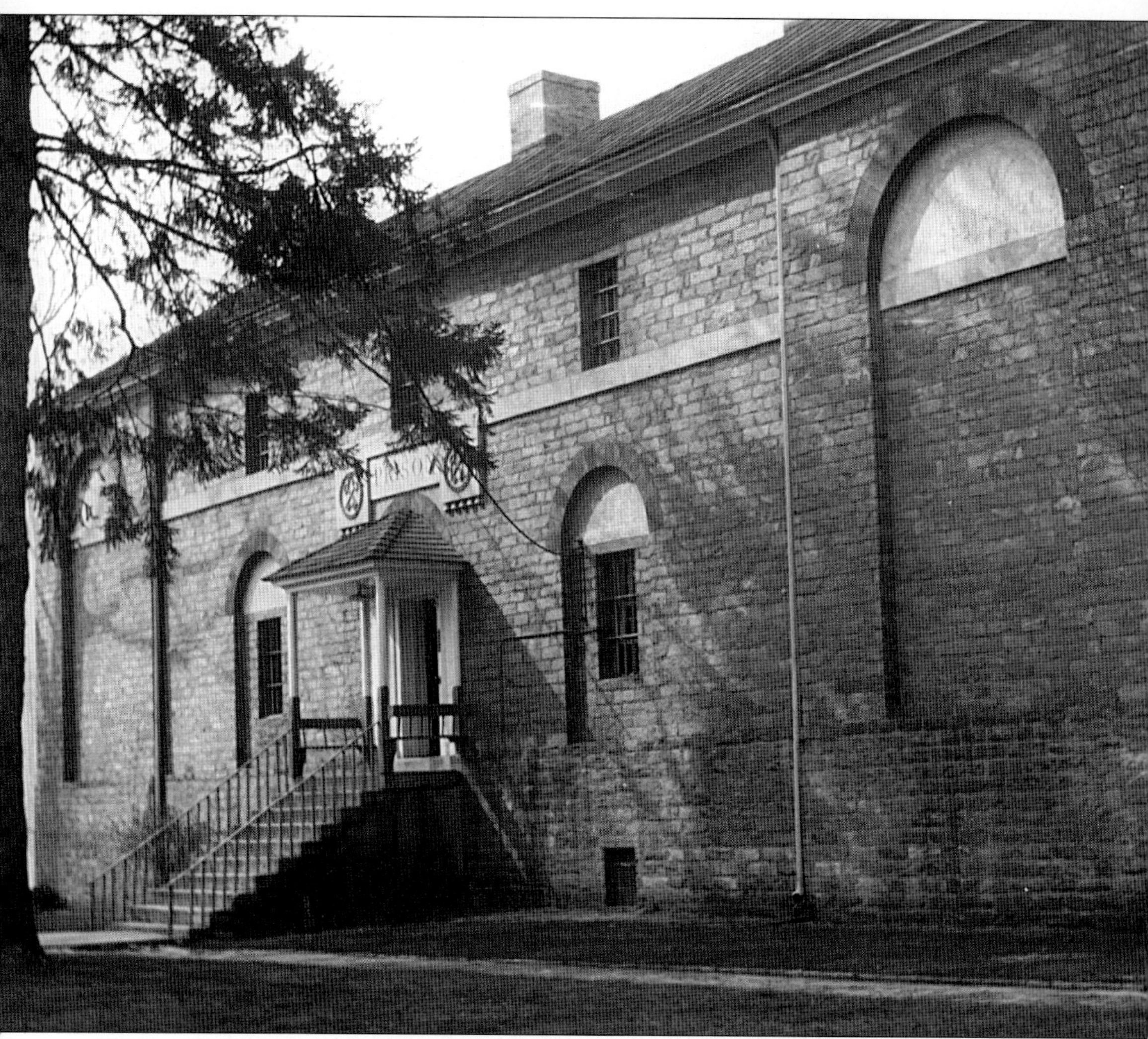

The Burlington County Prison (now the Prison Museum) was completed in 1811. This prison was in use until 1965, making it the oldest in continuous use in the country. It was designed by Robert Mill, who also designed such landmarks as the Washington Monument. The dungeon (maximum-security cell), in the center of the top floor, was complete with a permanent iron ring to chain down prisoners. Each prisoner was supplied with a Bible or prayer book to improve the soul. The prison museum is open for tours on the fourth weekend of each month and for group tours.

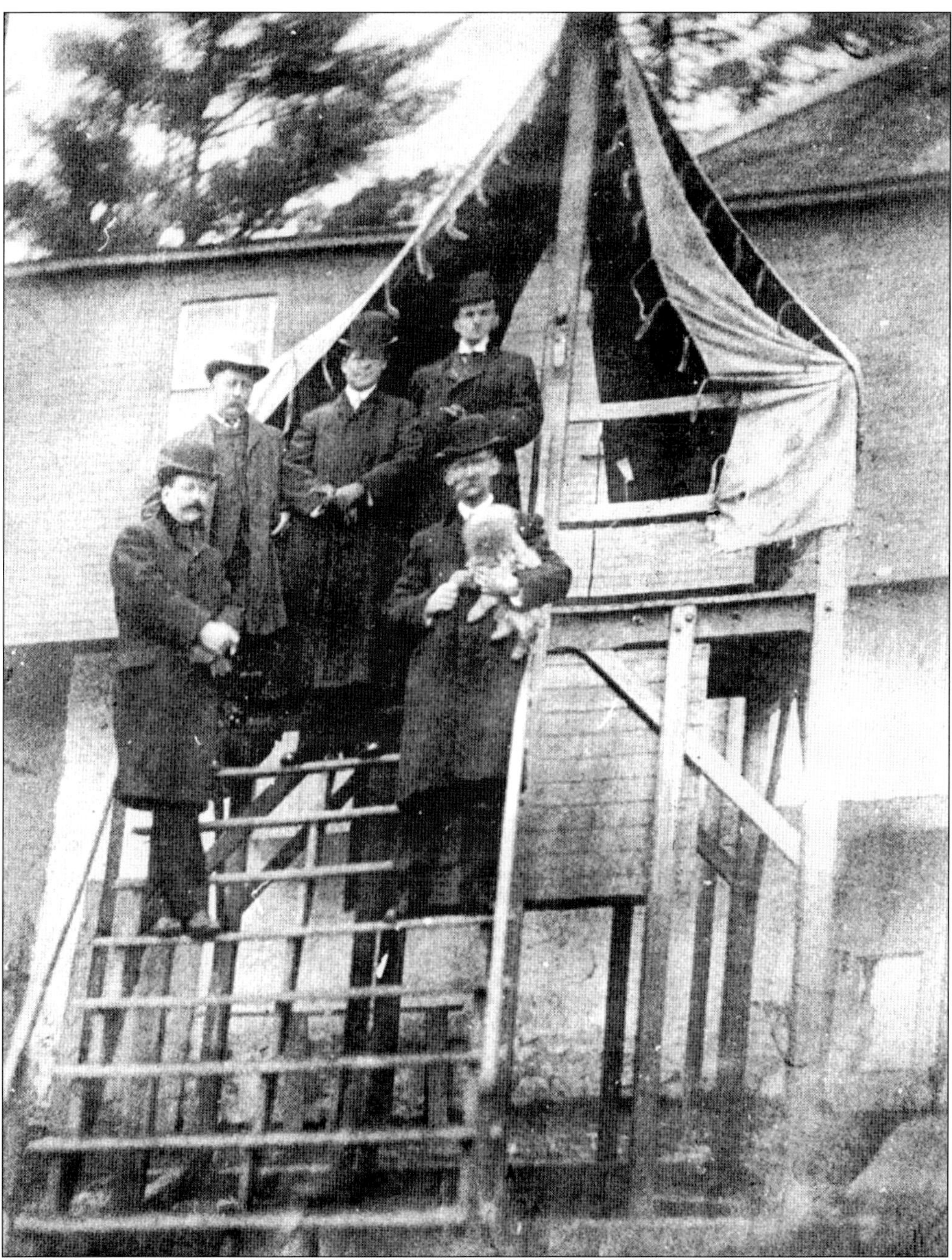

The gallows behind the prison was dismantled between hangings. During the early 19th century, four murderers were hanged in Burlington County (not all at this prison). At one hanging, spectators crowded into the yard where the scaffold stood ready to hang Wesley Warner, who murdered Lizzie Peak by stabbing her in the neck with a carving knife. A leather strap was placed on Warner's legs above the ankles. A black cap was adjusted over his head, and the sheriff pulled the lever, opening the trap door below. Shown from left to right are prosecutor Eckard P. Budd; Sheriff W.A. Townsend; prison physician Dr. W.P. Melcher; coroner Enoch Denworth, and jury foreman Joseph C. Kingdon, with the dog.

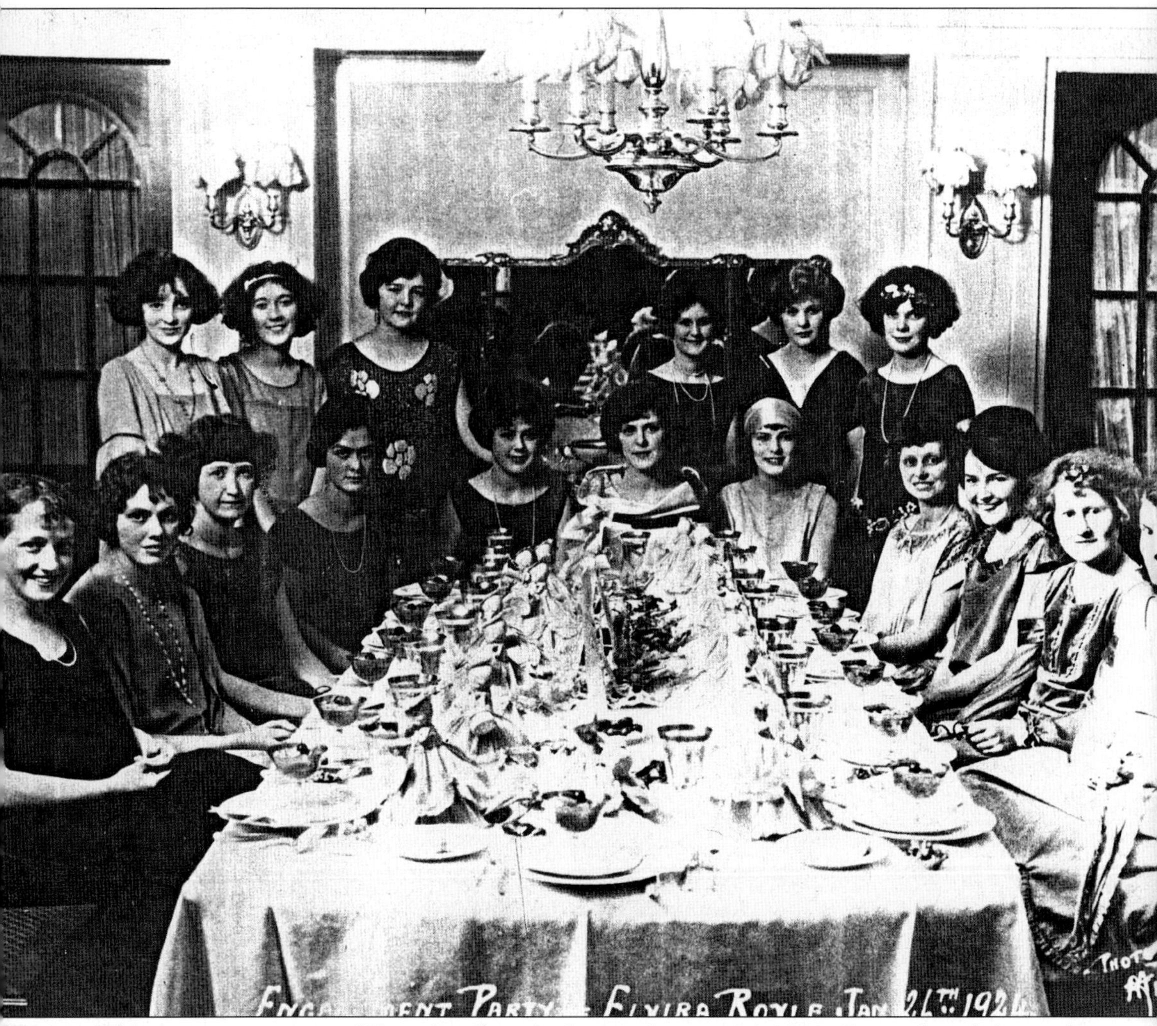

The engagement party of Elvira Royle took place on January 26, 1924. Shown from left to right are the following: (sitting) Mary Coles (Irons), Charlotte Long (Parker), Beatrice Haines, Mildred Budd (Rudderow), Eleanor Sleeper (Rogers), Elvira Royle, Gladys Royle, unidentified, Helen Bradley Gilliam, Ruth Van Stork, and Grace Budd (Graham); (standing) Clara Crippin, Margaret Lavery, Alice Clarke (Dunham), Elizabeth Gaskill, Dorothy Hillman, and unidentified.

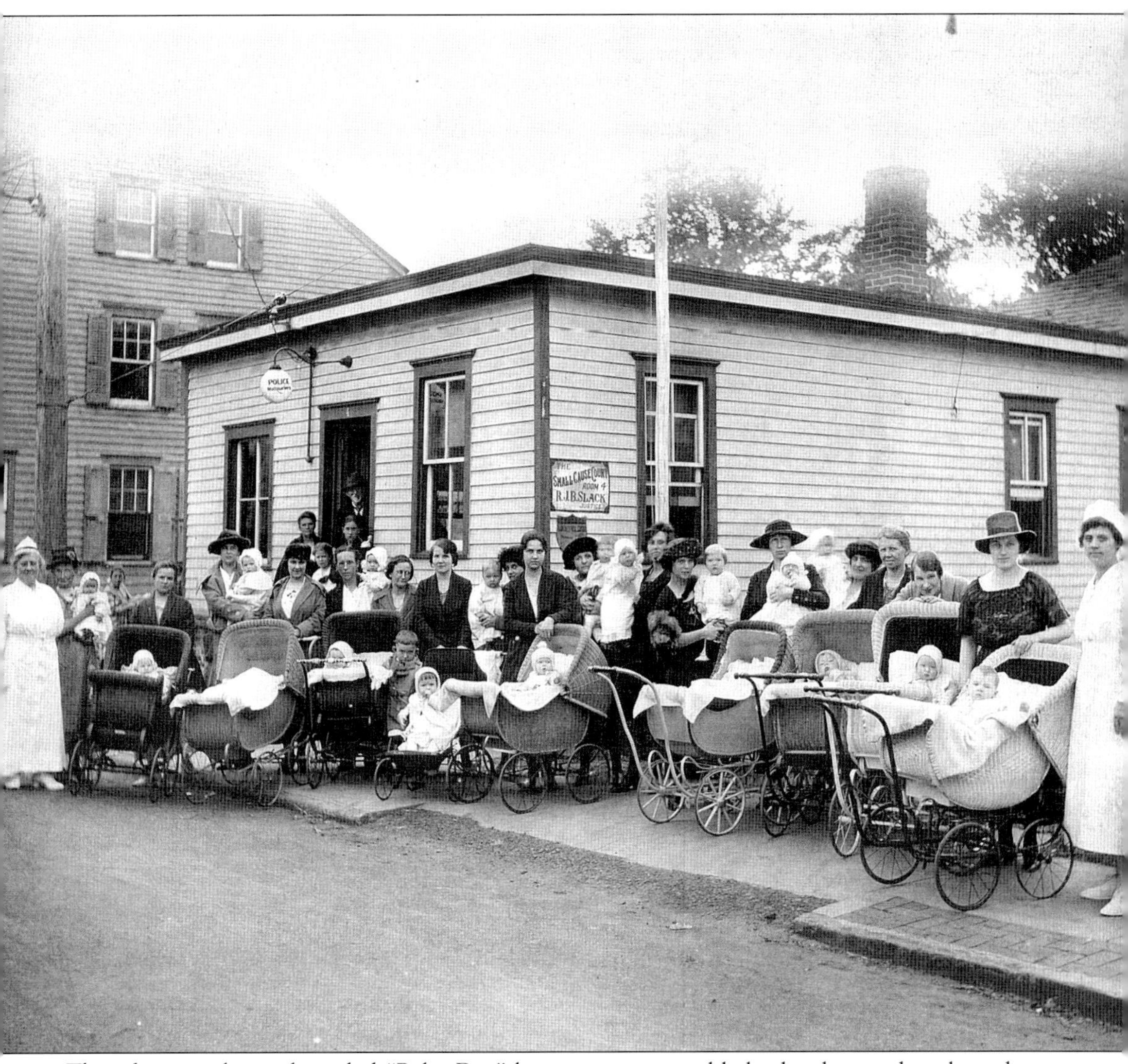

This photograph can be titled "Baby Day" because it is most likely the day mothers brought their babies down to the town hall for immunizations of some sort, judging from the nurses on hand. The building behind the group is 4 White Street, the first town hall, police station, and lock-up; it is now the Robin's Nest Annex Bakery.

THE GREAT

Mount Holly, N. J., Fair,

October 8, 9, 10, 11 and 12, 1888.

PREMIUMS, $20,000.

The most noted fair on record. The *largest* and *most elegant* of *Grand Stands;* one of the finest Race Courses; hundreds of commodious Stables; everything in *Art* and *Agriculture* to please the eye and cultivate the mind.

Every variety of amusement. Trotting, Running, all kinds of Equestrian and *Wild West* Performances. Entertainments between the races on stage in front of grand stand.

Public Sale of Refreshment Stands on Monday, September 17th, at 1 p. m., on Grounds of Society.

Excursion from Philadelphia and Trenton, including admission, $1.00; other points at same low rates.

To Ladies. One of the chief attractions will be the exhibit of JAMES PYLE'S PEARLINE WASHING COMPOUND—where every lady who has used Pearline can express her opinion of it, and in return receive a Souvenir. In case you cannot go yourself, send your message by your husband or some friend.

The Burlington County Fair (Mount Holly Fair) was really a sight to see, and people did see what was there by traveling from miles around. The grandstand was built in 1887, and the first fair was held in the courthouse yard on October 28, 1847. In 1856, 24 acres of ground were purchased on Burlington Road and the corner of Woodpecker Lane for the new, larger fairgrounds. It was so popular that Pres. Woodrow Wilson attended several times. The fair was discontinued in 1926.

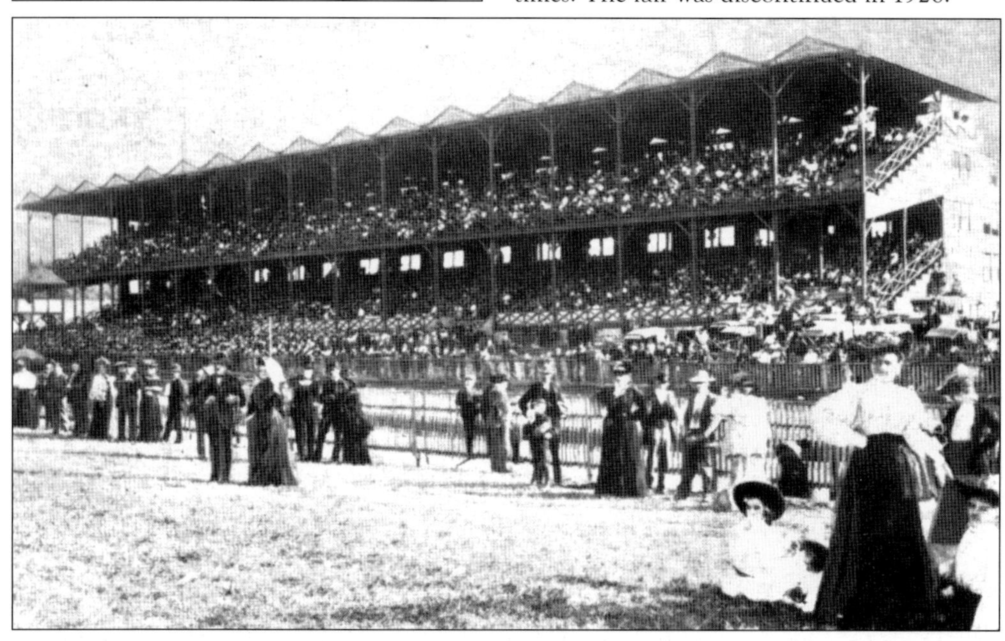

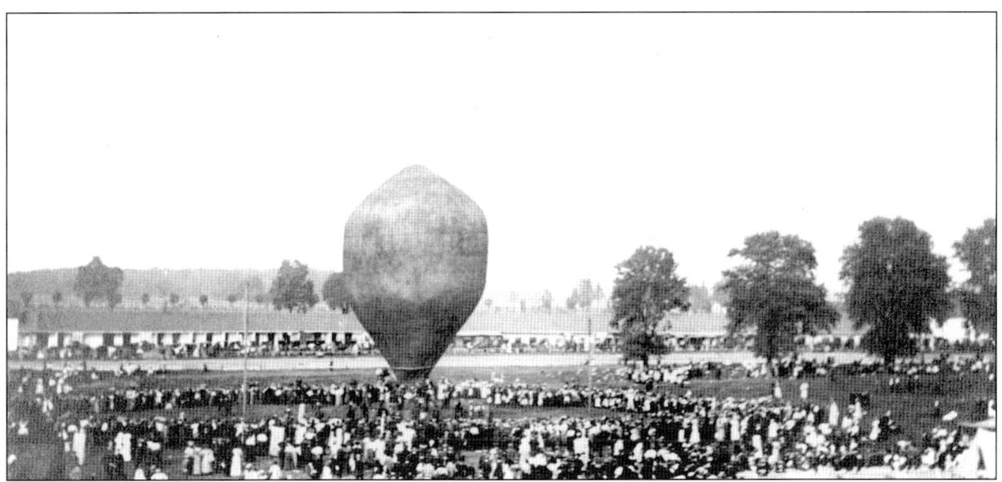

A balloon waits for riders at the fair.

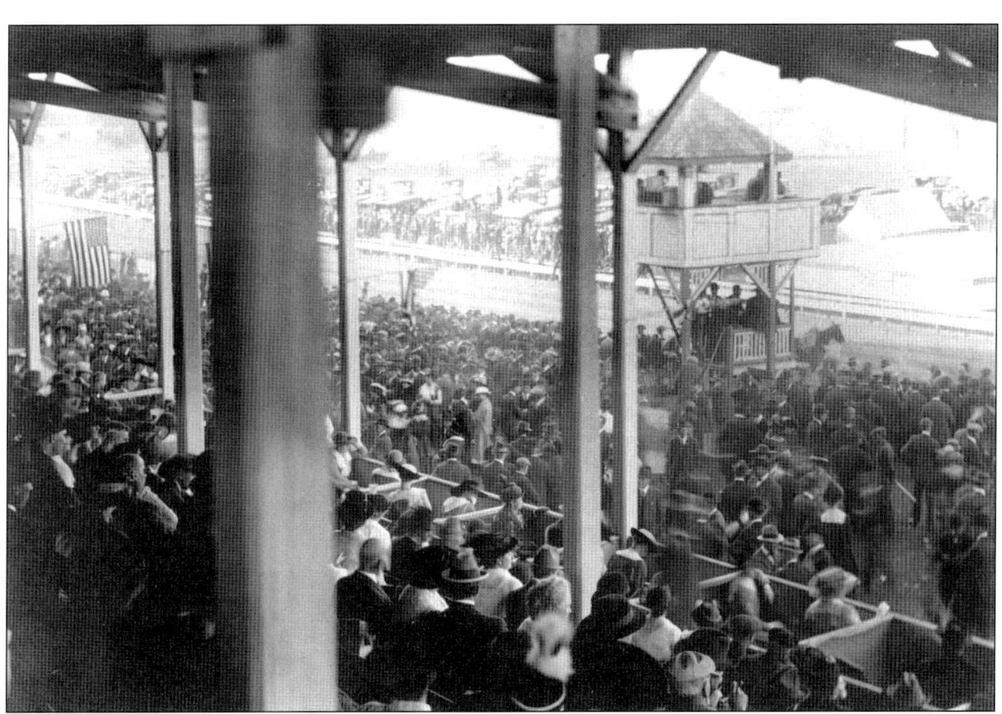

A crowd watches a horse race from the grandstand.

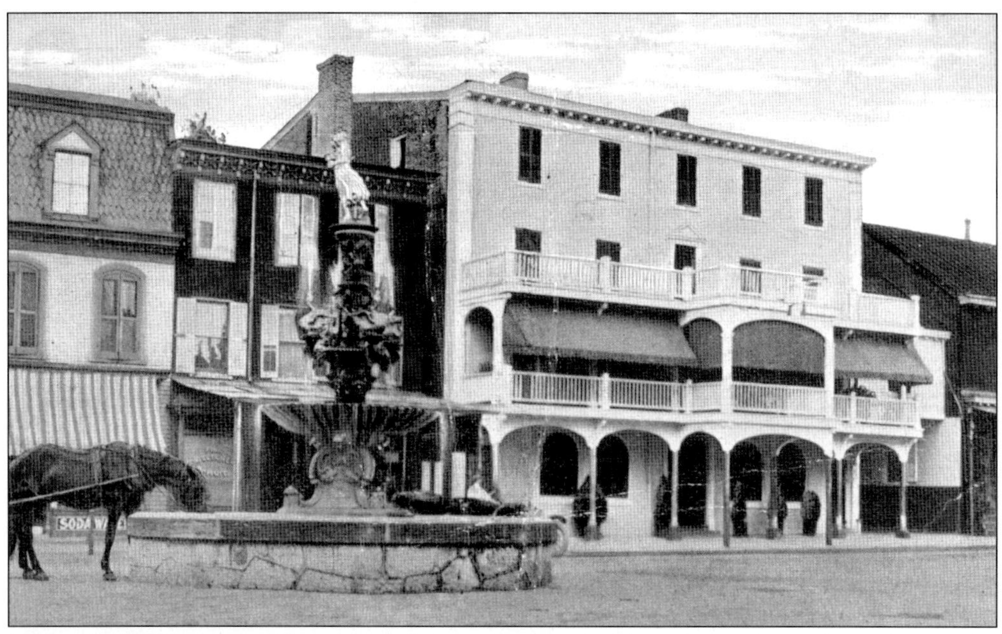

Mount Holly's Fountain Square and the surrounding buildings have changed much over the years. The Arcade Hotel (with balconies in three shots) was known as a fairly rowdy place, with

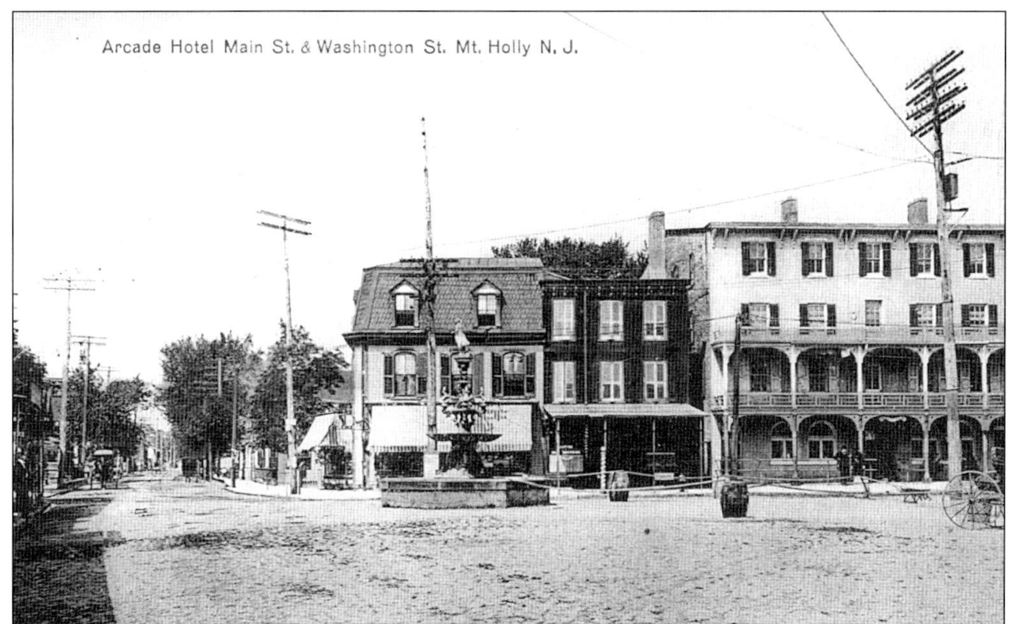

a pool room on the ground level. Notice how the fountain used to be a large flagpole in the center of the square.

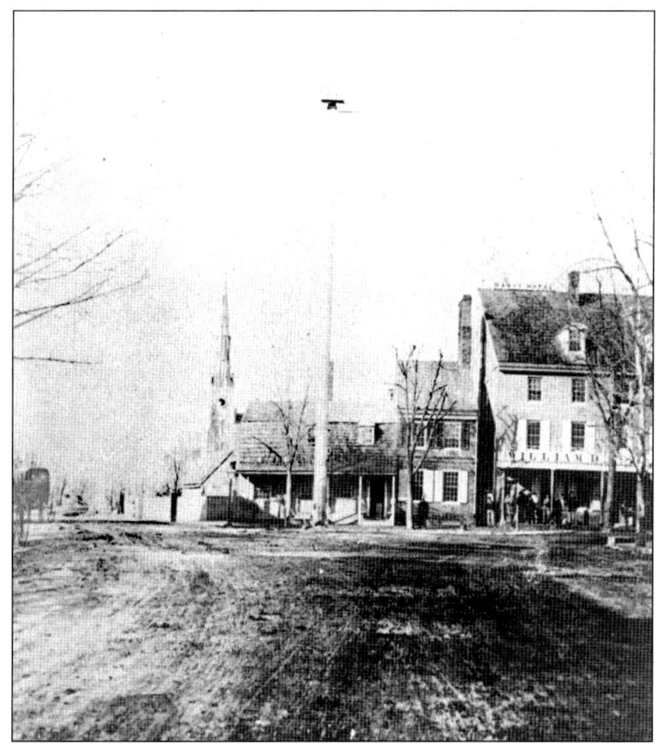

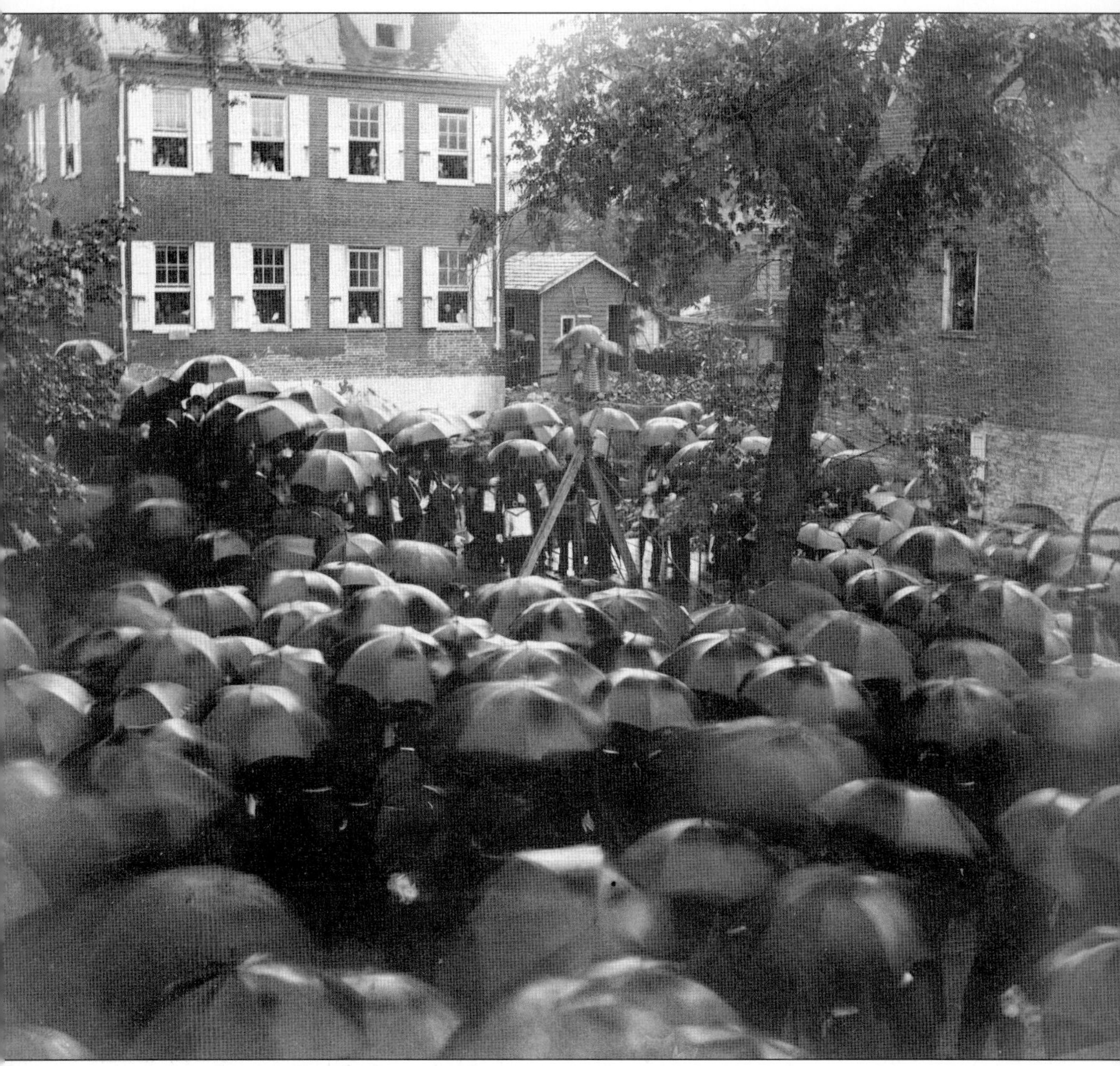

Laying the cornerstone of the new Masonic Temple on the corner of Main and Brainerd Streets made for an incredible photograph in 1891. On this dismal rainy day, all the Masons were under black umbrellas, and onlookers peered out windows of the house just beyond. That house was moved in order to make space for the new temple, which was destroyed by fire on January 28, 1925.

Six

TRANSPORTATION

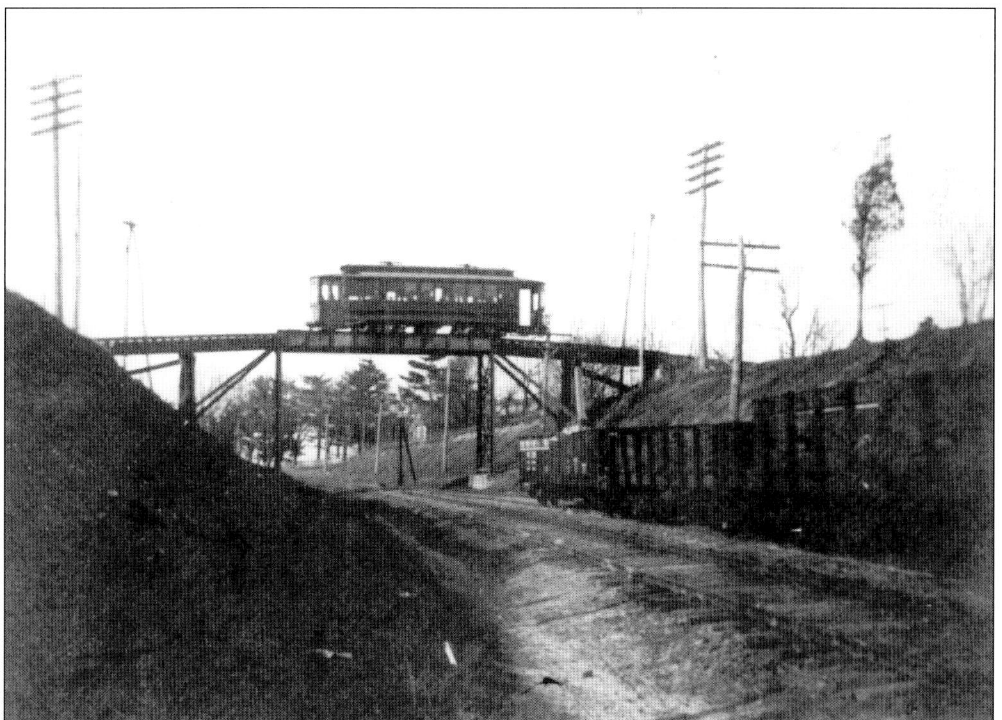

The Mount Holly Trolley provided a convenient way to travel around the area. Here it is shown crossing over High Street, where it followed the tracks all the way to Burlington, seven miles away.

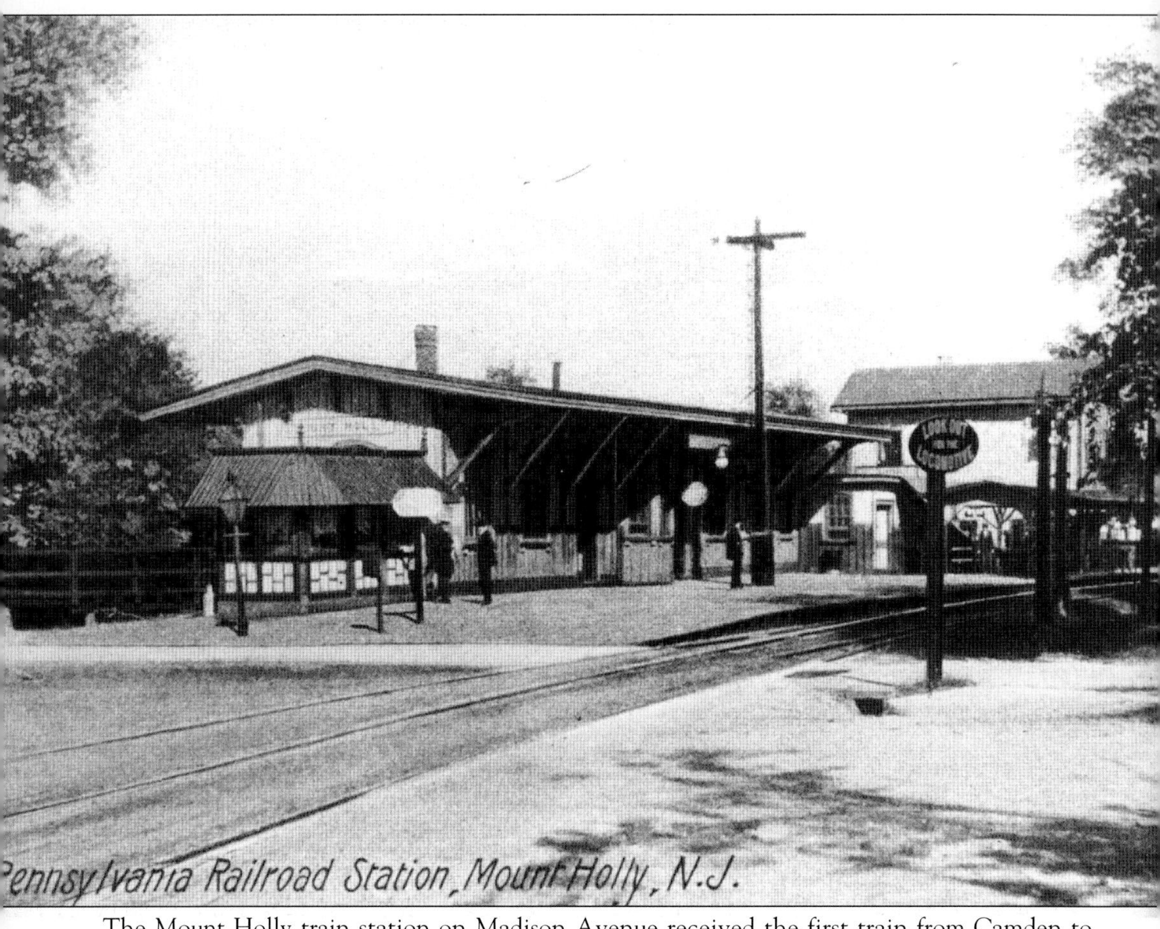

The Mount Holly train station on Madison Avenue received the first train from Camden to Mount Holly on the opening day of the Mount Holly Fair in October 1867. More than 50 trains a day stopped at the station in the busy season. Across Madison Avenue was a round, brick house and turntable, which enabled locomotives to receive minor repairs. Unfortunately, there

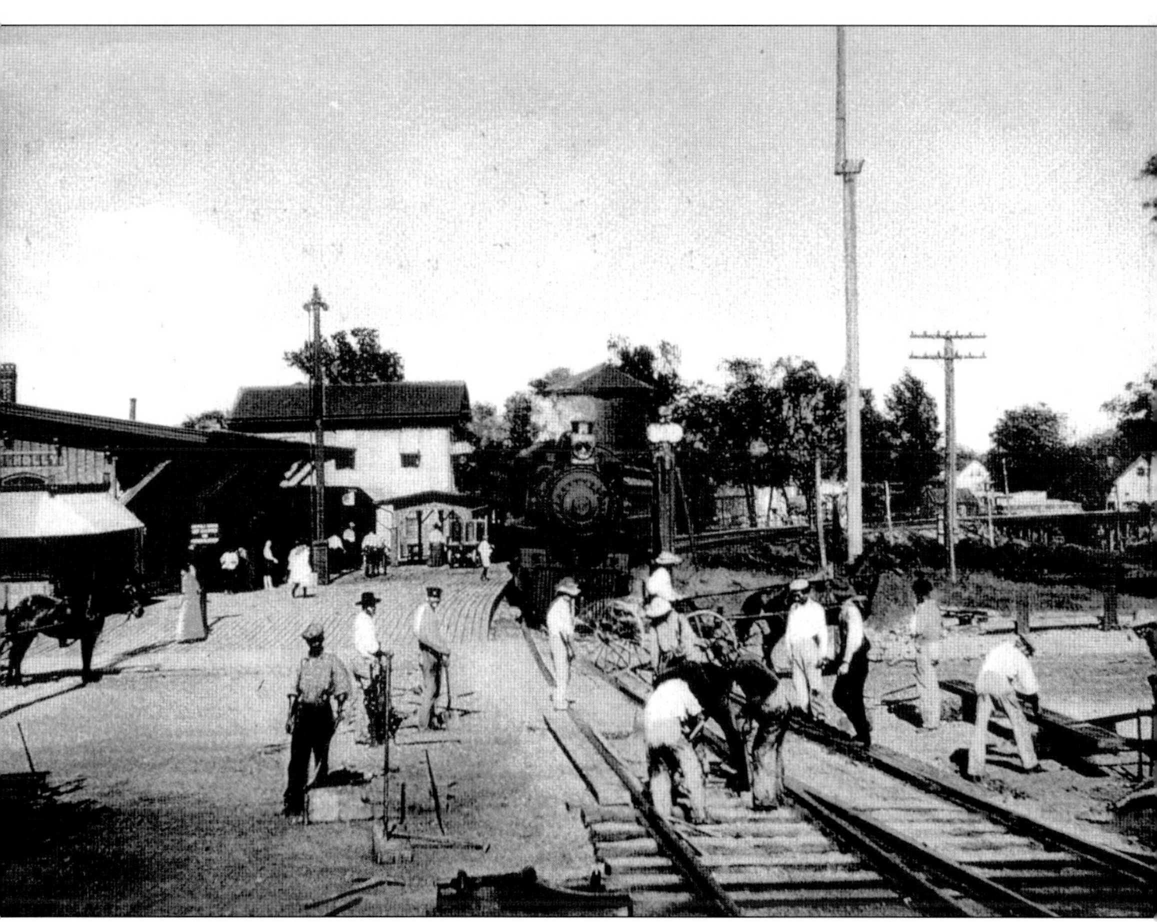

is no passenger service to Mount Holly now, just an occasional freight delivery. The train station was later used as the Burlington County Hospital Thrift Shop and has recently been turned into a delicatessen. Plans are under way to convert the train track from Mount Holly to Pemberton and beyond to a bicycle trail.

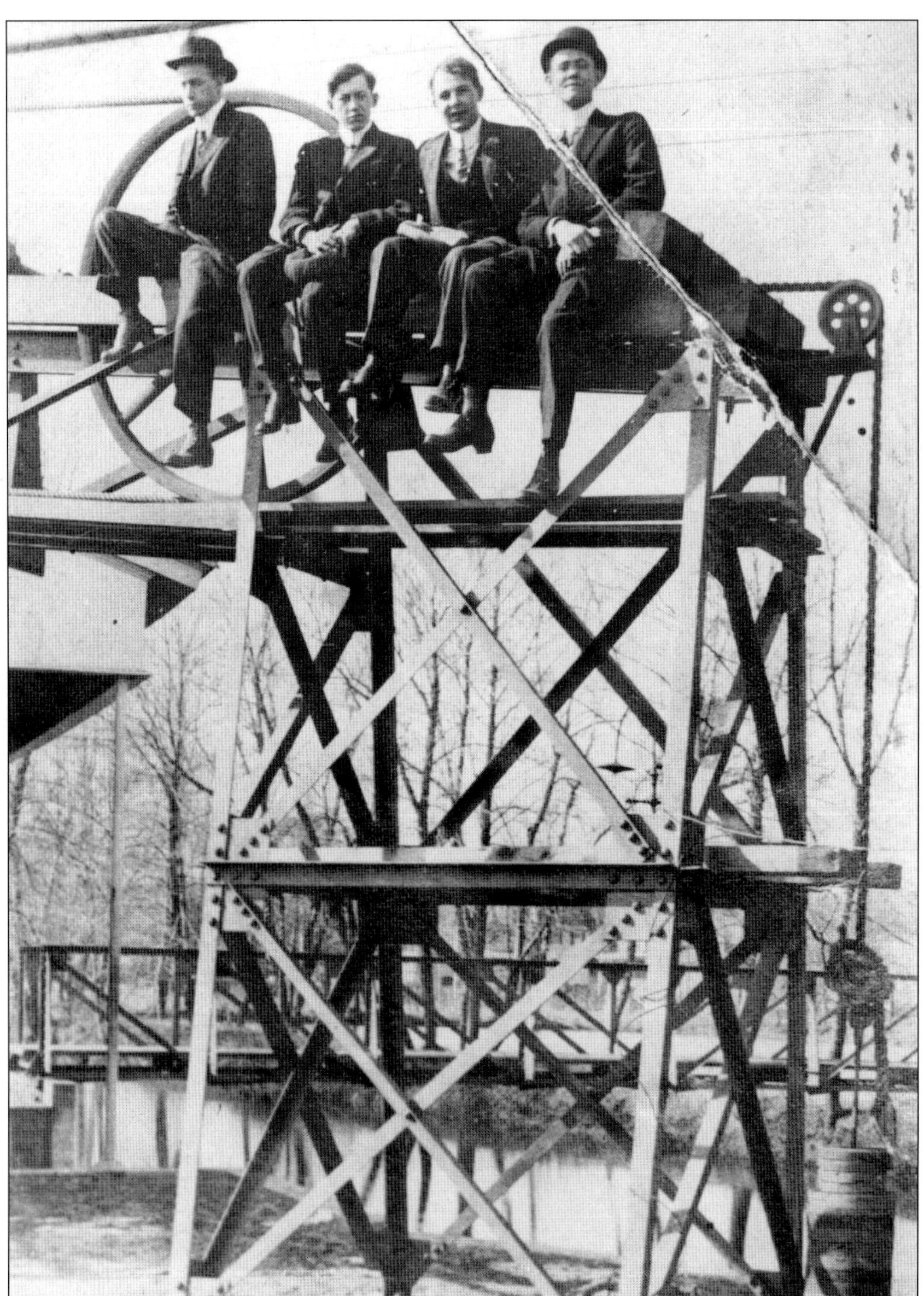

Sitting on the bicycle railroad apparatus, William Haines is second from the left. Later in life, Haines was a member of the Mount Holly Township Committee and served as chief of police. This unique bicycle railroad from Mount Holly to Smithville was probably the only one that ever existed. It was invented in 1892 by Arthur Hotchkiss of Hartford, Connecticut, to provide transportation for employees of the H.B. Smith Machine Company who lived in Mount Holly.

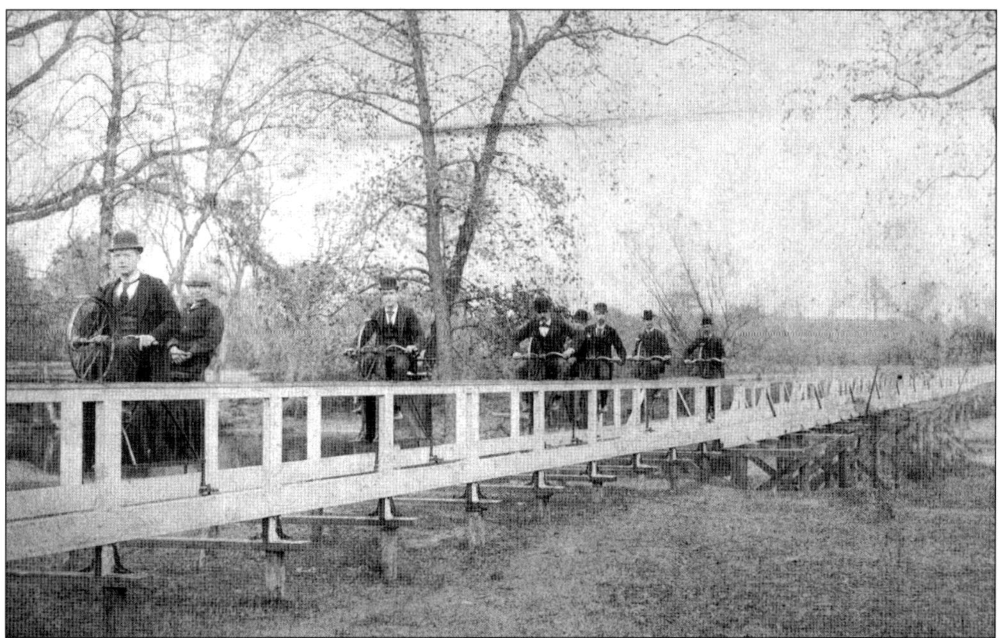

The terminal of the bicycle railroad was near the Relief Fire Engine House on Pine Street. A specially designed bicycle straddled a fence with grooved wheels running on an inverted T-rail on the top. The rail crossed the winding Rancocas Creek 10 times before reaching Smithville.

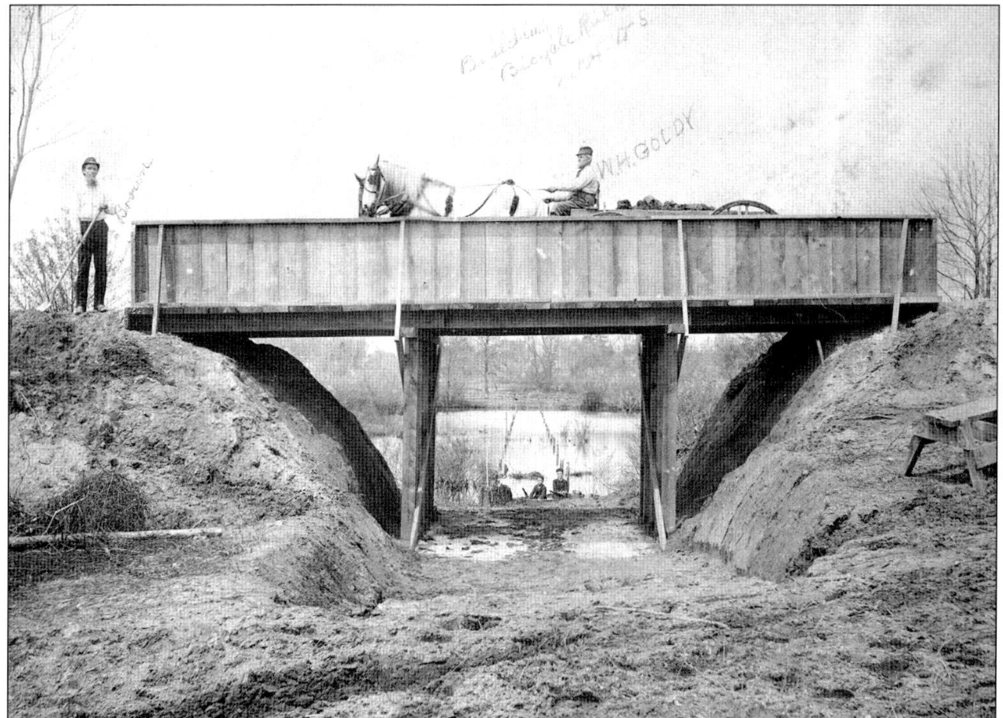

Building the bicycle railroad was a great undertaking, requiring much manpower and horsepower. W.H. Goldy rides the wagon and a Mr. Brown is standing just off this bridge they were building for the railroad crossing over the Rancocas Creek.

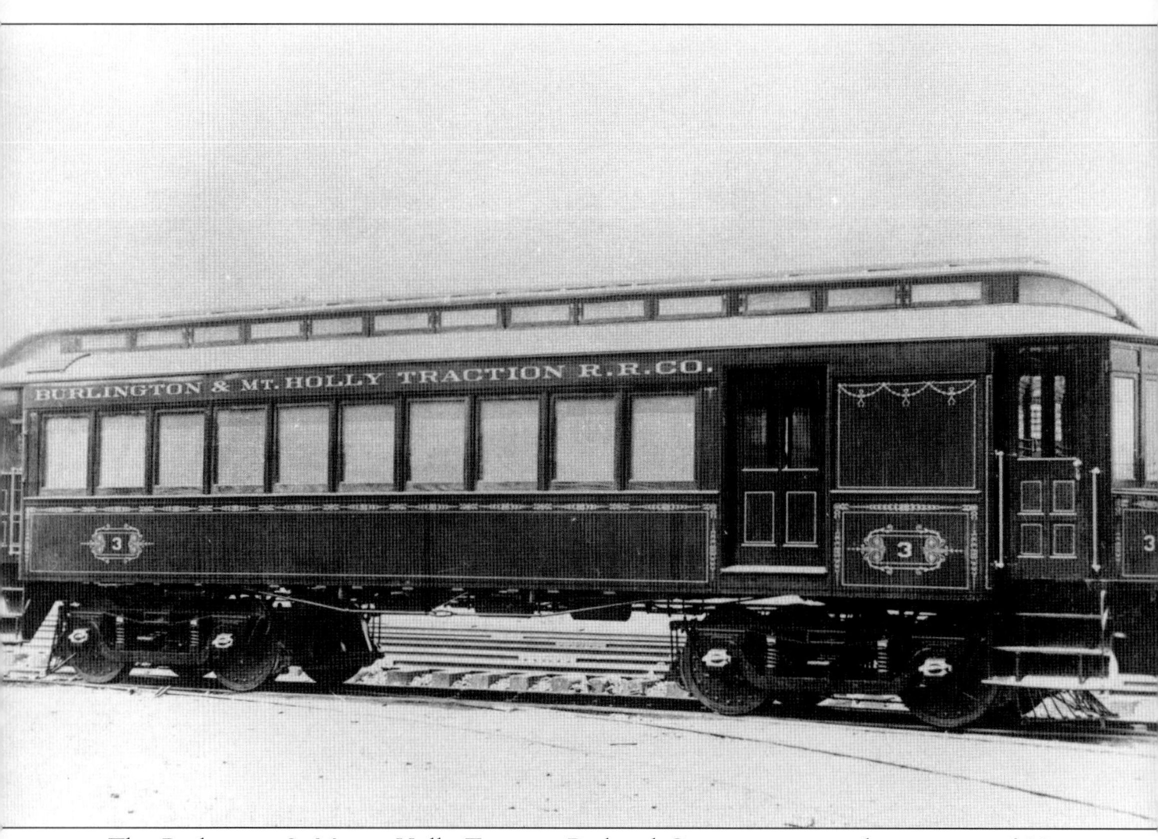

The Burlington & Mount Holly Traction Railroad Company operated trains out of Mount Holly and allowed folks to travel to Burlington, Trenton, Camden, Philadelphia, and beyond by simply stepping on the train here in town. It would be nice to have that kind of public transportation available in the seat of Burlington County today.

Seven
POSTCARDS AND SNAPSHOTS

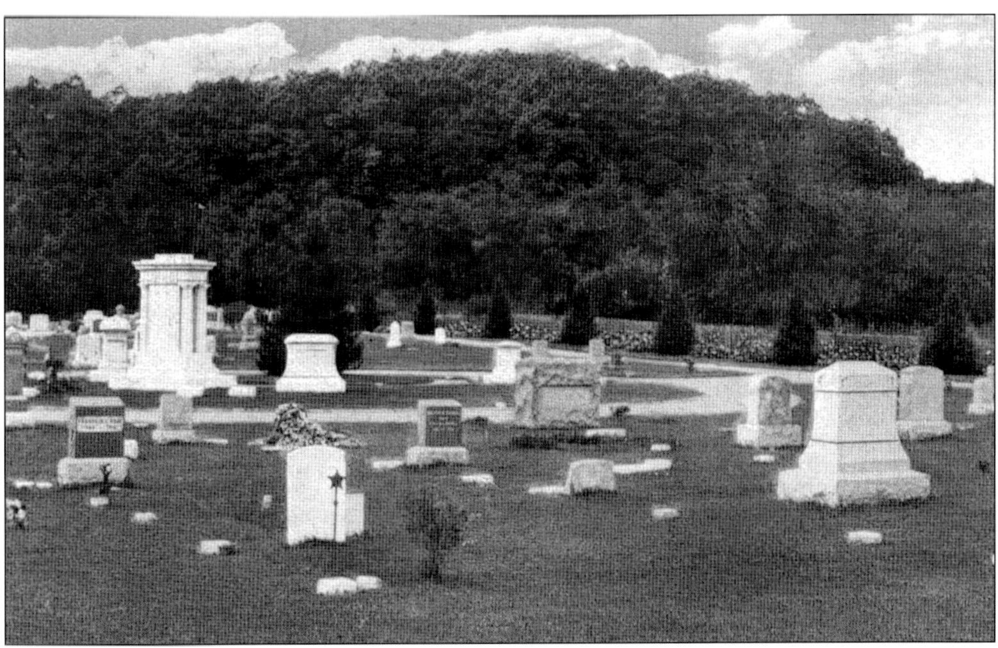

The Mount Holly Cemetery (shown with the mount in the background) is a lovely, peaceful burial ground with many ancient headstones bearing the names of people who lived in Mount Holly. This cemetery was established by Isaac Risdon in 1841 and dedicated by the four clergymen of the town representing the Methodist, Baptist, Presbyterian, and Episcopal churches.

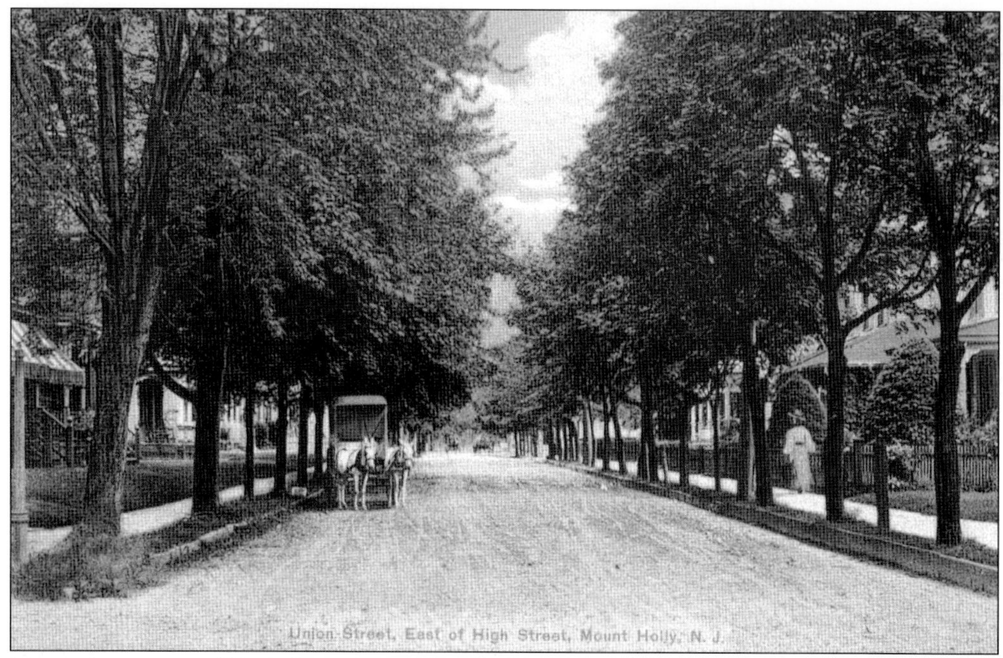

Union Street east of High Street is still lovely; however, this postcard is enhanced by the lack of motor vehicles parked on the street.

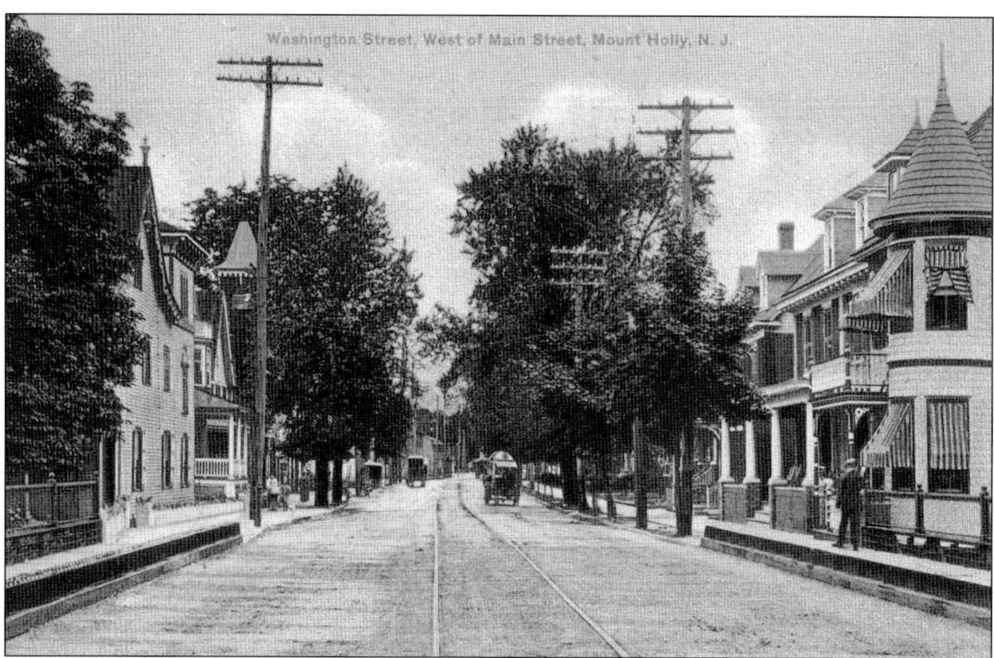

Washington Street was photographed looking west from the bridge over the Rancocas Creek. Notice the trolley tracks, striped awnings, and nice, big trees shading the sidewalks. By this time, the Trinity Church was gone, but there were still lovely homes on the left, which were later demolished.

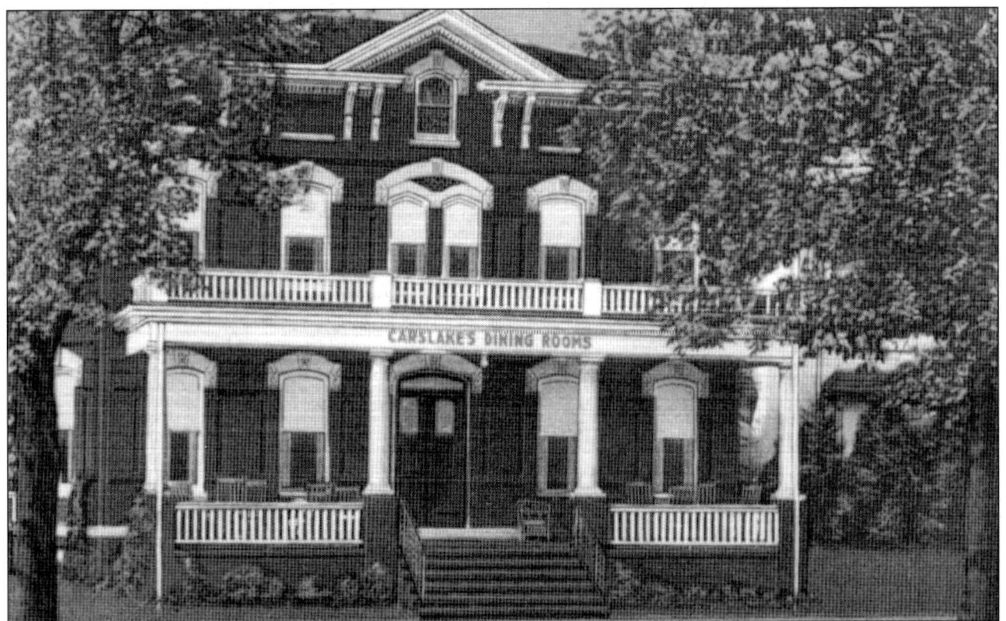

This was once the residence of the Roberts family. From the 1930s to the early 1950s, it was known as the Fireside Dining Room. After it was purchased by Edward Carslake, it was known as the Carslake's Dining Rooms. This building is now part of the Alaimo Engineering office complex.

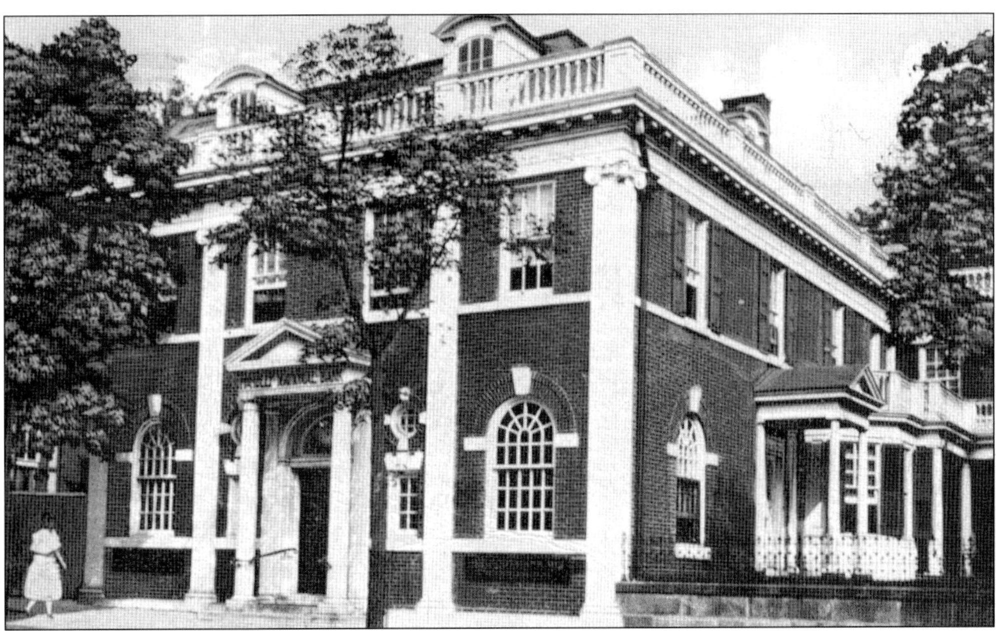

The Mount Holly National Bank was organized in 1857 and closed in 1929. It was located on the northeast corner of Brainerd and Main Streets and was eventually demolished to make way for a Bell Telephone building. The telephone company later moved to offices on Brainerd Street, and several small businesses occupied this site.

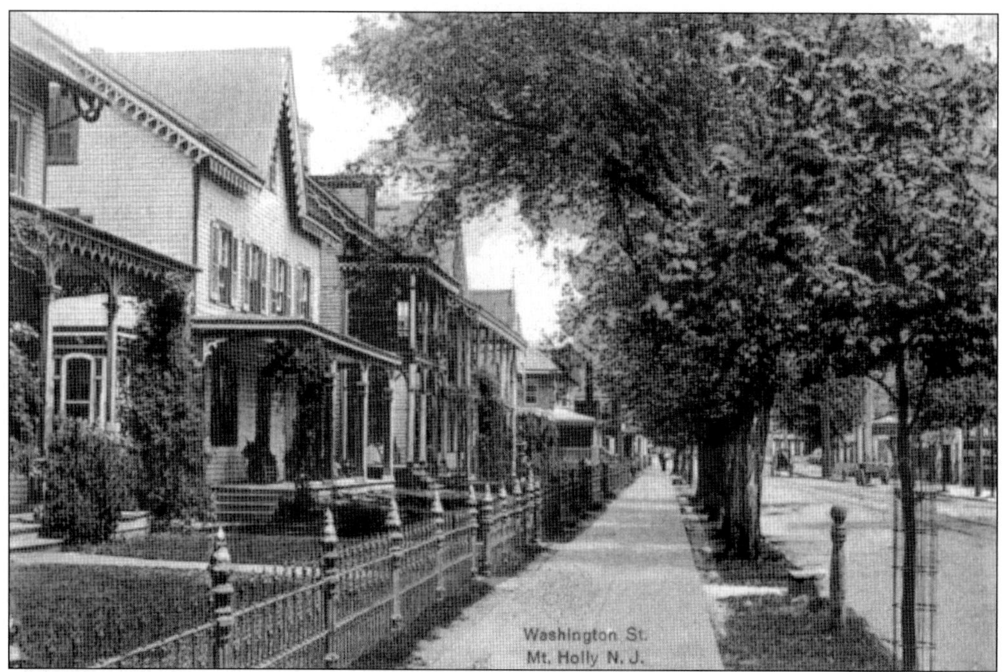

This postcard shows Washington Street between High and Bispham Streets. Washington Street was also known as the Great Road to Philadelphia. A few of the Victorian homes can still be spotted.

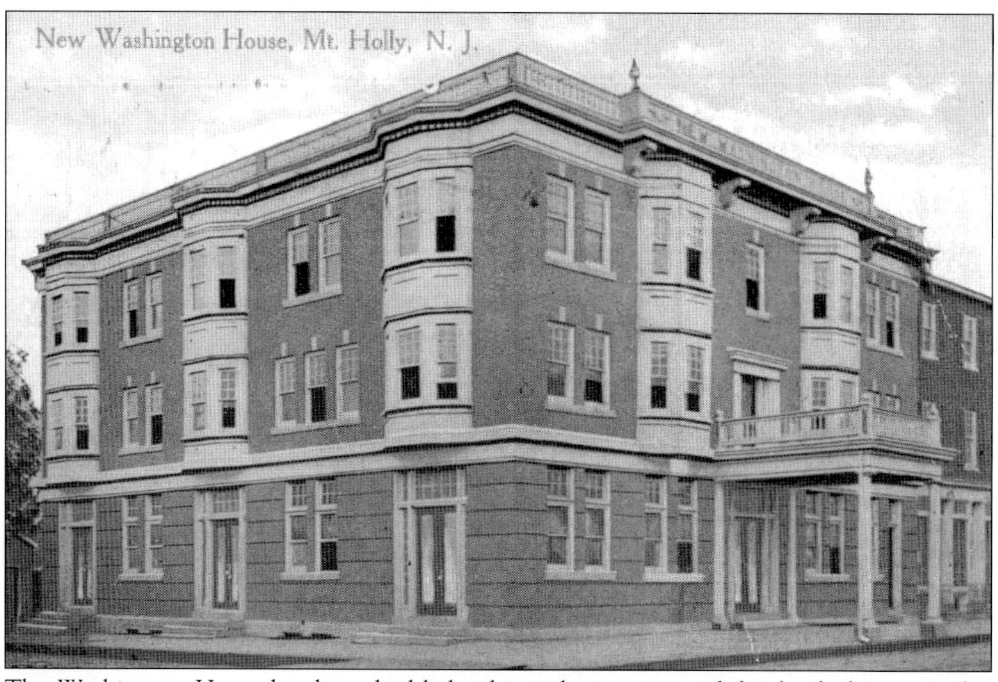

The Washington House has been highlighted in other sections of this book; however, this photograph is worth noting because it shows the doorways that used to exist along Rancocas Road. The doorways are now windows.

Although Bessie Pease Gutmann was born in Philadelphia, she spent her childhood and early years in Mount Holly. Her artistic talents were discovered early on and were encouraged by her parents. This eventually led to a career in illustration. When she was 12 years old and in the Mount Holly school system, a teacher asked the young girl to instruct her in art. She eventually had some of her work exhibited and went on to further training at the Philadelphia School of Design for Women in 1894 and the New York School of Art. She created art for prints, imagery for advertising, calendars, books, magazines, and postcards. It was hard to select one of the many famous prints to show, but "In Disgrace" was kindly given for use in this book by the Balliol Corporation. (The Balliol Corporation; Bessie Pease Gutmann is a trademark of the Balliol Corporation.)

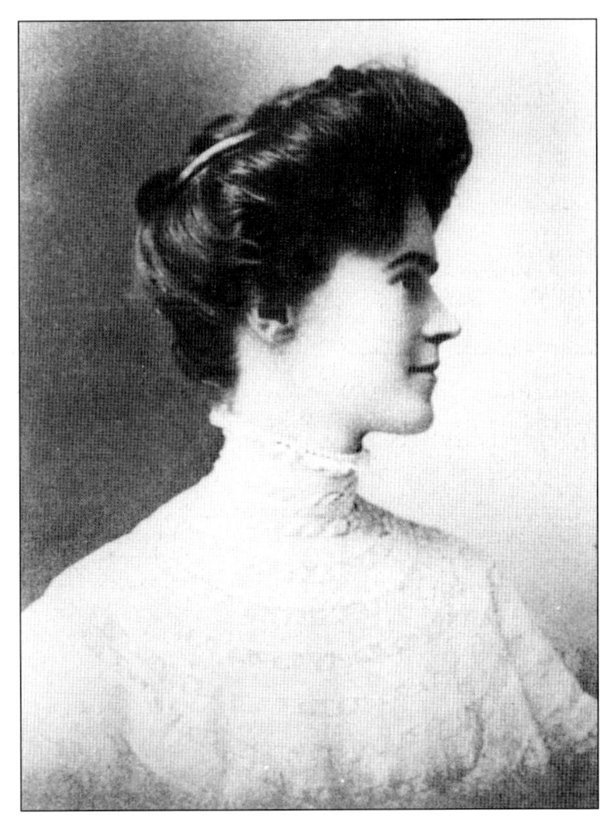

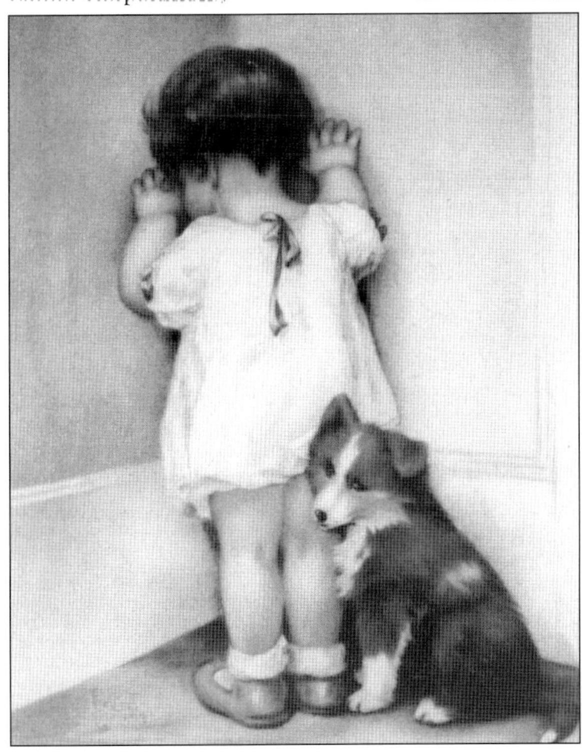

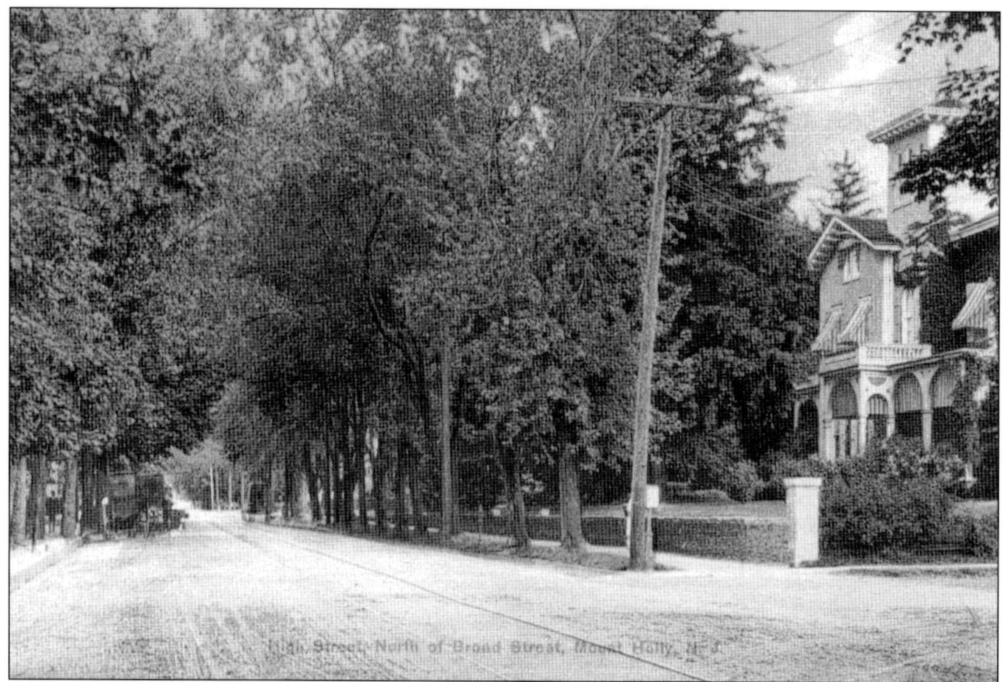

The Moose Home, located on High Street at the corner of Broad Street, was known as the Old Wardell Brown home. It was later occupied by Judge Frederick Lee. The property was demolished in 1916 by Herbert Killie, a great loss to the historic district.

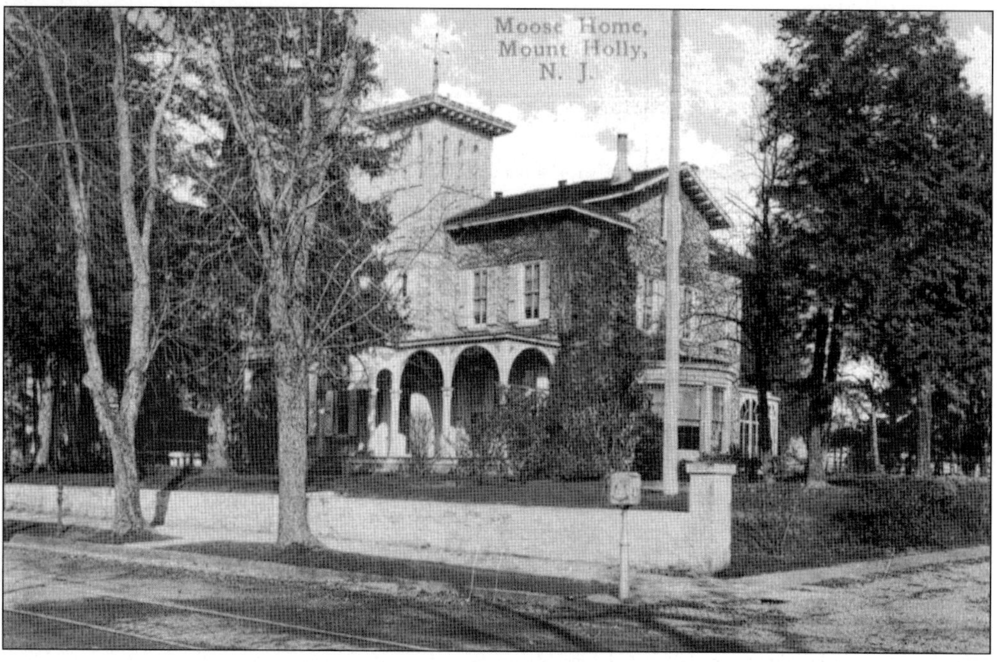

Eight

RANCOCAS CREEK

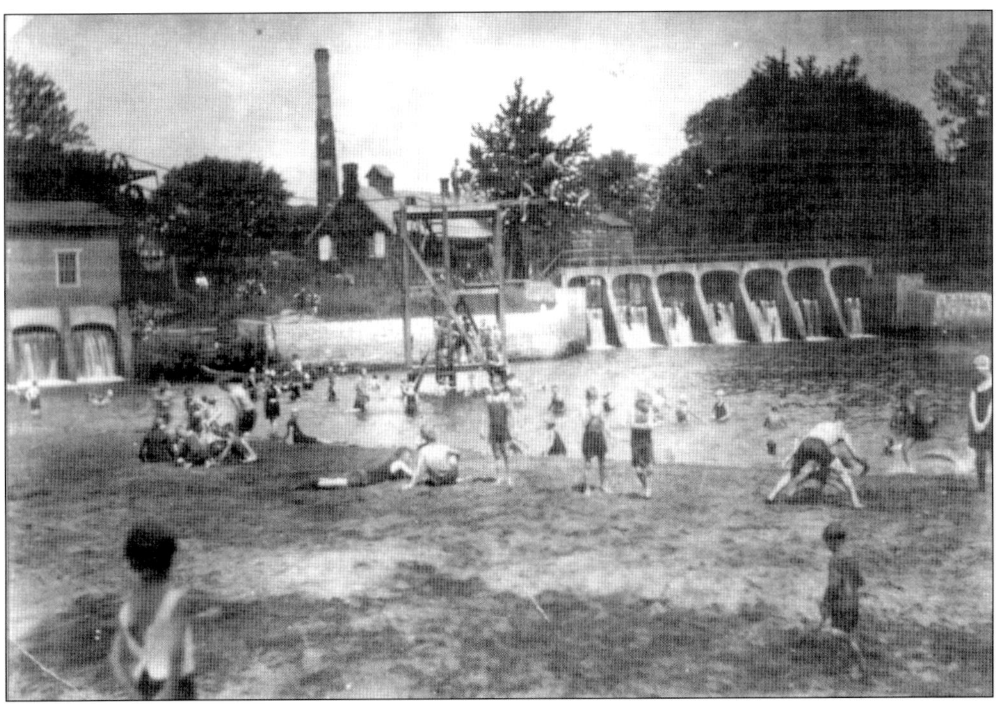

Mill Dam Park once had a great beach and diving platform just below the Mill Dam or Seven Gates Dam off Pine Street. The Rancocas Creek provided some wonderful recreation for youths, who would play in the water, swim, canoe, and socialize the days away.

This photograph, looking east toward Pine Street, shows Mill Street during an early flood. The stores on the right were also flooded from the millrace behind the buildings.

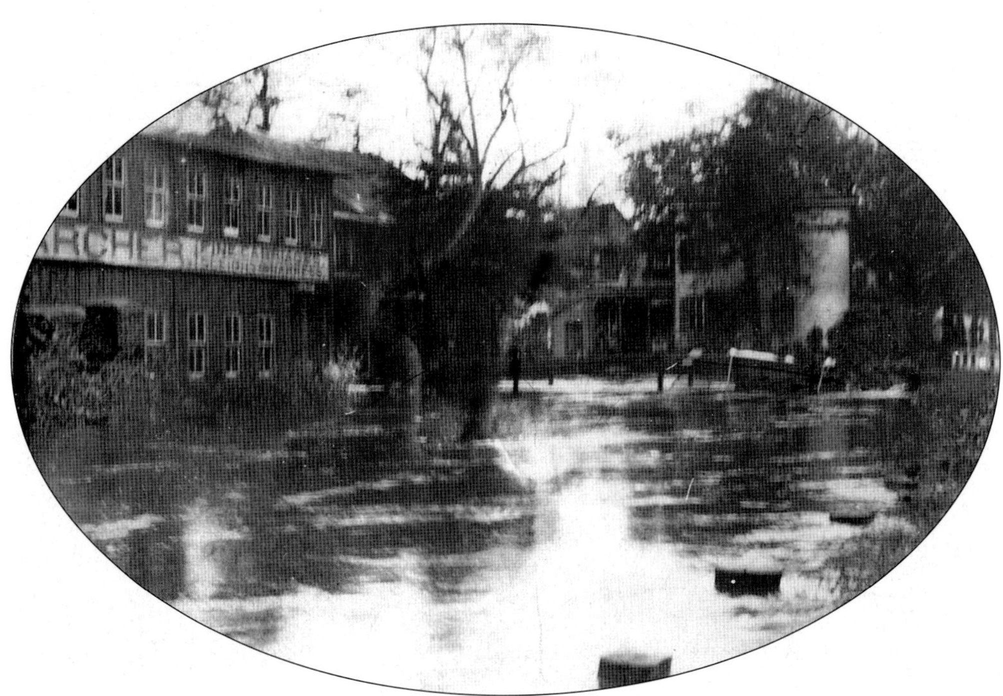

Washington Street was not immune to flooding. Here, John Archer's Carriage Shop on the south bank of the Rancocas Creek near Lumberton Road (now Madison Avenue) takes on water.

In this view looking south from the Washington Street bridge, the first building on the left (a barn) is now the Robin's Nest Restaurant outdoor dining area. Next is the outlet of the millrace and then the rear of 10 and 14 White Street.

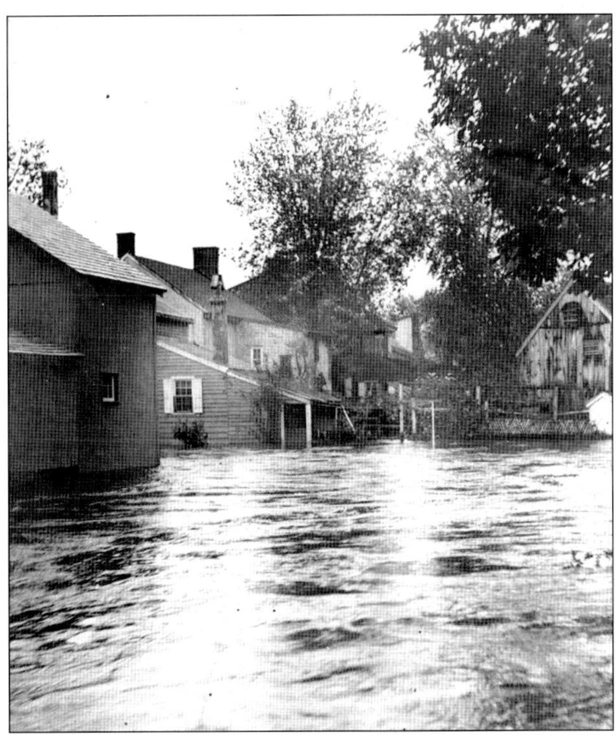

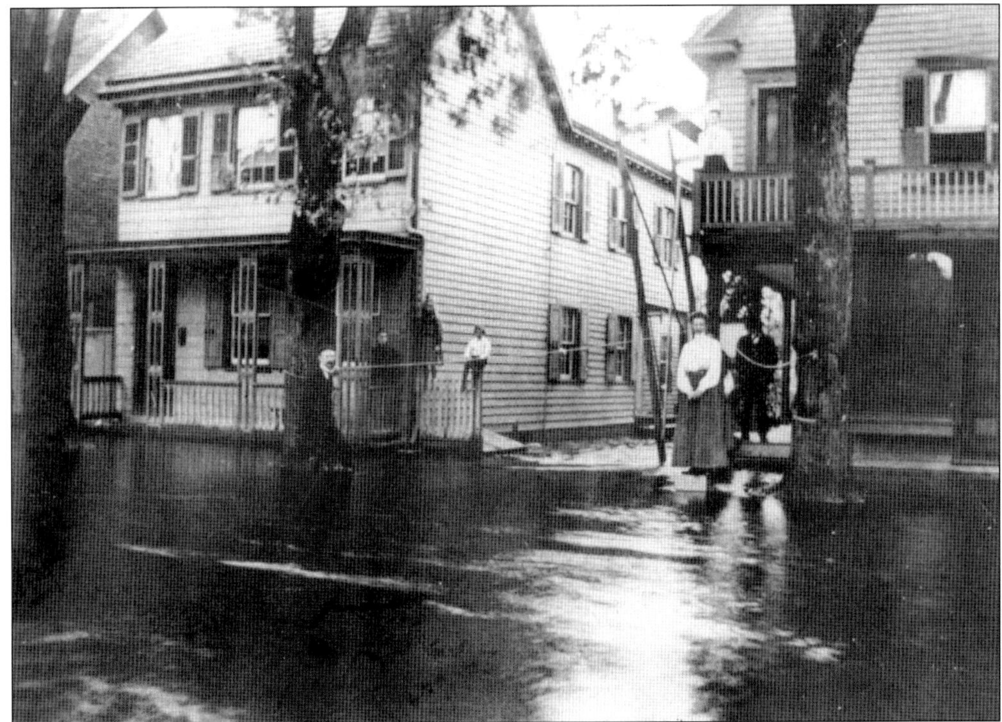

This is a freshet (flash flood) from a stream to the left of the first house on Garden Street, No. 415. No. 417 is the house next door. The houses were built *c.* 1854 next to this stream, which empties into the Buttonwood Run and then into the millrace.

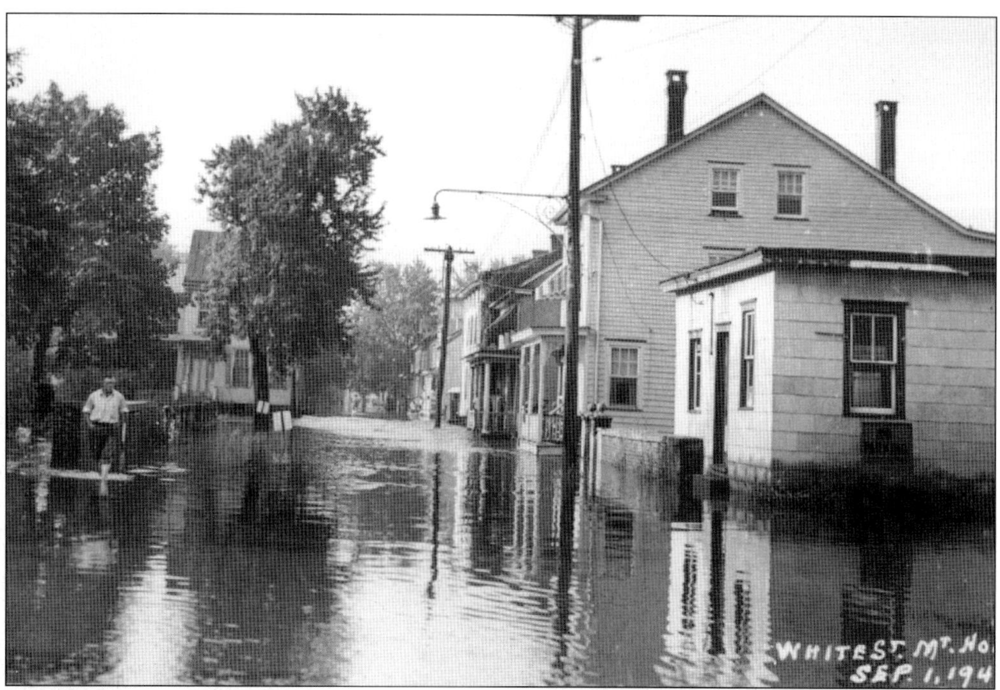

Ellis D. Megee of 8 Church Street wades down the street during the flood of 1940. White Street is the entranceway for the Millrace Village restoration area and home to some of the oldest buildings in Mount Holly.

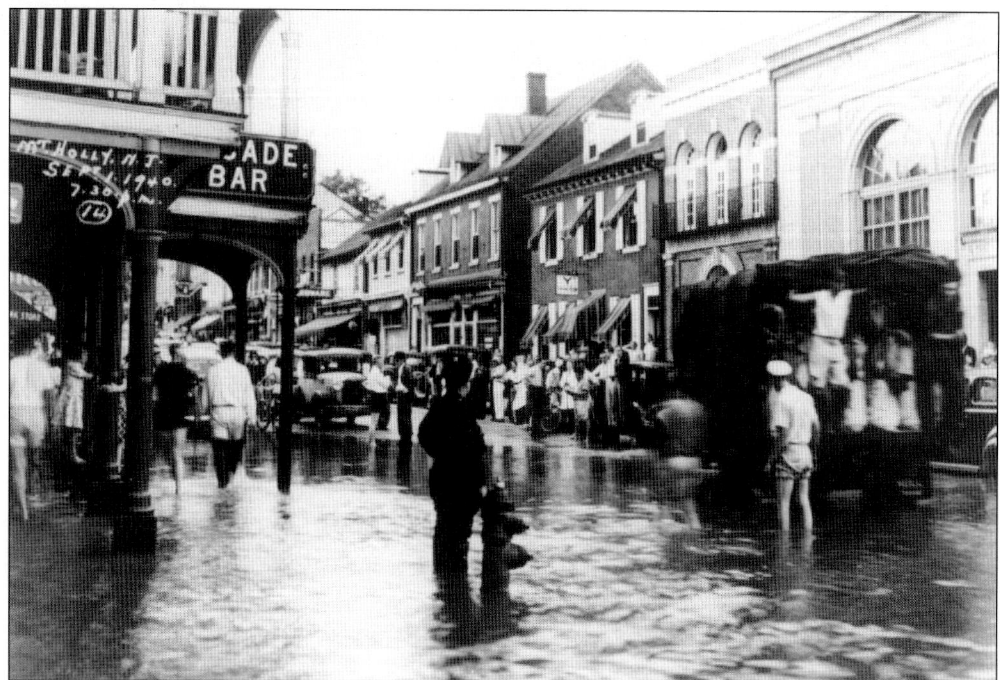

Many residents wade in bare feet in the streets during the flood of 1940 on High Street. They seem to get on with business despite the waters invading the buildings in the lower part of town. Note the Arcade Hotel and Bar on the left.

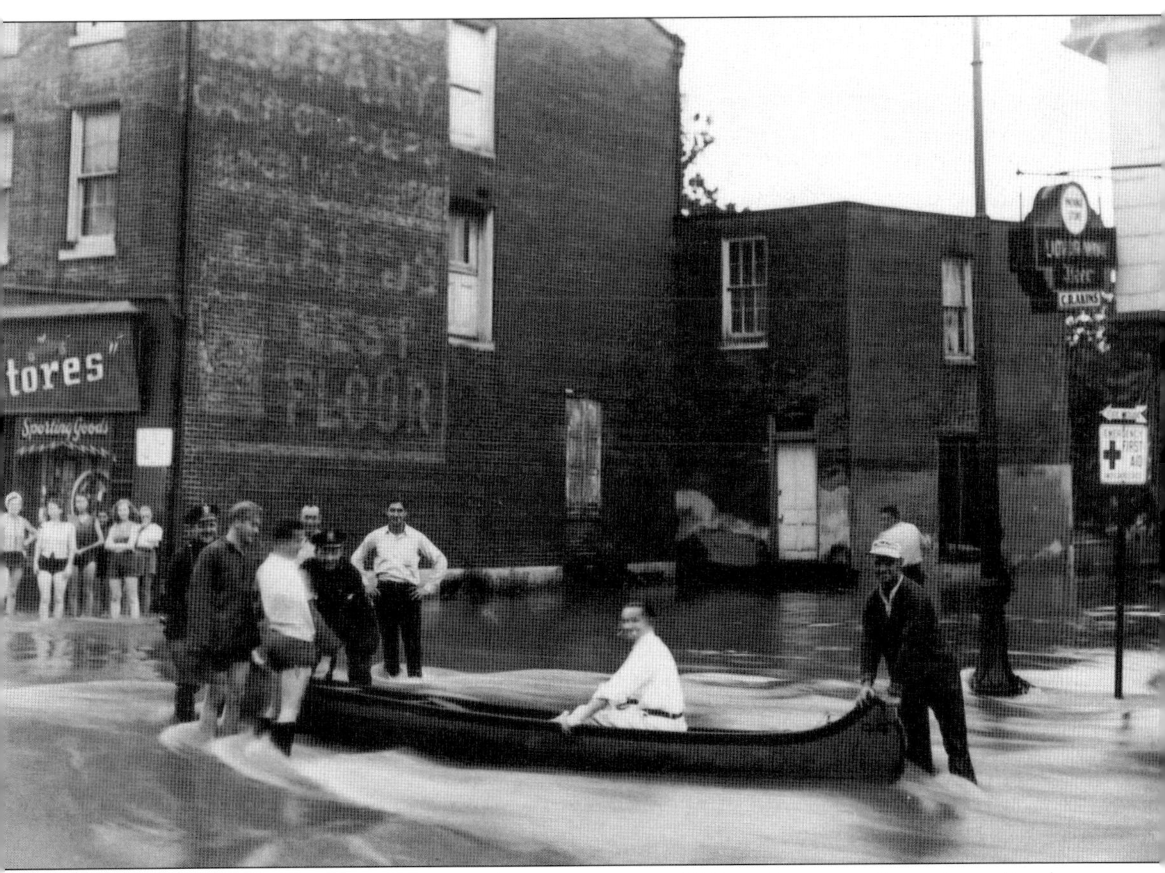

Canoeing along Washington Street at the intersection of White Street, police officers Frank Bowen and Edward Prince are on the left end of the canoe in uniform.

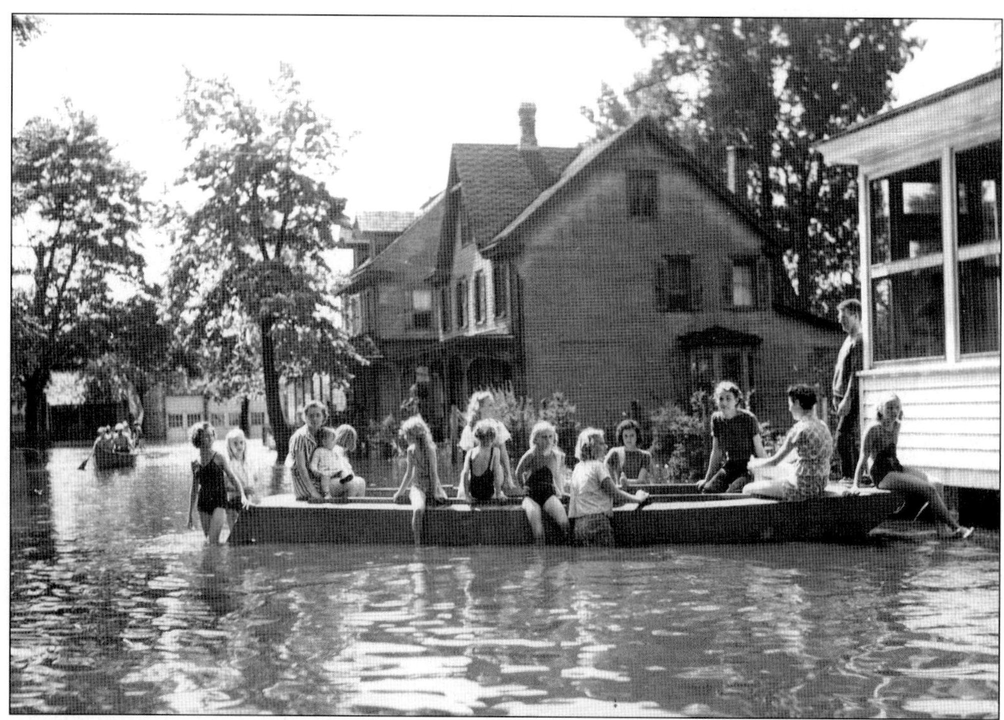

This photograph shows some girls and women making the most of the 1940 flood in their boats, paddling around from house to house.

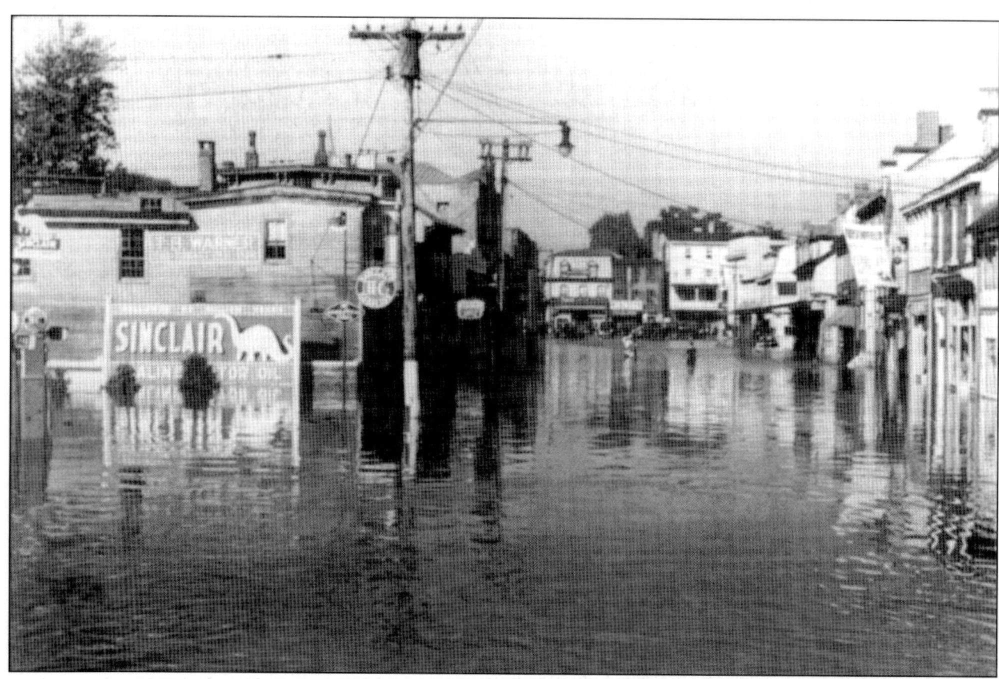

Floodwaters along Mill Street are shown in this photograph taken from the Pine Street area.

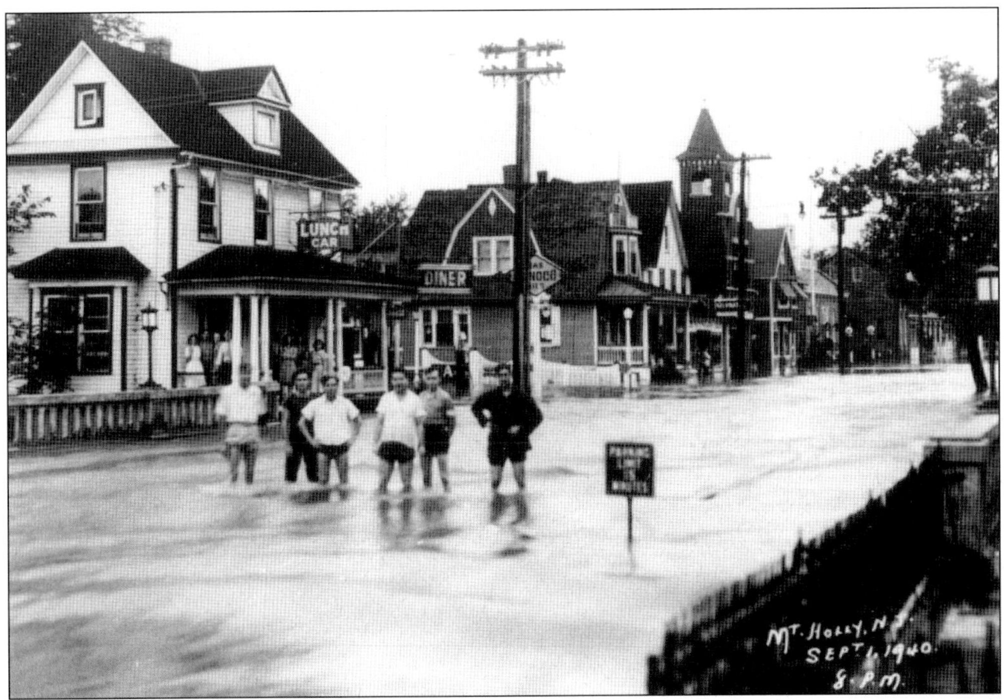

Posing during the 1940 and 1938 floods, respectively, the residents in these photographs are standing on the Washington Street Bridge. On the far left in both views is 8 Washington Street, which was a diner at the time. Next door was a gas station, which is now dentist offices. Notice the nice lights on the bridge.

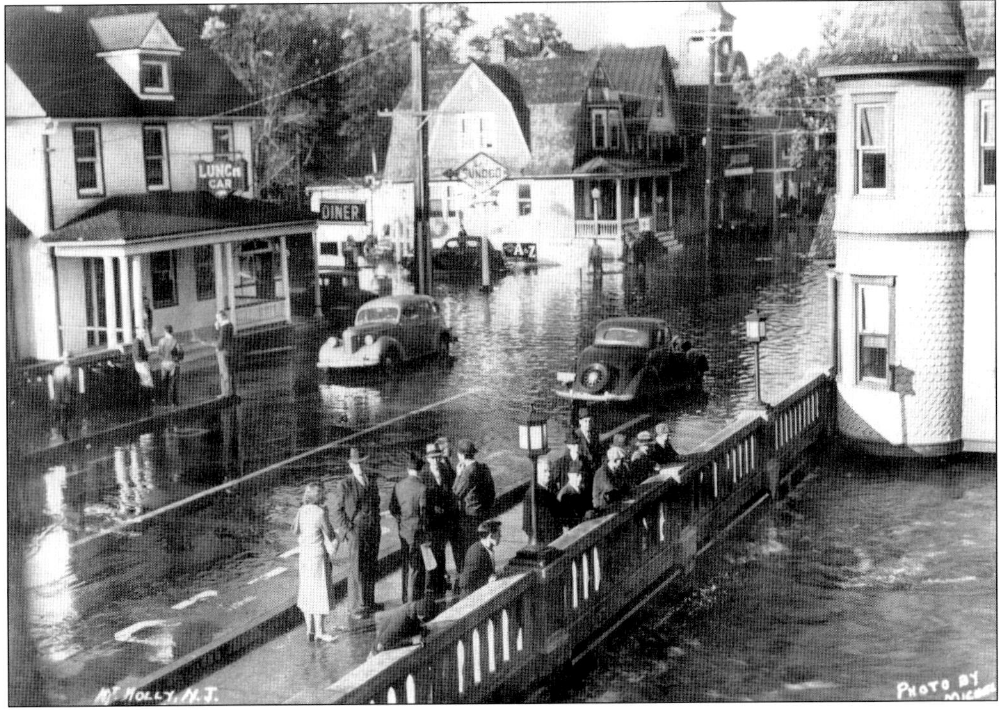

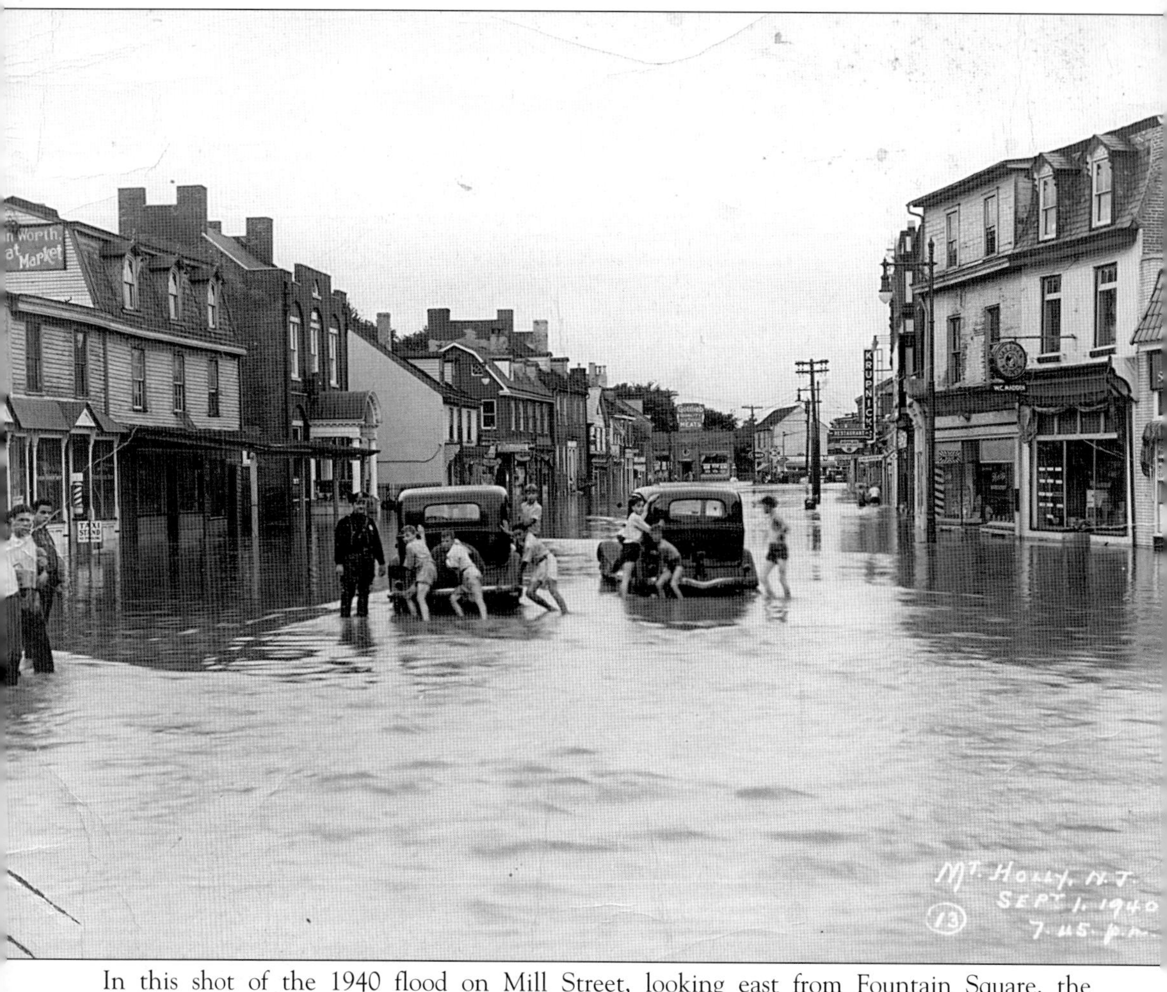

In this shot of the 1940 flood on Mill Street, looking east from Fountain Square, the Buttonwood Run is channeled under Mill Street and drains into the millrace. Not much water comes through since the construction of the dam at Woolmans Lake and the emergency management waterway along King Street. Here again is officer Frank Bowen.

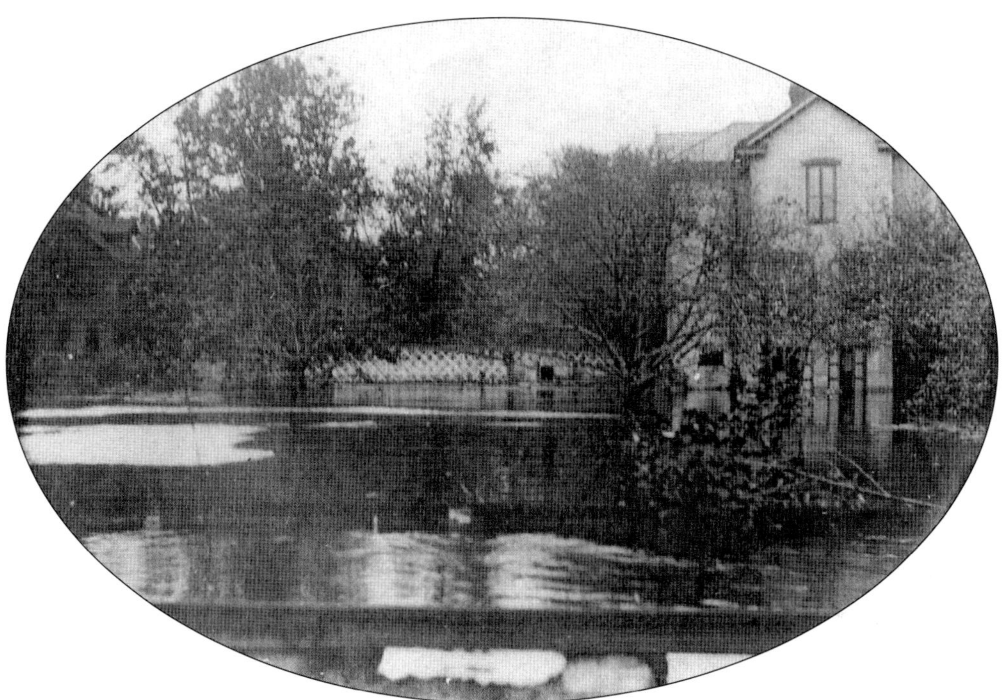

The house at 10 Bispham Street was built *c.* 1876. It is a great example of a mid-Victorian mansion with ironwork and fancy scrollwork common to that period. It is sometimes referred to as the Schrayshuen Mansion. The Rancocas Creek runs just next to the house. Here, the creek has flooded the property.

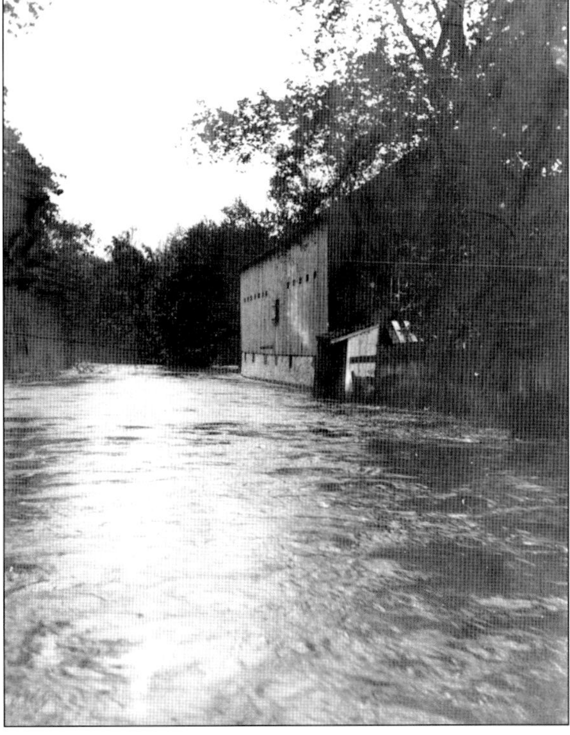

The Rancocas Creek was very high and ran along the back of the Arcade Stables, on the right. The stable was actually located to the rear of the Arcade Hotel fronting on Main Street. This shot is taken from the Washington Street bridge looking north.

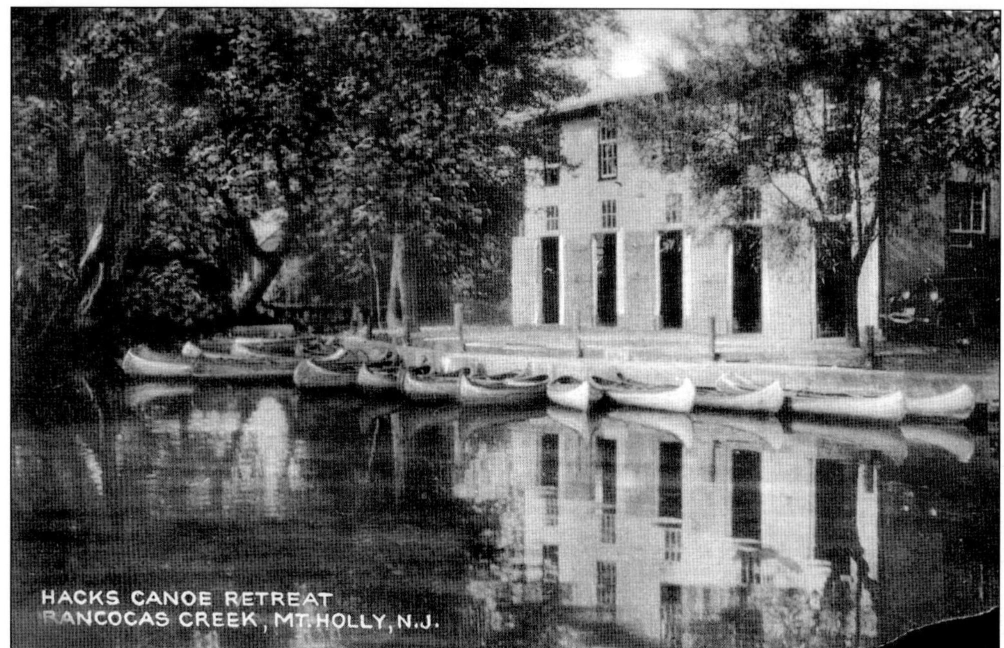

Hack's Canoe Retreat was established by Edward Hack in 1876 on the Rancocas Creek. The property is located at 100 Mill Street and was a famously popular pastime for locals and weekend retreat for city dwellers who would come to Mount Holly to canoe the Rancocas

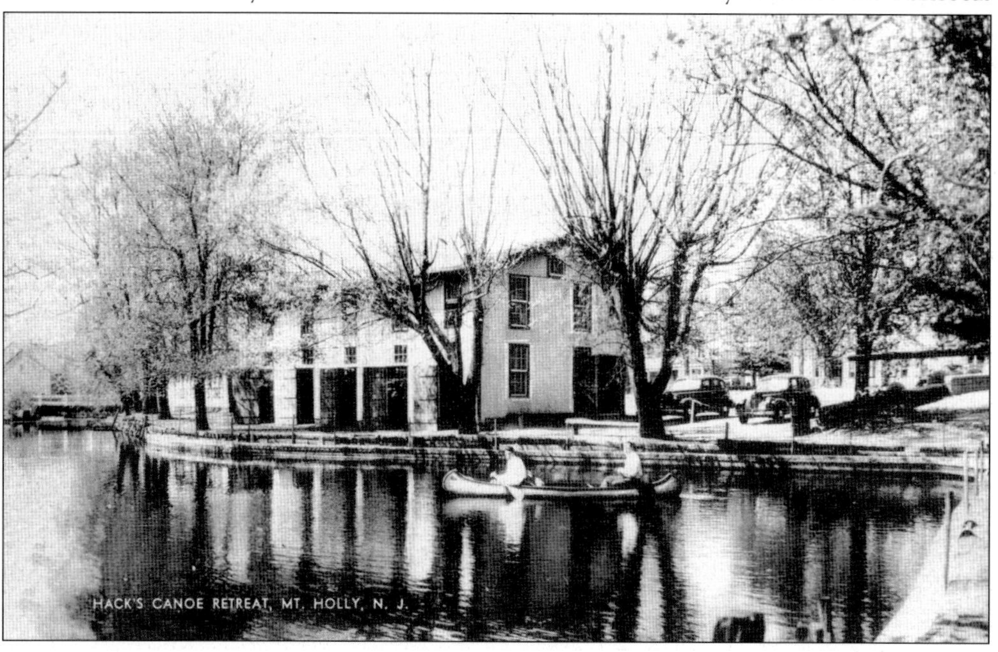

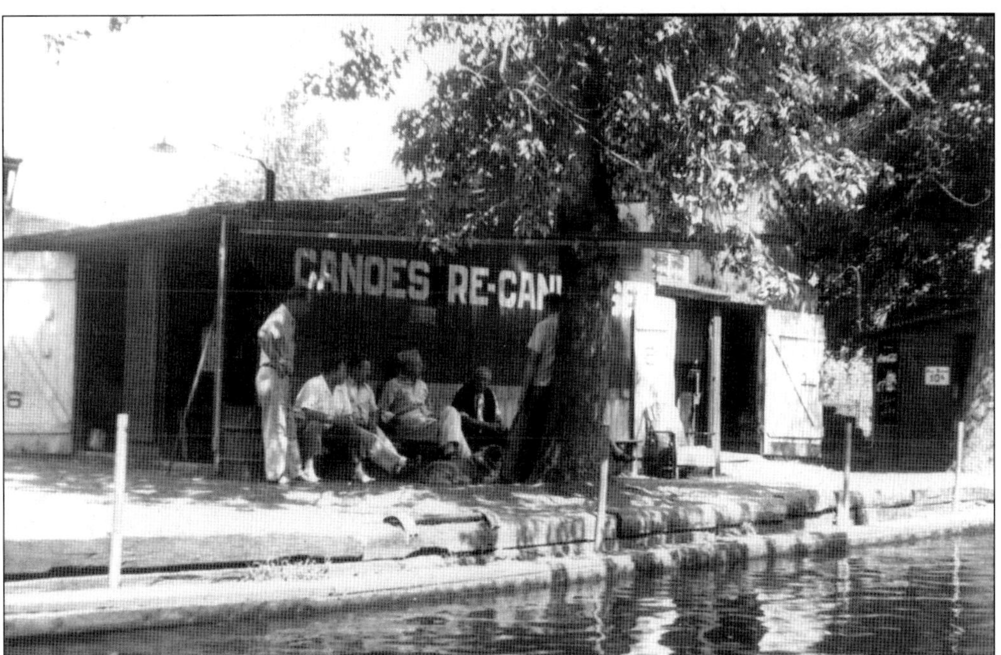

Creek and camp along its banks. Eventually, small cabins were built along the creek and people summered here under the shade by the cool waters of the Rancocas. Hack's Canoe Retreat is practically a landmark.

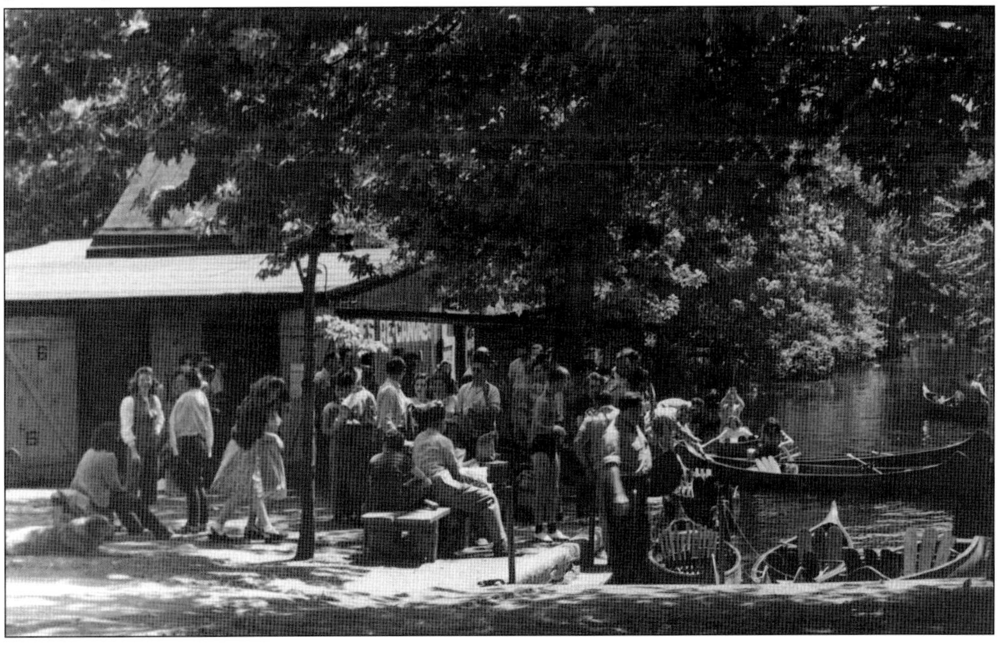

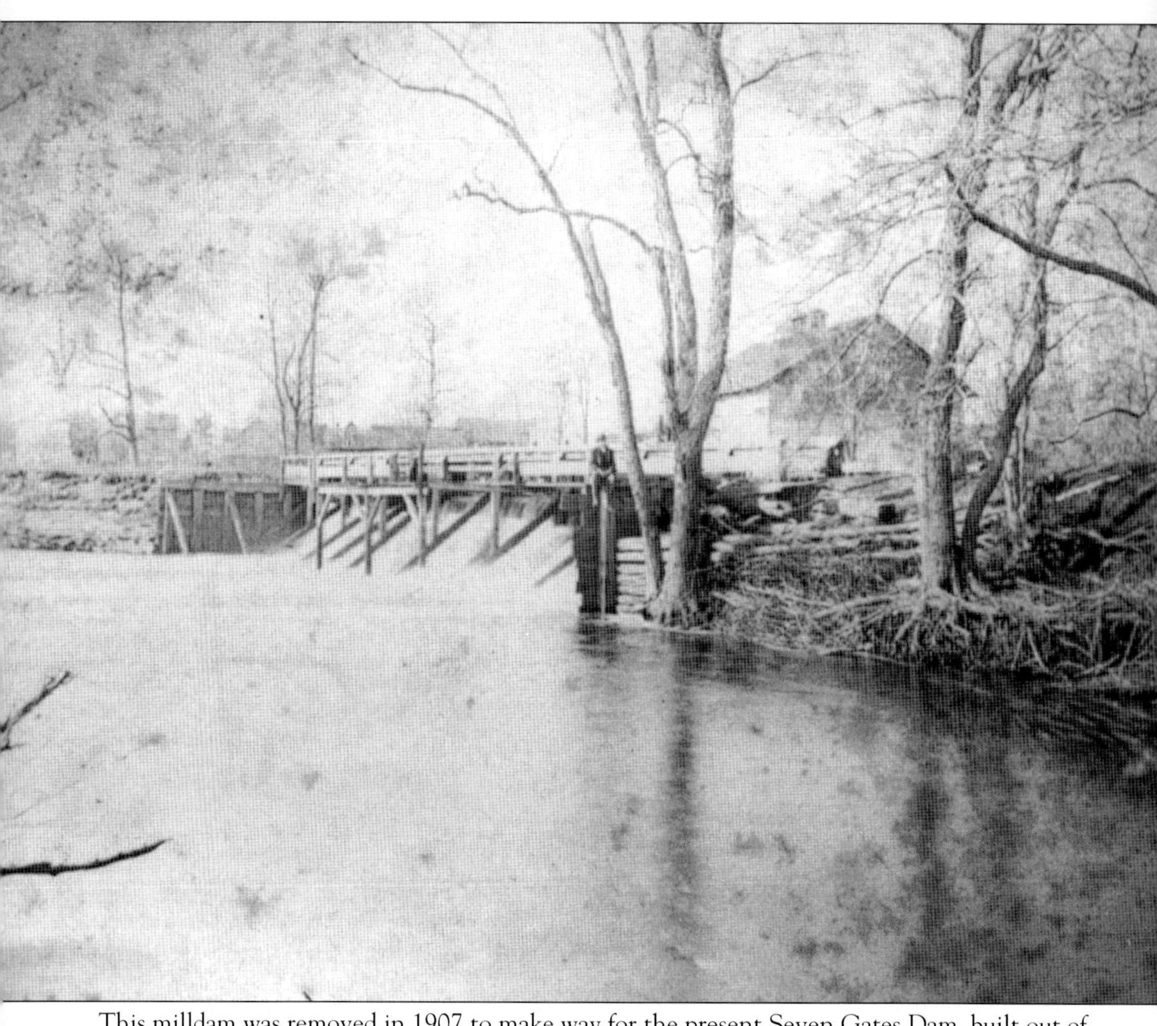

This milldam was removed in 1907 to make way for the present Seven Gates Dam, built out of concrete and finished in 1910. Behind the milldam is Durand Ice House across the creek where they would chop large blocks of ice from a man-made pond.

Nine
Early Times

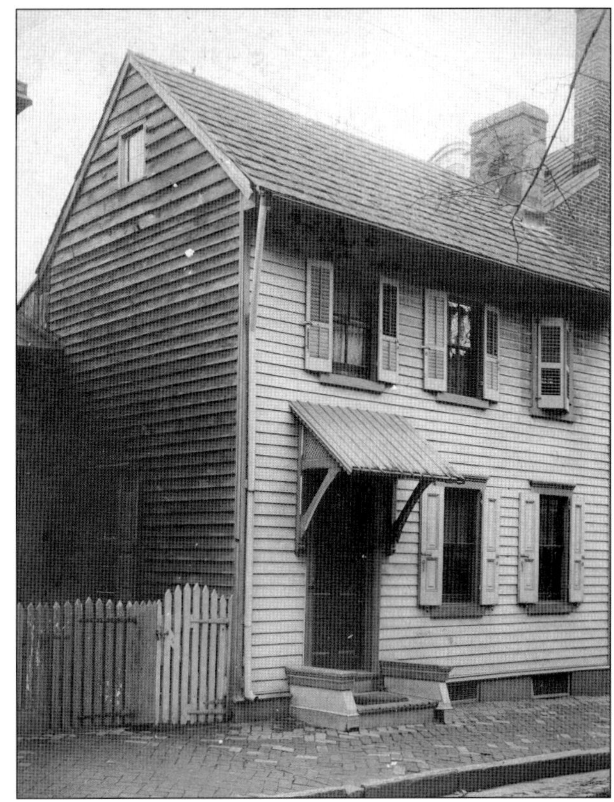

The house at 10 Brainerd Street, c. 1760, is a nice Colonial cottage and was the home of John Ridgway. He probably built the house for his bride when they married in 1760. He was a bricklayer by trade and built several brick homes in Mount Holly. He was also one of the surveyor generals of West Jersey.

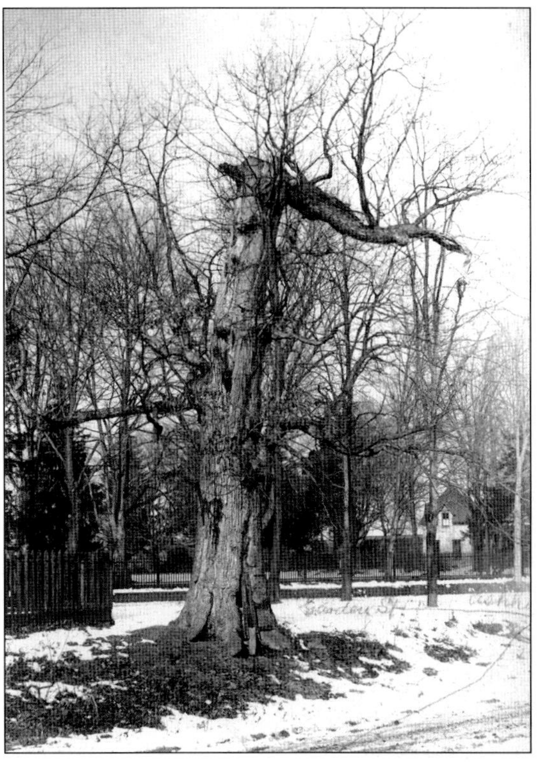

The Cripps Oak may not look like much, but it is a very important part of Mount Holly's history. Dating to 1688, the tree was used as a base point for most of the first surveys of Mount Holly. It stood at the intersection of Branch and Garden Streets.

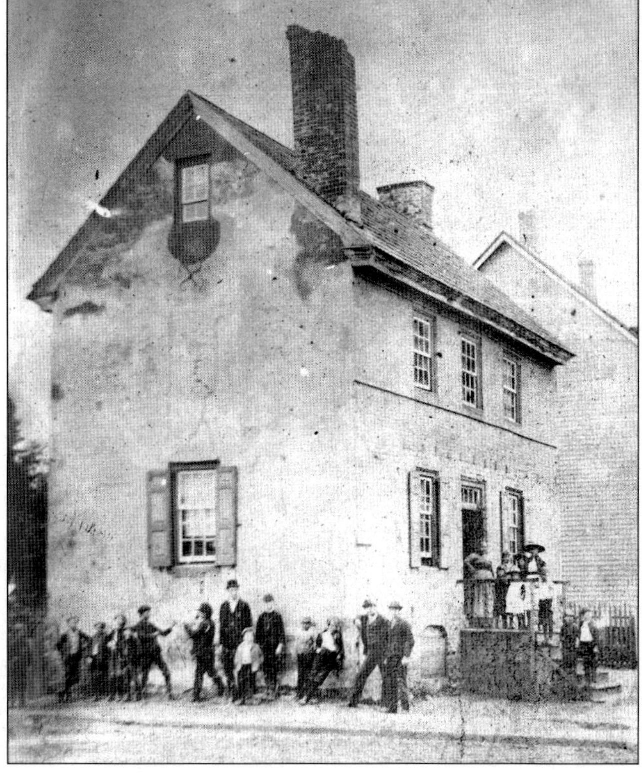

The northwest corner of Church and Pine Streets was the home of Josiah White, who built this house in 1730. He operated the Halsey Cotton Mill (destroyed by fire in 1881) and was a prominent member of the community. Note the two boys duking it out on the sidewalk.

The old iron bridge on Washington Street had a great deal of character, even with a dirt road. Washington Street was called the Great Road to Philadelphia, and people would come from miles around to cross the Rancocas Creek here in the center of Mount Holly.

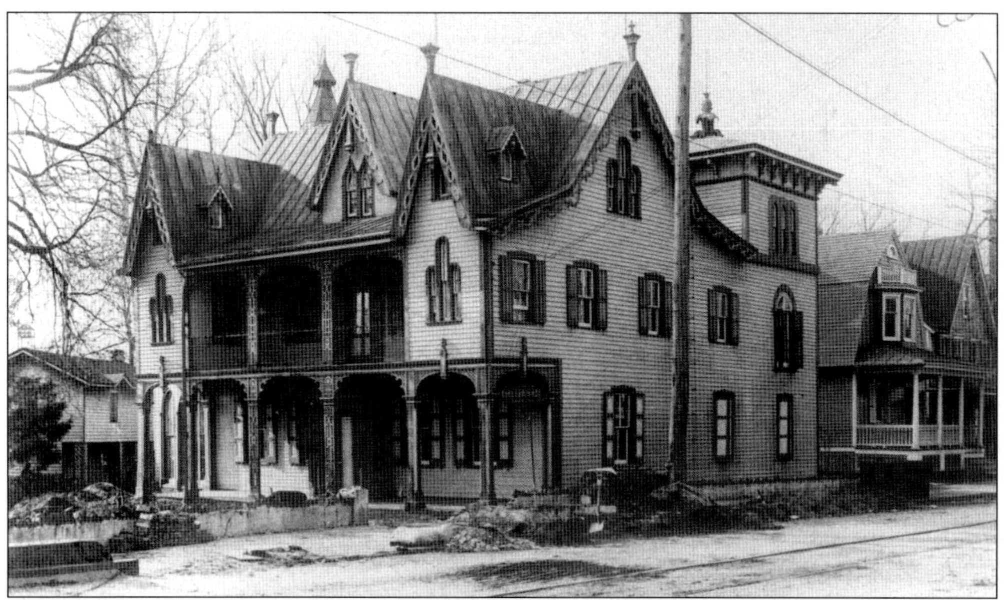

Sadly, this home, the Charles Bispham House, is no longer standing on Washington Street. In its past, this building was the parish house for the Trinity Church and was later used as a boardinghouse, called the Ivanhoe. It was eventually demolished, and this site is now occupied by dentist offices.

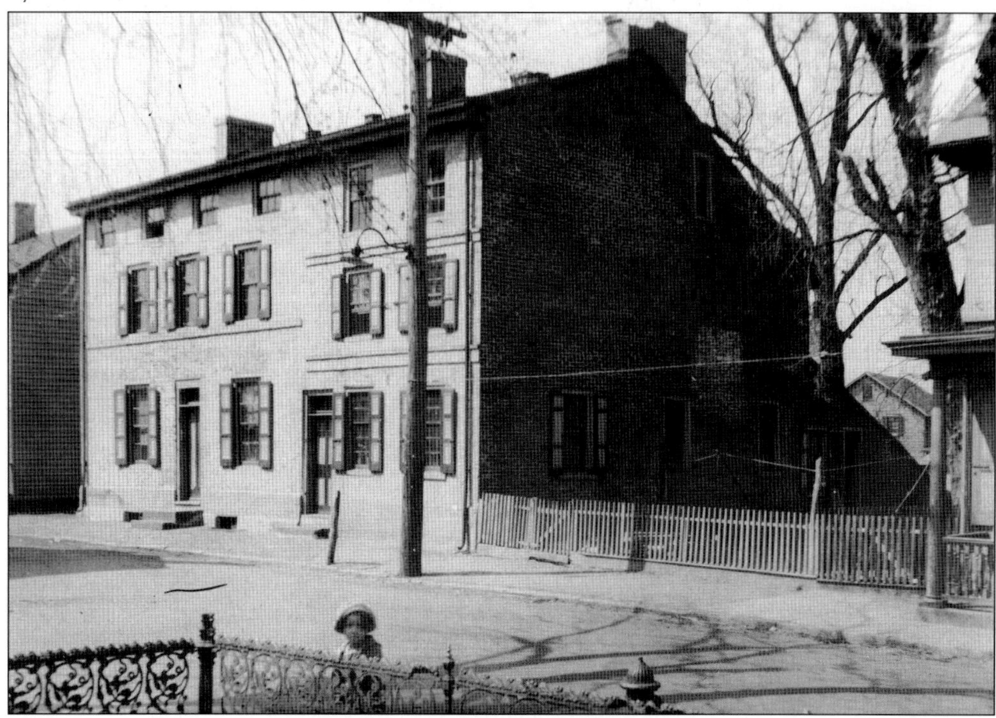

The Thomas Budd House is located at 20 White Street and is considered to be the oldest dwelling in Mount Holly. The right half was demolished and only the left side stands today. Charles Street is next to where the lawn was once located. This building is now part of the Millrace Village restoration project.

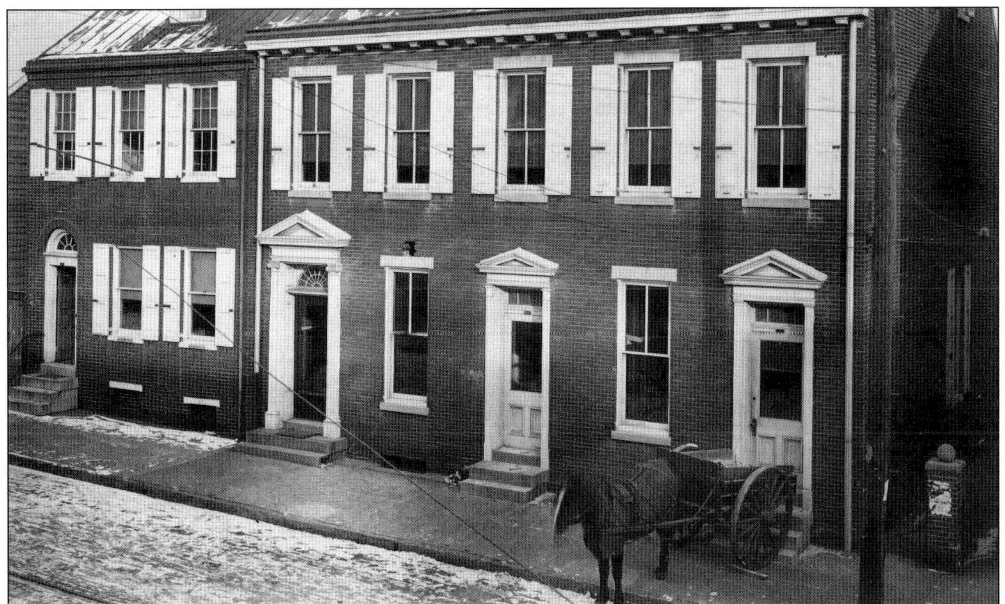

The former residence of Hulme Carter was photographed before it was changed to Wollner's Bakery. The door on the left opened into the residence. The center door was that of G.A. Rigg's office, and the next was the door to the Burlington County Fair Association office. Ewan Merritt erected this building at 25 High Street in 1927 near the Grant Store and Don's Barbershop.

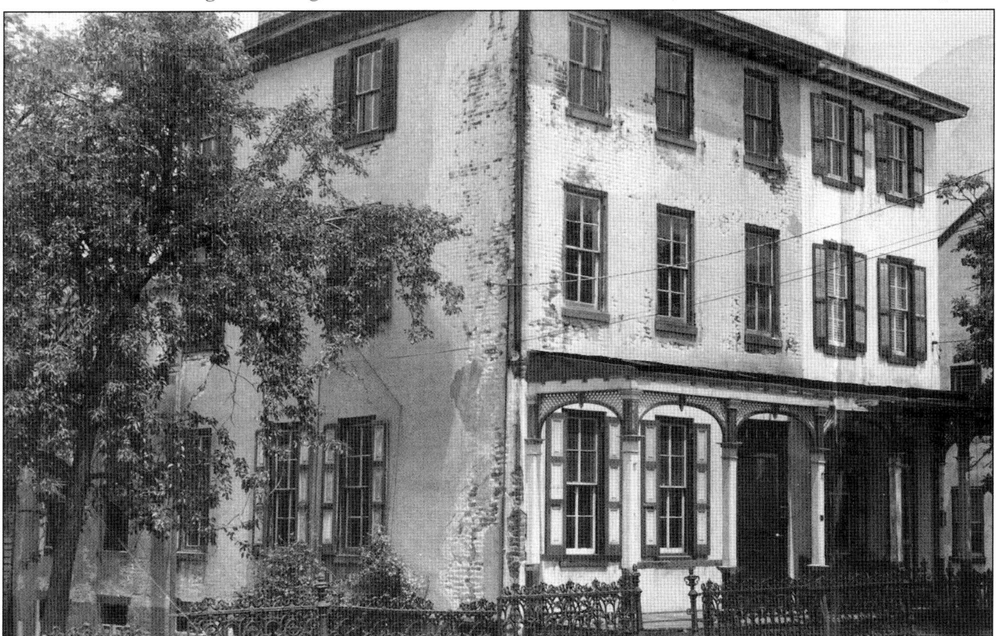

The Thomas Foy House at 25 Church Street was built *c.* 1840 on the site of the old Bass Brewery by Isaac Risdon. At one time, a Catholic mission was conducted in this house. Thomas Foy was the first person buried in the Sacred Heart Cemetery in 1857. The wrought-iron fence in front of the property was made at the Risdon Foundry. Over the years, it has slowly disappeared. Thomas Foy also operated a soap and candle shop in this area. Currently this building is part of the Millrace Village restoration project and will be fully restored.

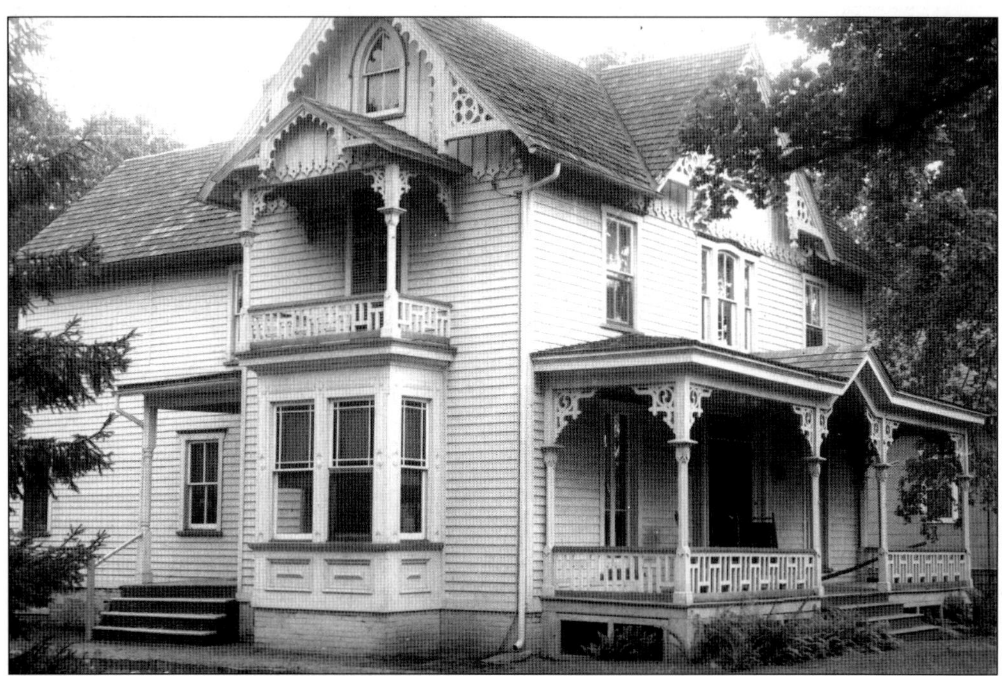

This was the home of Dr. Joseph Still, son of a famous Negro herb doctor, James Still. Dr. Still was never as famous as his father, but his early advantages and education were far greater. When he lived in this house at 97 Madison Avenue, he kept rooms for professional use (behind the bay window where the porch is now). Sometimes patients would stay on in the house for treatment.

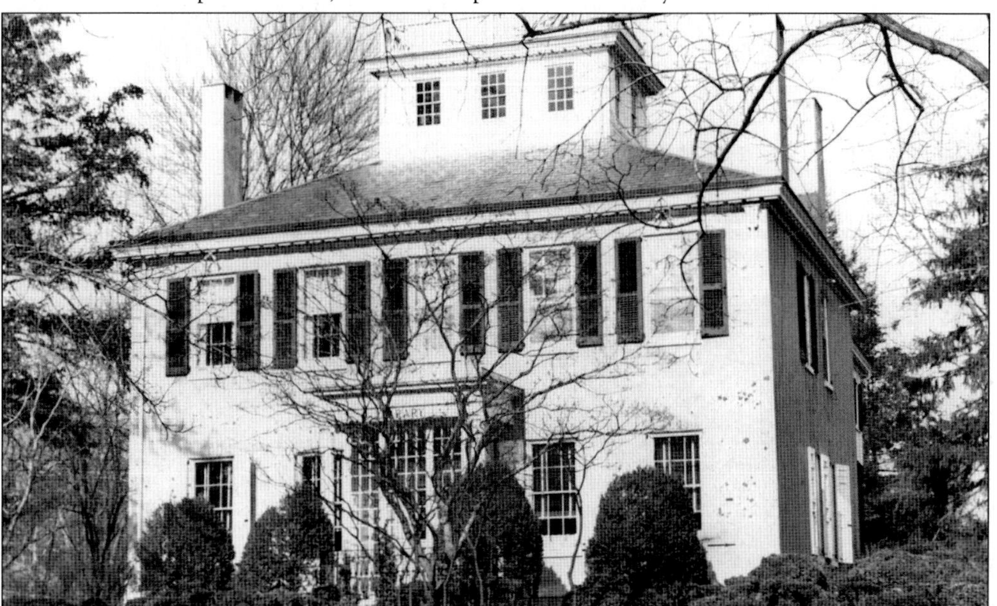

The Mount Holly Library was the James Langstaff Mansion, built *c.* 1829 on High Street near Ridgway. The library purchased and occupied the mansion in 1957, providing for its permanent home. In 1882, the library received a gift of $10,000 from Nathan Dunn, and the fund is its principal support. King George III of England chartered the library in 1765 as the Bridgetown Library.

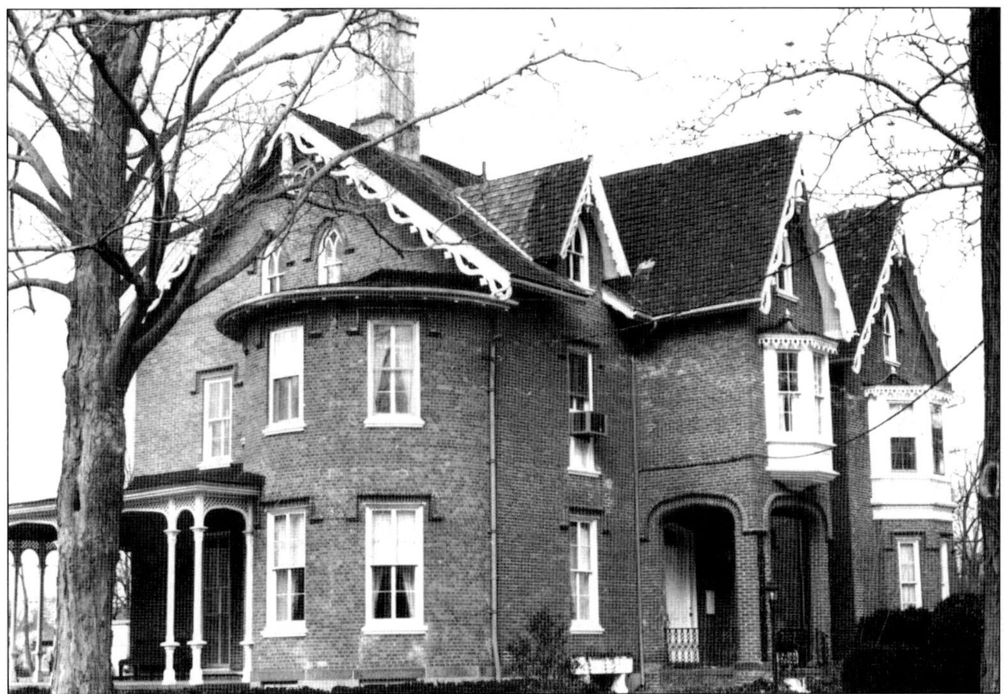

The Ashurst Mansion was built in 1857 by Lewis Ashurst, who was born in New York in 1806. He founded the Philadelphia Trust Company in 1857, married Mary Hazelhurst, and came to Mount Holly to build his home. His son Francis became a doctor and started a movement to erect a hospital in Mount Holly, which eventually led to the establishment of the first Burlington County Hospital located at 130 Mount Holly Avenue in 1882.

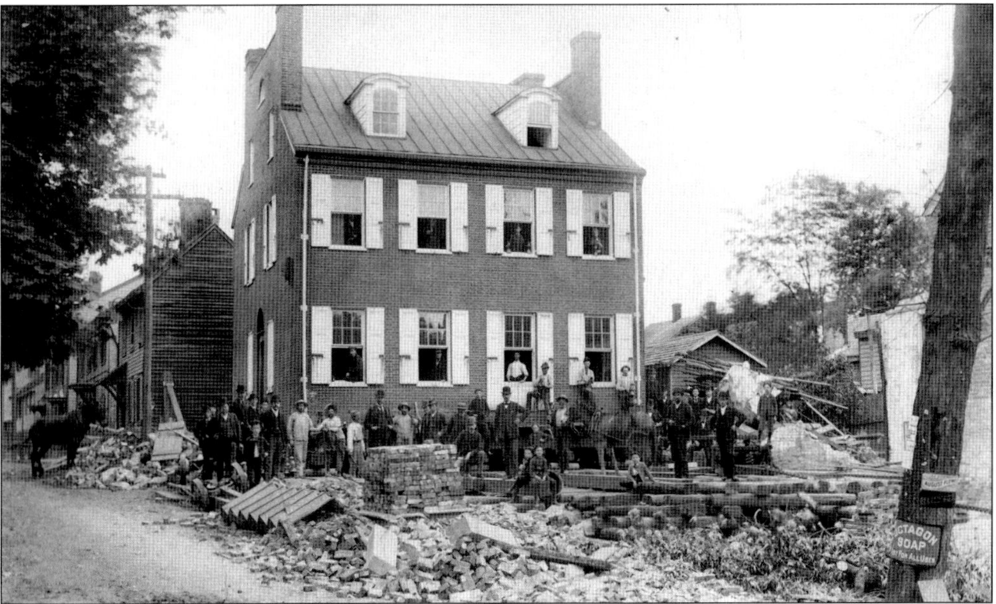

This home can still be found on Brainerd Street just off High Street. The Bainbridge House once fronted Main Street but was later moved back to make room for the new Masonic Temple on the corner of Main and Brainerd Streets in 1891.

ACKNOWLEDGEMENTS

There are many people to thank for helping us create this book, giving residents and visitors the opportunity to glimpse into Mount Holly's past. We have both been thrilled with the help neighbors and friends have given us in identifying scenes, naming people in the photographs, and digging up images to share.

A big thanks goes to Mark and Cheryl Deans of Deans Graphics on Mill Street, who volunteered to scan and save historic photographs in CD form so they will never be lost or destroyed. Everett and Barbara Turner, who collect old photographs of Mount Holly, were gracious in sharing them with us. Dorothy Bedwell McGrath, Francis Durand, Brooke Tidswell Jr., Harold Bozarth, Dr. Arthur Steitz, and Lew Morse spent hours reviewing photographs, identifying the places and people, and sharing their memories and their own photographs. The Burlington County Library, the Mount Holly Library, and the Burlington County Historical Society Library kept excellent records and photographs on hand. Trustees of local estates donated photographs to the Mount Holly Historical Society from the estates of Franklin Kates, Alice Jones, and Beatrice Harker Haines. The *Mount Holly Herald* and Kenneth Brewer (a photographer for that newspaper in the early 1900s), the Henry Shinn book *The History of Mount Holly*, George DeCou's *The Historic Rancocas* (which always shed light on historic facts), and the words of Joseph Cowgill (a Mount Holly historian in the early 1900s) were invaluable resources. There have also been many people who have dug up interesting photographs for us and allowed them to be scanned and saved. We thank all of you for taking the time to help preserve Mount Holly's history.

We have tried our best to identify photographs accurately and to include a wide variety highlighting Mount Holly's diverse and unique history. Proceeds from the sale of this book will go directly to the Mount Holly Historical Society.

Recommended books:

DeCou, George. *The Historic Rancocas.*
Greiff, Constance M. *Burlington County Historic Sites on the State and National Register.*
Shinn, Henry C. *The History of Mount Holly.*
Smith, Mary L. *Mount Holly Women Who Cared.*

Activities:

For a Mount Holly self-guided audio tour, pick up a CD player at the Robin's Nest Restaurant.
A Mount Holly driving tour is available through the Mount Holly Historical Society.
Tour the Historic Rancocas Valley Tourism Region on the Web at www.RancocasValley.com.
Visits to local historic sites can be made on the fourth weekends of each month from April through October.
Visit www.MountHolly.com for local event information.

Baiting the Void

Penelope Scambly Schott

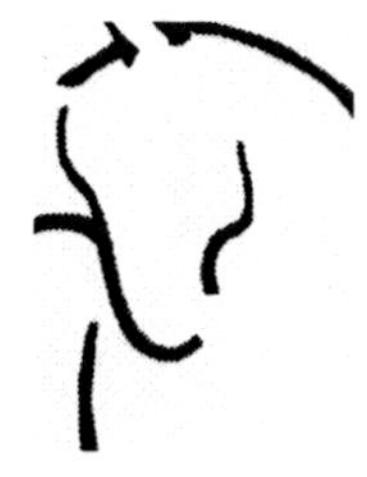

Dream Horse Press
California

Library of Congress Cataloging-in-Publication Data:

Schott, Penelope Scambly
Baiting the Void

p. cm

ISBN 0-9659307-9-3
1. Poetry

10 9 8 7 6 5 4 3 2 1

First Edition

Frontispiece: Briggs by Diana Ludwig
http://www.geocities.com/diwigy

Table of Contents

I

II

I

Introit

We placed on the high altar a glass vase
with sprigs of rosemary and wild purple phlox.

We shucked bushels of fresh corn, enough
to cover the floor, the slabs over dead bishops.

We carried the husks in a basket
down to the crypt.

When the great chestnut stallion lowered his muscled neck
to enter the sanctuary,

his ribs glistened like copper.

How could we not believe?

Tiresias in the Winter Fields

All afternoon, earth darkens.
Trunks, stumps, cold stones. The hush

of fresh snow. This one moment
is the path I am going,

me and my dog stalking together
over sharp indents of rabbits.

And what pre-canid thing am I?

Once,
like Tiresias, I wanted to switch my sex

in the act of love. Instead,
I am tracking past species.

Being half
of a pair.

Where the dog snuffles, I peer into
darkness.

There, among frosty soybeans,
five deer sleeping.

I am ready to nest
in the purple councils of the air, asking,

How are the categories rightfully derived?

because I can't disconnect
my own flesh from the grace of beasts—

my mothers and fathers being birds or fishes
or the creased and whistling stems

of movable grasses.

Life as a Dream

Because the rabbits of twilight were thinking my name,
I didn't want to come in

I kept on playing among the rabbits, our damp tracks
hopping through dew

In the boathouse of fireflies, someone has opened
the double doors

Now

I am rowing my heart like a dream of standing water
under the syntax of stars

As a cockle boat glides among rushes, that softly,
I am risking my whole soul

Starvations

Famished, I want to clasp the hand
of some creature fashioned handless.
Someplace my cells replace my cells
and are not mine. And some mute star
ignites my body's driftwood ribs.

Fireflies double in cisterns, ponds,
and pupillary wells that draw
us in; grapevines silver with dawn;
stony trilobites swim in the pines.
What mother tongue was ever enough

to feed us? What else is there to eat?

Convolvulus

Twisting, twining, writhing,
a live and convoluted vine
like the fine rolls of the vulva—

oh, morning glory, evening glory,

ingenious adaptations of the seed,
as rhinoceros maketh rhinoceros

while snail maketh snail.

Under the hedge, a green finger of will
wriggles through interstices, clamping,
climbing, winding its tubular way.

                                        Who knew
the flesh of plants possessed
such rich intention?

I tried to explain it
to Hitler or Stalin or Genghis Khan
or the nameless man with his hot gun.

I said, *Here's what we do to survive:*
hack the tendons to our own paws,

suck sugar out of the sweet stem.

Convolvulus over the porch lattice,
and under that same porch, worms,
and back and forth the wicker swing

slicing narrow swaths of moonlight;
the bone urge to twist this whole life
into interlaced words, or only an owl

winging above the intricate stubble,
cruising for voles.

The Wealth

All there in the bloody straw: the messes
of birth and death, awkward leakings

of fluids, the double waters of the earth,
river and isthmus, wellspring and tide.

The rotting of straw: tiered hayloft
invisibly aflame, dust motes afloat

in the striped, ascendant nave of the barn
where plumed snuffles of plowhorses

the grandfathers greeted each morning by name
still soften the hewn rafters, muffle

the wind. Throaty odors of baled hay,
leather harness frayed on its hook,

a readiness to mount, the rusty taste
of blood like molten iron at the earth's

hot core, yellow trumpets of sunlight
on winter afternoons, this great wealth

for us who came with nothing in our hands.

The Kiss

Almost the hour to gather the sun
like the yolk of the great egg it is,

to carry that loose yolk
in my closed hands;

almost the moment to drop it gently
down the rim of the world.

Time for you to lean and drink
from these cupped hands.

Your sinuous tongue on my twin palms
is the hot tongue of a white dog

named *Daylight*,
but soon the tethered underneath

of your night tongue
will move like a path in a forest

where each leaf is lifting up
its sacrament of moonlessness,

its one black fragment.

I Am

I am somebody small with gray-brown fur

I live in a round hole under the hood
of a blue pick-up which has stood a long time
rusting in wind beside a silted pond
in the country of overgrown fields

I nibble wine berries juice sack by juice sack
They burst in my mouth like tiny pricks of thought

I drone on in the morning *Oy-ya-oy-ya-ah-ah*

In the tender pauses I open the claws
of my white paws

                                        I like touching the damp earth
and the smell of my parents under black soil
where evening doesn't snap shut like a knife

My parents made me under Queen Anne's lace

I have been me in this same place and exactly
my same age for all of my life

I never think about my abortion except when I visit a new gynecologist

and someone hands me a clipboard
asking me to list date & outcome
for each one of my pregnancies.

It was back in the 50's—I was fifteen—
but it was completely legal,
because I was upper middle class.

The two requisite psychiatrists
concurred I was crazy,
so I could go to a good hospital.

Masked men painted the insides
of my thighs bright red. Afterwards
I screamed in my private room.

I wanted to die.
People are dying here, said the nurse,
and I knew she hated me. Later

my father sat in a straight chair
by the railed hospital bed
and tried to teach me to play bridge.

He had put himself through law school
on poker and bridge. I never learned
to play any card game but *Go Fish*.

Washing Moon

Under her serge dress, those are her briny ankles

Every full moon she washes her knives in the sea
to keep them sharp

She hones each blade on the sandy sole of her foot

With a hot mouthful of straight-pins,
she is pinning a lace collar of tatting and open work

to the full slope of her bodice
It swells and falls like foam on water

Before her, sea wrack and one lost fork
whoosh and retreat with the casual pebbles

                                        Tonight in a blue town
she will dine with that fork,

its barnacles and tines salty as blood,
and beside her, at table,

in the place of a husband, these long-handled knives

The Fish

The years where his slicked hair
darkened the tops of the cushions,
their loose weave of eyeless fish—
            and I scrubbed.

Give me a bleached nightgown,
a mopped floor to lay myself down,
give me a way to forget his skin—
            and I bathed.

In the old squares of the calendar,
a bride spooned out applesauce
while a scholar memorized dates—
            and I studied

even in line at the U-bookstore,
my toddler stacking cigarette butts,
a thin chicken drying in the oven—
            and I cooked.

But that was in the other century
back where the little boy grew up
and stars kept spiraling down to hills
            as they still spiral

to drown in the flow of glacial melt
whose cool braids foam over rocks
where a water ouzel dips and lifts
          and dips again

as I lean forward to watch
over ghost water in which each fish
is a silver quarter I toss away
          like a fast year of my life

of my life of my one absolute life
as I stretch and reach and keep
on tossing.

Premeditations

1. At the last picnic of my present life

Be careful, I tell myself,
running a finger down the slope
of the mushroom, its thin gills underneath
like gauze in the lungs swelling in April air.

In the clicking of insects under the white oak,
in the minuscule stories of planets and stars,
in the brilliant speckles of dark,
be careful.

Where shadows of two bridges are stirring
the current over two black drowning-points
and the frayed thread of the river runs dry,
here I am truly dismayed.

As a skunk laps at the milky water,
trillium petals pinken and fall;
as crows caw for sinew and seed corn,
I fail to whistle on a blade of grass.

When I kneel on this black boulder,
kisses unstick from the moss and blow loose;
when I sip at my lukewarm coffee,
I am licking rock salt.

2. Si Deus Quizer

There are ten basic designs for leaves.
Conjugation means grammar or sex:
I will die, you will die, she will die.

Only the lovely Portuguese language
possesses a true future subjunctive:
If God in the future may be willing.

As I flip the sheets of the calendar,
I am dipping my quill into ruby port,
sketching fresh leaves for the cork tree.

For the next two weeks of my life
I shall speak only in Portuguese;
for the next two weeks of my life,
I am planning to live forever.

3. At the first picnic of my next life

Pale green spinners of seedpods
will drop from the Norway maple,
and the grass, a week past the mowing,
will ripple and ripple.

A warm June wind will dance down
until the yellow umbrella tips slightly,
and the frilly table cloth will curtsy, lifting
its yellow flounces.

Spring, sing the black-capped chickadees,
gathering at the feeder
as if they, above all, have been invited,
until, all in a rush, come

Phyllis and Alice and Candace
and Susie and Harriet in matching lace.
Dearest generations of daughters,
our beaks will be crowded with crumbs.

Waiting for Kay

The first rule in badminton: Never Apologize.
Okay to miss the return, but don't say, *Sorry.*
Knock the birdie up into the box elder trees
where the woozy perfume of centipedes
rises through branches, over early crickets
sawing their legs. Don't apologize for twigs
crashing; it's noise we breathe, whistle at night
across miles of dark trees, weave of the net
plucked by swallows who swoop at dusk
between twin metal posts. We slap racquets
past breakable white moths, mashing them
flat as Wonder Bread. We hope we will never
be hungry again, nor ever doleful, clacking
our racquets like freight trains rocking the ties
of the tracks that head south down to Kay,
my friend who doesn't visit.
                                        Twenty years,
but still, but if, but when she finally comes,
swallows will dart out from under the net,
trees will blossom, grass say, *Welcome,*
it's been your turn for a very long time.
Here is a new birdie with real feathers—
it cost enough to call it a shuttlecock,
it has cost us decades. Next, Rule Two
of this game: Never Regret. Rule Three:
Let the third hand extend a warped racquet,

its turquoise paint chipped, frame unstrung
from that endless game played with my sister
in all those blue twilights before we grew up
and I lost her.

The incandescence

under white clusters of cactus spines, the slag
end of another heartless day, where sundogs
on the sparse clouds double the heat over desert
tracks and pale husks of stalks I can't name,
pods and rattles slicing my bare shins,
and my skin the skin of a parched toad recalling
a cold rain on the porch floor you dragged
your bags across that day you left. Where now
is the grocery sack spilling your boots or the jeweled
buckle of a tooled leather belt beating the steps
as you went? That was hard music you sang me,
not love songs, not crickets, never farewell.

Where the Songs Come From

Eyes of the cool women are hot with zeal.
Our feet possess the ground we stand upon.

Each of our names drops a patch of shadow
on moving water.

Our own ripe daughters consort with sunlight
while ruby-throated hummingbirds hover,

hover

over their brilliant hair. Yes,
the cool women are getting old. But still,

we can taste
the clustered blossoms of black locust,

their ivory pleats such an ardent perfume
burning

through those arched bridal chapels
inside our throats.

Never Sweep a Porch after Sundown

August is a bad month
in which to buy a broom.

Now I must set our bed
crosswise to the world

—not east or west—

and sleep alone
with the moon in my face.

If you stir the milk with a broom
the cow will have sore tits

and a woman who falls from a fig tree
will never get well.

I am sweeping my heart
through a crack in the porch floor.

My Box Turtle

When I found you, I was younger
and prone to grief.

Dark oval on the double white line:
I braked and stopped.

I was scared of your curved claws,
your fingers of delicate manicure,

eyes expensive and leafed,
a shuttering lens.

I picked you up and plopped you down
in the grooved bed of my truck

and drove and let you go
in scrubwood behind the house.

I am never looking for you,
only finding you

under multiflora, poison ivy,
five-leafed Virginia creeper;

I am never losing you,
only forgetting you,

you talisman and incunabulum,
my old plight, you cradle

of lost works,

your high arched back
bright among damps.

In that year you leave me,
how will I know it?

There will be none
of the stern silence

of one just dead.

The Birds of Sorrow

Stand too long in tall grass,
and they will build their nests
in your uncombed hair.
With small twigs,

they will pick, pick at your scalp until
they unweave your cap of misgivings,
and give you up to pure despair.
A thousand sorrows

swoop and hover over bent grass.
For every clump of grass,
there are many sorrows
and each sorrow

is named *sorrow* or *bunch-grass*
or *flyaway-grass* or *broken thing*.
Winds rise until your eyes burn.
The round

black eyes of a meadowlark,
slit eyes of a barred owl,
shut and open,
open and shut.

Around you in frozen grasses
the feathers fall, unpreened.
You may say *shroud*
or *yes, white birds,*

come peck my eyes blind.

Three Short Questions

There is a solid parcel
I lug in my hand

hanging from a string
around my finger

a mahogany double bed
on a thread

in my old mind
was a bed—

after fifty-five years
my parents

buy a new bed
stretch their thin legs

sleep like sisters
in white cotton gowns

the parcel on the string
clinging

like a little girl
in a white nightgown

between her parents
on a Sunday morning

all of us cuddling
under the fluted wooden

headboard, my well-
scrubbed finger nails

click-clicking in the ridges
of the headboard

of the bed, of the bed
of my young parents

kicking their bony feet
now in a new wide bed
before the last.

Where is the milk bottle
        half full of pennies?

Since when can't I smell
        the stink of grownups?

And why, at the ends of my wrists,
        am I wearing again

        such small moist hands?

Practicing

All across America, the widows
sleep with their radios on,
        the sonorous announcers
        speaking only to them,

and my mother, who has never
been cold, is always cold,
        until the sky finally lightens
        as the widows plan lunches,

as they phone married children
to come sleep in the guest bed
        which is always ready
        with fresh sheets.

After each visit, the widows
empty their waste baskets.
        not sniffing the sticky wads
        of Kleenex, knowing

that the kind man on the radio
will murmur all night,
        holding them close
        with the gentlest music

until a huge sun erupts
out of the black woods,
          and the sky
          unfurls so fast that from my side

of our rumpled bed, I practice
returning to girlhood
          where I slept alone
          with the Lone Ranger.

Turn up the old radio. Punch
down the quilt. Pound hard
          at the stuck
          door of the heart.

Who is that masked man
always coming toward me?
          Who is that man
          riding away?

Two Days in a Seedy Airport Motel

This nest is made of dull brown scrapings,
frazzles of strangers' hair, damp indentations
in the carpet or the skull, pin feathers
loose in the odor of singed stubble.

When I tuck my head under my wing,
poor thing, the white blizzard and the soiled,
the downward blizzard and the slantwise, snow
which is neither white feathers nor cotton balls

nor starched sheets in a linen press, snow
which is neither soap foam nor redemption, snow
which nails crows to the covered asphalt, snow
confounding the down with the up, until

there is only one gray substance in a gray world,
and the whole day is cold and sharp and grainy,
and if I were to lay my unfeathered self in a drift,
my skin would burn before it froze. How I barely

remember, or don't, what manner of bird
I was.

The Green Longings of Upstairs Windows

These are the signs: slam of a screen door,
spiky cucumber warm from the vine,
sadness of cherry pits spat into grass,
illumination of the fireflies.

At open windows behind white curtains
the children are not sleepy:
　　　　Mommy, I'm not sleepy
　　　　I'm not　I'm

How stern the tutelage of Fall:
　　　　purple eyelash of the fringed aster,
　　　　gartered snake in yellow poison ivy.

What you don't learn comes round again
until you do, but you can be kept back
until you're too big for the chairs.

Blue Mother

1

She, she   my honey child
slammed my hand

she slammed my hand
in the car door
thumbnail's turning black

she, she   my own child
slammed my hand

my only daughter
mashed my hand
yes, she mashed it

and she ran from me
and she won't come back

2

Slap-slap   slap-slap
Wet night   black road
slap-slap   of the wipers

slap-slap

I took his car   and I ran
slap-slap

up at the house
the man in the hat
is bolting the door

slap-slap
mark of his hand
on my cheek

slap-slap   slap-slap
crush of two hands

on my neck
slap-slap

3

Gonna ink my girl's name
on the back of my fist

If I ever forget
the feel of her curls

somebody   slice off this hand

No point in crying
I was dumber than water

Go ask my daughter
I was broke a long time

and wasn't it   a crying shame

4

Never took my kid   to the Petrified Forest
didn't have any   automobile

never took my kid   to the drive-in movie
cost me enough   just to buy her a meal

Well, now I can afford   to hit the road
so I drove on down   to the Petrified Forest

handed them a ten spot   at the iron gate
great big gem stones   lying on the dirt

but hey, I'm sixty   and I've come too late
she's all grown up   and doesn't own shit

so I bought her   this little piece of rock
I put it on my   Gold Card

5

Most of my fibs
sound so real

Knock-knock.
Who's there?

I love you, honey
I love you too

Back in that blue city
we ate moldy bread

My Daughter who Was Once Eleven

No, said Sappho. *You adore her flesh*
too much. Be this your punishment:
she must get old.

A long black coyote
skulks through my unplowed pasture.

Each dark night the ten pearl moons
of her fingernails orbited my heart.

The black coyote has not yipped, yet,
but he approaches. The white sheep
know nothing about him.

Now I race back to Sappho and ask:
Where is your Cleis in yellow ribbons?

The moon sinks.

She got old, says Sappho,
and wrinkled. Her velvet cheeks
sank over her teeth.

Coyote sneaks closer.

Lady, you offer me no sweet answers.

No, says Sappho, *but I don't lie.*

The Trail of Giant Cedars

They go marching, the great red cedars,
striding the ancient forest, their silver roots
toeing down into the green understory;

and I want to follow these peaceful giants
into high caverns of birdsong and hemlock,
into the place before iron and motors

and more stuff than anyone needs. Even
their sepulchers are taller than two loggers
or the huge double saws those men hoisted

to fell them. I love that woman who dwells
in the broad stump of an old-growth cedar,
its vaulted chamber fragrant and tender

with soft brown needles, and the whisper
and taste of a thousand winters of rain.
Under the fog she wears as a garment,

the sheen of her skin is a twisted skein
of slowly folded patterns, and the knots
of her old hands touch my own knuckles

and grow warm. When she tells me,
Come home, I open my clenched fingers
and now I rush toward her, almost as if
I had always known how.

The Man and the Boy

On the day DiMaggio died, I stood
a good ten minutes under the ash tree

holding, loosely, one end of the leash
while my eager dog dug for a mouse.

I glimpsed it a couple of times scrabbling
under the root, and then she caught

the gray field mouse and closed her teeth
and shook it and turned away, and the game

was over: *One to Zero,* and I thought
about great fame and how even the heroes

go down to death, limp as wet mice
and silent, and later I went to art class

where a nine-year-old boy posed for us
holding his bat, a crackerjack little boy,

delicious and bright with grace. He held
his stance and we sketched as fast

as we could, and then he shifted and stood
looking the other way, as if down the road

where Joe had gone, and the boy's eyes
and his wooden bat grew heavy

and heavier, and slipped downward,
and for his last pose he sat in a chair

and his soft bangs fell over the bat
and the boy slept.

The Necessity of Lemons

The lemon pulsed in the nest of her two hands.

Its tip rose up green above the cool and dimpled hide while the yellow of the rind hid inside the nest of hands.

It glowed in her hands like a lantern in a nest of straw, and its hide flared with a yellow fire like the sun.

She lifted her hands toward the hollow of her throat, and her neck sparkled with sunlight.

Lemon oil scented the skin at the hollow of her throat, and she breathed lemon like morning air.

Her two hands rose along with the rising sun, and the lemon soared above her and became the reflection of a goldfinch or the yellow beak of a black-backed gull or one round eye of a barred owl or else, over an island, a high canary star.

In each and every valley of the world just such a woman is holding her single lemon. From each lemon, one taut thread shoots straight up to the sun.

Each woman walks in a great circle in her own valley, around and around, and each thread, connected as it is to the sun, continues to weave its own tall funnel in the yellow air.

The women with their lemons will keep the sun from abandoning the earth.

If ever we learn to speak in the words that are native to this place, perhaps we will know how to thank her.

Listen here in our valley. I think you can hear her walking.

Siesta

On the last afternoon of his life
my father slept by the sea.

In the midst of sleep
he lifted his head

and said,
Hello?

as if
he were being called.

II

Fern

Spines of a cactus,
bones of a trout—

deep
in the great north forest

over the gorge
of a huge river

I combed my hair
with the shadow of a fern

and then I swam home
through the gloom

and the trout returned
to her ancestors

with one wet word
in her peaked jaw:

fir, or *far*, or *fern*

    If I live a long time
    I may learn it, that word,

    or not

Fear as the white pith

I sucked two lemons under a full moon,
each tipped like the aureole of a nipple.

The squeezed juice of the lemon
stung all the cuts on my fingers.

I gave my daughter a dimpled lemon,
I gave my daughter my yellow heart.

Ripe lemons hung heavy as testicles
until the lemon tree dipped into the river

and all her cowardice was washed away.
In my next life I will worship turnips,

depth of a hard winter,
heartstring into the earth.

Almost Learning to Live in this World

Children crouching in stairwells, the treads and risers,
embers of blankets under soldiers' boots.

Something I expected in this life, a neighborliness, not
the hacking of skulls. This poem,

like a twelve-year-old girl, is burning to dance.
Like the beaded neck of the painted turtle, it starts

at shadows or ripples. It pulls itself in.
What does a beak mean or a tender claw reaching

like a child's arm out the window of the school bus
waving at Mom on the sidewalk

and saying *how brave, how brave, to go to a room*
with so many chairs?

Shadows of willows on the plated shell, each branch
dowsing for a partner, because dancing

was all that we did, Judy and Polly and Winifred and I,
who wanted, above everything, to discover ourselves

mysterious, as we were, and deserving and clever,
as four new moons rising clean and safe

in blue hoop skirts over a beat-up planet.

The Collaborators

Loud waves opened and closed
over the jetty; and the family
in the little white sailboat
and our hands scribbled *oh,*
oh on the foamy sheet of air,
and one man came up for us
but he preferred his dead brother
drowned or maybe a son
dead in the womb; and all the gulls
bending and crying *woo, woo*
and *oh*; and we stood and noted
from the salt end of the jetty
how we kept on breathing, dry
and frantic as crinkled paper,
each of our separate breaths.

Usual Objects

The slant shadows of chimneys
across a roof

or leafless rose stalks
scratching windowpanes

a wind coming

bellies of flying birds lit by a low sun
immense reaches

of one human mind

finding itself
crowded with worlds and still alone

But here is a bowl carved from a burl
and elsewhere, a rock and a stone pestle,

its top polished round
by the palms of a woman

usual objects exquisite by use

Torture the birch's pendulous catkins
into a fine brown powder

Scream down a well
until the stars answer;

you won't live long enough

Rather, may *things* comfort the needy,
the standard artifacts:

all the wings of all the insects
the dark hearts of the rocks

the fact that anyone
gave you a name

First Spring

Wind, do you know me?
April without my father;
my hair has blown white.

Beneath the plank bridge,
pale petals of the pear tree
float over slick stones

like thin white lockets—
one untranslatable word
inside each petal.

Succulence

Daddy Sun & Mommy Moon & all the baby stars,
a bone teapot & six matched cups, a ruffled wedge

of ducks;
Oh succulence, the hen & chicks.

Even our stories crammed full of family:
Oedipus & Jocasta, Grendel & Mom.

To belong forever, be loved
in the comfortable clutter of others,

not Joan alone at the fiery stake,
but rising together and whole—no edge to our souls.

On a slope in a mountain meadow
lives one tree in multiples, joint root at its cloned trunk:

the great aspen. It quivers a leaf
and an acre apart

quivers another. Pod of the closed earth,
contain each seed

so that I may be known.
Let stones tremble on one stem.

Under the Sun

I want to locate a landscape
where there has been no killing,

neither violence in the hedgerows,
nor on the roofs or trestles,

no human femurs poking from ditches
nor buttons rusted under loose rocks;

only cow parsley tall as my shoulder,
its umbrella of small blossoms

smelling of old cupboards
where dirt sifts down on a blue plate.

I want to paint light, how it flows
into grass like the winged shimmer

of ripe alfalfa, or the pink tinting
of clouds, a blush of unshed blood,

as if I, who hit a girl in seventh grade
and scraped my hand on her braces,

were trying to paint my own way in
to grace, or dash my whole inheritance

of English words at the moiling furnace
of our harsh and dispassionate star.

The Nature of Clouds

There is a cloud on my house.

The cloud has arrived in strings and wisps and ringlets. The cloud has wrapped my house away from the valley. When I step outside my house, the cloud is on me.

I stand outside my house in a place like rain. The rain moves neither up nor down, just very delicately toward the east.

What color is the cloud? Pink and opalescent gray. Maybe if I were outside the cloud, it would be black.

What does the cloud taste like? Rhododendron. Pink star rhododendron lifting spiky petals into the gray.

What does the cloud think? *Hill.* The cloud thinks about leaving this hill. The cloud misses the western ocean. Nobody has told the cloud that when it comes to the snowy mountains, it will break. The cloud doesn't fully know the nature of clouds.

When I open my front door, pieces of cloud waft into the house. The pieces float among sofas and chairs.

Now the cloud is stuck inside my house, and I am sad for the cloud. Therefore I open the back door to let it move on. The rest of the cloud streams through my house. It touches papers with its moist breathing. It swipes against walls and makes them shine.

My old dog lifts her head. She watches the cloud go out the door. Then she puts her muzzle down on her crossed paws and thinks the thoughts of a cloud.

Neither the dog nor the cloud will say what they are thinking. Maybe they are lucky and think only in wisps.

A wisp is coming to me now:

> *I am ten years old on the summer lawn and my father, who is still blond and gawky, is doing a somersault on the sweet grass. He has huge black shoes.*

My father has gone to where the cloud is going, all broken into molecules, and where my old dog will go soon.

When I am dying, I will try to remember the day there was a cloud in my house.

I will wait like that cloud for someone to open a door.

Telling my Husband Why I Do It

Why I tend the elderly:
Really for practice.

How I made the widow's bed:
Two bottom sheets, hospital tuck;
flannel rag across the pillow.

Why I tend the elderly:
For pay.

What her sheets looked like:
Patches on patches on patches
showing through holes.

Why I tend the elderly:
Pure fear.

How she sleeps in that bed:
Eighty-seven and hunched
in husband's worn pajama tops.

Why I tend the elderly:
So someone will love me
when I am old.

What I tell you in bed:
Nothing. Only my legs
talk to yours. They beg.

The Starving Heron

Witness the heron, fastidious of step.
How remotely from hunched shoulders, the neck
unrolls and jabs.
                    The stoop of him, the stolid
tread, the lack of any tiny thing
to eat, the sleet-wet air: he is doing his time
in the trenches, on the bank of the frozen canal.

As if in war, this irreversible knowledge;
what you learn to live without: hope,
like a birthday favor, or heat, or just your common
breath, that sweet repast.
                    Disconsolate,
that word I don't use, is what this heron is,
lifting and settling his outspread yellow toes
with mute intent along the crumbling ice.

Snail Path

Whenever I need forgiveness
I follow the path of the snail

up a stone wall. Her silver
trail glistens before me.

When she climbs the spine of a fern,
it bends as if it were wet;

to commit or receive evil
is not remarkably different.

However you choose to go forward,
the way of rocks and fronds

demands the closest attention.
You can learn a lot from a snail:

the will of a woman is stalwart
and forgiveness small and slow.

Signing for his Cremation

My mother sent me: what I saw in the coffin
was meat out of a long icebox;

even his white hair, though still elegant,
was not human, and after three days,

his cheeks had sunk. *Please leave me alone*
with him, I asked, and they all scattered,

but even while I stood in that small room,
I was without him. I called them back

and said, *Yes, do it*,

as if I were signing a chit. Now
I am reciting his name: *Elihu, Elihu Schott*,

but I hesitate to tell anyone, even you,
how softly my fingertip grazed

the cold lobe of his ear
before I untucked the blanket and lifted it up

to look at that withered and delicate place
I had come from.

I wanted to shape a poem

in praise of natural arrangements, but this year
I'm doing badly. I meant to endorse the solstices,
that matter of angles and slants. I intended to praise
the whole planet, out to galaxy's edge and universe,
into the life forms of carbon, all of them, algae, bugs
with intentions, the golden tamarin, women and men
who have tried to define a strategy.
Well, pardon me
if I can't do it, can't compose paeans, because I object
so violently to the entire contrivance, because I resent
each supernova, the burn-out of stars, the loose mantle
as it melts and shifts on the heat of our planet, the loss
of the great dire-wolf—just bones and no pelt, the gentle
parting of my old father who once would have read this
and now won't, and would chide me, were he still here,
because the whole world was so funny, so dear to him,
so beautiful, he would say he loved breathing the air.

Extra Innings without My Mother

The spotted backs of your hands, smooth
as the palm of a catcher's mitt, thump
of a called strike. We are two teammates
in an old game: the game of getting old.
How restful this scuffed field, the sagging
scoreboard. I need never be glamorous
or spiffy or sophisticated, never get rich.
I need only become your orphan up here
in the bleachers like the crotch of a tree,
peanut skins drifting to the dugout roof.

When I try to describe how safe I'll be,
I remember the white backs of her hands,
her slim fingers, towers of golden rings,
two strikes against me, my rough slide
home. Now I am stacking the top half
of a peanut shell, lid of a sarcophagus
expectant in the great museum, empty,
though inlaid with topaz.

Swimmer

To swim among lilies whose slick stems
entangle the thighs of the swimmer
in beads of light—

a pond of yellow stars, and beyond cupped
fingers, a watery sky that trembles
into wrinkled glass.

I meant to learn to breathe under pondwater
instead of being forced ashore
among weeds,

their golden heads so freighted with seed.
Who guessed a waxen lily pad
possessed sharp edges?

Instead I am watching my old dog sleep,
shallow breaths stirring the white
underhair of her chest.

I meant to memorize my constellations,
to tell one romping Brandenburg
concerto from another.

In the month of August, certain lilies bloom
an astonishing pink, much as when
the inner flesh

of a white-haired woman, unlike the slit
of an old bitch dog, will ripple again
with quick zest.

The Generosity of Pears

The small gravel of the brown Bosc
gritty between the teeth,

and a yellow Bartlett ripened too long
in a blue bowl,

its velvet flesh gone milky and wet
like custard before bed, juice

drawing flies,

plus one decorous Anjou
minding its pale green manners

in a cool metal lunch box—

> Remember how we knelt in the orchard
> between arched rows?
>
> How we pointed our wooden ladders
> into the rooms of the sky?
>
> How we crated up beauty
> side by side in its own perfume?

—as the rimmed sun touches noon
and three grown men in worn jeans

gone white at knee and crotch
straddle the stacked lumber,

unbuckle their heavy leather
carpenter's belts

and reach into the truck
for the packed lunch.

> Remember the wet tip of the tongue
> flicking the bow of the top lip?
>
> The full curve of the lower lip
> that slips over slick flesh?
>
> The sweet swelling and melt
> in the spaces between our bones?

You, I have loved completely,
your beauty like three pears

smooth in the hasp of calloused palms,
each man unshaven and fragrant

as the white blossoms of April,
each bud concealing its jewel.

The Eye-Stalks of Ghost Crabs Are Mobile and Long

I remember the first hour
your eyes moved into mine,
the heat in the room
and the painted walls vanishing.

A ghost crab can burrow four feet deep:
I have felt you so far inside me
that my lungs are lifted
and my heart is squeezed.

Ghost crabs produce stridulations
by friction against a skeletal ridge
causing squeaks, croaks, and twitterings:
you have heard me cry out surprised.

At low tide they emerge and scavenge,
catching small fish at the edge of the sea,
just as you've caught me tonight
here in your sleeping arms.

When I comb your hair with my fingers,
you mutter *I love you* and breathe aloud
while outside our bedroom windows
airplanes blink red in the night

as if everyone else has flown away,

until I cannot separate your face
from the impression of your face
on the dark pillow. The ghost crab

is best known for its shadow.

Looking Out at the Sourland Mountains

This is my own farthest horizon:
that blunt line of worn hills.
Long shadows of box elders
stipple the lawn.
I think I've gone
the whole day without looking
and am not proud of it. What's a window
for?
When you peer into the soul
of any hour, you note how fragile
your smallest minute becomes.
Imagine
a giraffe, her head in the tender tops
of branches, the delicate horns of her ears
ignorant of crickets sawing their bows
among fragrant grasses.
So I, having lost
one full day of loveliness
by not sufficiently loving the hills,
have grown a day older in misplacing
my attention, and am become most penitent.
Flash me across distance and I will come:

Twilight sparkles the shallow river
where it turns in the valley below the hills
and ferries the sunset away.

At last
I cook dinner, slicing a mountain of onions
on a green oval platter, doling out
knives and forks, picking my way home
through the long gestures of the work.

Welcome Home, Soldier

— on Veterans' Day

Thank you, America, for sending him home.
Thank you for drafting him mid-semester,
for rushing his first girlfriend into his wife,
        into his ex-wife.
Thank you, America, for teaching him loneliness
in this man's army and everywhere he goes.

Thanks, Uncle Sam, for selecting a shy boy
and shoving him into a scared space
so his eyes are neither blue nor gray,
even as his hair grays over the smooth
forehead of that boy I never knew.

Thanks to the officers of provision and supply
who fitted him for war.
Personal thanks for his bald middle-aged legs
here in my bed, calves rubbed hairless
up to the tops of his combat boots.

Thanks for assigning him to Signal Corps:
whenever he wants to kill, he remembers
he never learned how and is still guilty
for being grateful.
Thanks for that, too.

Thank you for teaching him to be too careful,
to imagine every worst thing.
Thanks for a whole life of hesitations.
Thank you, America, for his nightly crouch
in the electronic foxhole of his study

where every signal is virtual,
www.dot.Vietnam, and no one got hurt
but the ones in the Wall,
and in hospitals and shelters
and alleys and jails

all over the Land of the Free
where we still keep pretending,
God Bless America,
my husband is perfectly well.

River-Woman

In a boat like tomorrow,
the current furrows before her.

In a boat like tomorrow,
she slowly unbuttons

the round pearl buttons
of her high-necked silk blouse.

She rows, breasts bare,
in this boat to the riverbank

where she puts on her moccasins
blue with beads

and leaps over gunnels
to lie face down

among shore grass
and blue camas.

Under the black silt
waits a deeper boat,

a dug-out canoe
fitted with raven wings.

In this boat
made of many long sleeps,

the current is breaking behind her,
and her body,

as sleek as a salmon,
ascends to become a pink cloud

the exact shape of the boat.

During the Long War

I walked around with an upturned thumbtack
inside my shoe to prove I was brave.

When I was born I was one hundred years old
and I killed my grandmother three times.

When she put her bony hand on her bony chest
and was hauled away to the emergency room,

I played the piano and was happy.
When I was a child I was ten feet tall.

I owned the whole Hudson and the Broadway IRT
and two howitzers, and I strung the white lights

of the George Washington Bridge around my neck
and flew off to my victory party up in the sky.

Nobody ever smacked me with a hairbrush,
nobody ever called me stupid,

nobody convinced me there was no safe place
on the planet for someone unworthy as me.

I didn't spend years proving otherwise:
I didn't raise my babies on nickels,

I can’t see hungry children in rubble,
I can’t taste the chemical reek of smoke,

I don’t inhale the heat of my dog’s fur,
I have never wanted to go back to sleep.

Les Neiges d'antan

Where are the mice of yesteryear?
Humus underneath leaf-shred.

Where are the mice of yesterday?
Bone chips in the pellets of owls.

Where are the mice of an hour ago?
In the clean mouth of the cat.

Where is the mouse of now?
In the dim kingdom behind the wall.

After the framer, electrician, painter
lock the door, scoots the mouse

on her delicate pink feet, that thief
who stows away below the decks

of expectation and will shorten
our voyage from buoy to buoy.

What courage it takes us
to make anything of nothing

when only this nothing
clangs with importance,

while inside our walls, mouse
is mincing the new insulation

into a loose nest for a handful
of hairless pinkies waiting

to smell of cellar and shed,
ready to bait the void.

Inchworm, Inchworm

You're dead a long time, said my uncle,
tipping port from the garnet decanter,

same old uncle who flicked his fat finger
under the strap of my double-A bra

decades ago when I turned twelve,
same uncle a long time dead.

Who knows where the soul goes
in the hard earth or the soft?

A little green inchworm is measuring
the weathered edge of a picnic table

where a tin milk can fills up with rain.
We are growing a new crop of uncles,

weeding and hoeing. A young girl
runs through the drizzle, ducking

under the hedges. We shout for her
without opening our mouths.

Replenishment is her name
and yes, she is lovely

beyond any measure.

My Father's Employment

Such a demanding job: another ordinary Wednesday
and you're still dead.

This weekend, you'll be dead too. Don't you ever get
a day off?

I am shaking the dry coins of the Chinese money plant.
Look,

you can see through each disk into the bright kingdom
of precious objects

that don't exist. I would spend every leaf in my garden
to cover your wages

for half an hour so you might knock off and sit with me
here in the striped shade

of stripped branches and we might sip our tea in tall
glasses of air.

Suppose I go put the kettle on. A painted chair
waits under the big maple. Now I am pouring the water

over your ashes.
Let us drink tea together after they steep.

September Kite

On invisible string, the rainbow kite
swims in the sky on black wings.

The grass of the dunes
spills small moans on the wind.

Rewind the string on a round stick
tricking the kite into buzz, flicker,

and dive, down, down into flightless
collapse. Gather up the loose

plastic cups. Shake out the towels.
Fold up the great yellow umbrella.

The body re-absorbing its failures.
Telling the children to empty their pails.

April, Again

The most brutal movie I ever saw
was time-lapse film of fruit in a dish,
all that tender ripeness caving in
on itself: the collapse of *is* into *was*.

When I glimpse my face in a mirror,
I remember a chipped colander
mounded with yellow cherries,
some rotting and some just dried.

Remarkable, all remarkable,
like this loose pebble in my palm,
its sparkle of mica, speck of lichen
thinking of nothing but *cling, cling*.

My fists are clusters of blossoms,
and inside them, the stone knuckles
with whatever of flesh will adhere,
adhering. Yes, I am old enough

to discuss April with a certain
earned authority: how pale petals
on the cherry tree guess nothing
about the hard pit.

Acknowledgements

Grateful acknowledgment to the contests and publications where some of these poems received prizes and/or first appeared in print.

American Poetry Review, "The Collaborators"
Atlanta Review, "The Generosity of Pears"
Bitter Oleander, "The Geology of Flesh"
Chester Jones Contest, "Looking Out at the Sourland Mountains" (second prize)
Clark College, "The Birds of Sorrow" (first prize)
Columbia Riverkeepers, "Fern" (third prize)
Cool Women, Volume Two, "Where the Songs Come From", "Inchworm, Inchworm", "Washing Moon", "Almost Learning to Live in This World"
Cool Women, Volume Three, "Practicing", "The Nature of Clouds", "The incandescence", "Swimmer", "Fear as the white pith"
Dogwood, "My Daughter who Was Once Eleven"
Fireweed, "Extra Innings without my Mother"
Florida Poetry Contest, "The Starving Heron" (second prize)
Footworks, "Welcome Home, Soldier" (editor's choice)
Georgia Review, "Three Short Questions", "April Again", "Under the Sun"
Grove Review, "Les Neiges d'antan"
Inkwell, "Tiresias in the Winter Fields" (first prize)
Inventing the Invisible: Art on the Air, "The Man and the Boy"
Manzanita, "The Fish"

The Oregonian, "The Incandescence"

Passager, "My Box Turtle"

Peregrine, "Fern"

Runes, "The Nature of Clouds"

Sow's Ear Review, "The Necessity of Lemons", "I wanted to shape a poem", "Washing Moon"

US 1 Worksheets, "The Eye-Stalks of Ghost Crabs are Mobile and Long", "Never Sweep a Porch After Sundown"

Verseweavers, Oregon State Poetry Association, "The Fish", "Blue Mother"

Visions, "My Father's Employment"

Willapa Tidings, Friends of Willapa National Wildlife Refuge, "The Trail of Giant Cedars"

Also "Never Sweep a Porch after Sundown" was included in *Wave Amplitude in the Mona Passage* (chapbook, Palaquin Press, 1998), and several other poems were included in *Almost Learning to Live in this World* (chapbook, Pudding House Press, 2004).

Thanks to the New Jersey State Council on the Arts for four fellowships as well as to the Lannan Foundation and the Fine Arts Work Center in Provincetown, Massachusetts, and to the Dodge Foundation and the Vermont Studio Center in Johnson, Vermont under whose auspices some of this work was begun. Plus ongoing thanks to the members of the Cool Women of Princeton, New Jersey, and to the Pearls and Portlandia Collaborative of Portland, Oregon. Special thanks to my longtime friend Susan Gubernat who helped me arrange this manuscript.

Biography:

After receiving four fellowships from the New Jersey Council on the Arts, Penelope Scambly Schott moved to Portland, Oregon where she plans to stay for the rest of her life, not counting occasional writing jaunts elsewhere. Along with writing, she paints, hikes, indulges her family (especially her dog), and teaches poetry over the internet. She has also worked as donut girl in a cider mill, home health aide, and artist's model. Her writing residencies have included The Fine Arts Work Center (Provincetown, Massachusetts), The Vermont Studio Center (Johnson, Vermont), and most recently the Wurlitzer Foundation (Taos, New Mexico) where her next book was dictated to her by a philosophically argumentative magpie.

Printed in the United States
69001LVS00007B/159

9 780965 930796